Aging and Loss

٨

Global Perspectives on Aging Series
Edited by Sarah Lamb, Brandeis University

This series publishes books that will deepen and expand our understanding of age, aging, and late life in the United States and beyond. The series focuses on anthropology while being open to ethnographically vivid and theoretically rich scholarship in related fields, including sociology, religion, cultural studies, social medicine, medical humanities, gender and sexuality studies, human development, and cultural gerontology.

Aging and Loss

Mourning and Maturity in Contemporary Japan

JASON DANELY

RUTGERS UNIVERSITY PRESS
NEW BRUNSWICK, NEW JERSEY, AND LONDON

Library of Congress Cataloging-in-Publication Data

Danely, Jason.
  Aging and loss : mourning and maturity in contemporary Japan / Jason Danely.
    pages   cm.—(Global perspectives on aging)
  Includes bibliographical references and index.
  ISBN 978–0–8135–6517–0 (hardcover : alk. paper) — ISBN 978–0–8135–6516–3
(pbk. : alk. paper) — ISBN 978–0–8135–6518–7 (e-book)
  1. Aging—Japan.   2. Older people—Japan.   3. Death—Social aspects.
4. Mourning customs—Japan.   I. Title.

  HQ1064.J3D352   2014
  305.260952—dc23   2014014273

A British Cataloging-in-Publication record for this book is available from the British
Library.

Cover. Portrait of Ono Sayaka's grandmother, *Rōba wa ichinichi ni shite, narazu* (*Rōba*
[old woman] wasn't built in a day). Japanese pigment on gold leaf. Used with permission
of the artist.

Visit our website: http://rutgerspress.rutgers.edu

Manufactured in the United States of America

To Robin

Contents

PART IV
Hope

Acknowledgments

The lifeline of ethnographic research is the generosity and trust of a handful of individuals willing to share their time and their stories with a curious stranger. In particular, the twelve older individuals at the core of my interview group have been and remain a source of encouragement and inspiration, without which this project could not have come into being. My first and deepest gratitude goes to all of the individuals whose identities I keep in confidence, but whose hearts I have tried my best to express with honesty and dignity in the pages of this book. Most of all, they have taught me the joy of listening, and to each one I owe a debt of gratitude.

I would not have embarked on a study of aging and loss in Japan were it not for the guidance of my mentors and advisors who saw in me a potential that I could not have uncovered on my own. I am especially grateful to David K. Jordan, whose thorough, insightful, and always humorous comments on draft after draft of this book have taught me an immeasurable amount about the ethnographic process. No man has ever spilled so much red ink on my behalf.

I also would like to thank Carl Becker, who has extended himself far beyond what he would admit to create an intellectual space for me to conduct my research in Kyoto on several occasions. He has been an invaluable role model for his passion, rigor, and kindness.

Steven Parish was the first mentor to suggest old age as a research focus, and his curiosity and openness led me to examine in greater depth the themes of abandonment and loss from a psychodynamic perspective. Mel Spiro took the time to read some early case studies that became the backbone of this book, and helped me explore more about the significance of family dynamics and religious symbols. As this ethnography began to take shape, I relied on the responses and reflections of Roy D'Andrade, Keith McNeal, Christena Turner, and Richard Madsen.

I am grateful to Anne Basting and Thomas Fritsch at the Center on Age and Community, University of Wisconsin–Milwaukee for recognizing the importance of qualitative, descriptive research on aging and supporting my initial work on writing this manuscript and keeping me engaged in work with older adults. I am also grateful to Erica Bornstein, Paul Brodwin, David Moberg, and Susan McFadden for helping me talk through my ideas in ways that spurred my writing during my time in Milwaukee.

Much of my education in the anthropology of aging has come from colleagues and friends whom I have had the good fortune to get to know through the Association for Anthropology and Gerontology. I would especially like to thank Caitrin Lynch, Samantha Solimeo, Frances Norwood, and Jay Sokolovsky, all of whom donated their time and expertise to read various portions of this book at many different stages in its development. I admire their examples of clear and compelling writing on aging and culture. Other readers and listeners whom I would like to thank include Hikaru Suzuki, Jean Langford, Bambi Chapin, and Brooke Huminski. Yukiko Taniguchi helped transcribe many of the conversations that I have included in this book, and patiently sat with me on many occasions to describe the nuance of the vernacular with keen attention. I owe a tremendous thank-you to the two anonymous reviewers for taking the time to write such thoughtful, detailed, and honest responses.

The hardest decisions in writing and editing came in the final months, when it seemed more and more difficult for me to see things with fresh eyes. There are few words to describe how grateful I am to have had the chance to work with the editor of this series, Sarah Lamb, and with Marlie Wasserman, editor at Rutgers University Press, for shepherding the manuscript along, for the many close readings, and for trusting me with their vision of a new book series. My best decisions and clearest, liveliest passages in this book are all thanks to them, and it was much easier to snip out pages (or chapters) under their wise and caring guidance.

This ethnographic study was made possible by a number of grants that I would like to acknowledge here: the IIE Fulbright Graduate Student Research Grant, University of California's Pacific Rim Mini-Grant, the Melford E. Spiro Dissertation Award, and the Association of Asian Studies First Book Subvention Grant. Portions of transcripts and anecdotal material have appeared in previously published work, including "Art, Aging, and Abandonment" (Danely 2011), "Repetition and the Symbolic in Contemporary Japanese Ancestor Memorial" (Danely 2012b), and "Temporality, Spirituality, and the Life Course in an Aging Japan" (Danely 2013). Some material has also been presented at academic conferences and workshops and to other groups; all of these presentations have been essential for developing my sense of audience and keeping me aware of many perspectives and bodies of work.

Paul and Jan Stoub cooked meals, watched children, and generously lent me a place to stay, relax, and work. Paul Stoub lent his design skills to produce the map of Japan in chapter 1, and helped with last-minute formatting matters. Fenna Diephuis labored through the manuscript, and her experience in hospice kept me attuned to both healing and hardship. My parents, Richard and Rebecca Danely, have always offered love and support through the many highs and lows of early academic life. My deepest and most meaningful connection to life comes from my wife, Robin, who has patiently accompanied me since the beginning of this journey.

Aging and Loss

෫ᢙ

Introduction

The mid-July air hung, heavy and lazy, in the low bowl of the Kyoto Basin. The heat had forced a slowness on the city, but fortunately, I was nearing the end of fieldwork, and after a year and a half of interviewing older men and women about aging in Japan, I felt that I could use a break. I pedaled my bicycle through the narrow alleys of tightly packed houses enjoying the breeze. Occasionally I would recognize neighbors and acquaintances along the road and bowed while smiling and pedaling on. I caught flashes of the lilting local vernacular as I passed the open storefronts and bus stops, finally stopping in front of the tall stone staircase in front of Kyoto University of Art and Design.

I had arranged to meet there my friend Kato-san, a painter and student. Not long after we arrived in Kato-san's large shared studio space, however, Kato-san quickly introduced me to Sakaya Ono, a tall, rail-thin woman in flowing garments with large, magnetic eyes. Ono-san was the senior student in the group, and as we spoke, the other students began buzzing around the room, preparing tea and setting out some chocolates and cookies, before eventually settling down in a neat semicircle, like devotees before a guru, on the cool concrete floor. Ono-san sat on a low platform across from me and folded her legs into a half-lotus position. When I asked about her work, she brought out a folder of photographs taken of some paintings she had just completed, all portraits of her grandmother.

I had not set out that day expecting to discover something new about aging in Japan (I was deliberately trying to take a break), but there I was, notebook and pen suddenly materializing in my hands, talking about old age with a group of young art students. In Japan they might say this meeting was a matter of our *en*, an often mysterious or destined affinity and bond between individuals. En may arise as the result of encounters in past rebirths, and once established it is hard to break. En is sometimes glossed as "fate," and was sometimes used by my interviewees to explain my arrival in Kyoto, and the chance it provided them to tell their story about growing old. If en was the reason I was in Japan, listening to stories about aging, it was those stories that secured and deepened this bond as I continued to return to Kyoto, most recently for a yearlong stay in 2013–2014.

When I think about the years that had passed since my field research began in 2005, I remember all of the chance discoveries that helped me and continue to help me see aging from new perspectives. The afternoon looking at photographs of portraits of Ono-san's grandmother was one of these moments. As we looked at these photographs, I felt as if I had been looking into the eyes of the men and women whose life histories I collected for my research. Ono-san's portraits told stories—of aging, of loss, of human connection—but it was how the story was told, the process it unveiled, its unmistakably Japanese aesthetic, that made them so remarkable. In each portrait, the face of her grandmother was delicately rendered in gentle pale hues, the muted color of sand-polished seashells. This old woman in the portraits gazed back directly at the viewer, unsmiling, seemingly aware of being viewed, waiting rather than posing.

The most dramatic piece stood about one and a half meters tall, and was gilded with dozens of squares of gold leaf (cover). In the painting, Ono-san's grandmother wore the bright vermillion cap and kimono of *kanreki*, a kind of coming-of-age ceremony that marks five complete revolutions of the twelve-year zodiac cycle and a symbolic return to the point of one's birth at age sixty. The color of the fabric was so intense that the folds and wrinkles disappeared into a solid, flat block of distemper pigment. Even without the cultural clue of her dress, her age was apparent in her face; the corners of her lips and eyes sagged gently, and feathery tufts of silver white hair peeked out from underneath the cap. Her thin knees were drawn up to her chest as if sitting on the floor, bent into a small bundle of red, in almost a fetal posture.[1] On her thin, pale fingers she had wound a long string of golden thread, a symbol of en.[2] Neither slack nor taut, the thread catenated naturally between her hands, then leapt up in looping curls at the knobby joints of her fingers as if animated from within.

The gold leaf squares surrounding this older woman shone like the walls of a medieval palace or the light of the Buddha's Pure Land. There was no ground or shadow drawn onto this regal expanse of space, giving the subject a sense of lightness, as if she were suspended in luminous amber.

I asked Ono-san why she chose to paint her grandmother, and she replied matter-of-factly that she wanted to "put grandmother out into the public—to give her life." She explained to me that her grandmother was not well, that her memory was fading and she had only her daughter to care for her. After a pause, Ono-san continued, "When someone dies, the memory lives on through someone else's life, but in the case of my grandmother, we're the only ones that can understand her. After the family dies, she'll die. I wanted to memorialize her. To show that old people have some meaning."

I nodded. Then Ono-san asked me, "Do you know the word *oiru*? I think they use it more in the countryside these days, but it means something like 'becoming old and wise.' I think it's an interesting word. Maybe it only exists in Japanese?"

The word *oiru*, commonly translated simply as "aging" or "senescence," implies both a weakening body and, almost as a matter of natural course, the development of what Ono-san called "wisdom," but more specifically an inward turn to face one's personal suffering and death with detachment and grace (Takenaka 2000, 11–12). When Ono-san asked if oiru existed only in Japan, it seemed that she was speaking not merely of the social or biological process of senescence, but of a particular aesthetic quality of Japanese aging, more akin to what Japanese writer Junichirō Tanizaki called the "glow of grime" or a "polish that comes of being touched over and over again" (1977, 20). Although everyone (if fortunate) grows old in a biophysical sense, this luster of imperfection does not come naturally, but has to be painstakingly developed and cultivated by following ethical and spiritual principles (Rohlen 1978). Ono-san's painting was her way of recognizing this quality of oiru, a recognition she called "memorializing" her grandmother. The portrait of her grandmother as a woman entering old age somehow made it aesthetically appropriate to deem an object of memorial.

Memorialization of the dead is a common practice among Japanese people, but it especially evident among older adults. In Japan, memorialization of the dead can be broadly defined as practices that recognize the mutual interdependence of the living and the spirits of the dead. Typically these practices include different techniques of offering, petitioning, and visualizing deceased individuals at sites such as home altars (*butsudan*) and graves. As was the case with the portraits, memorialization functions to reimagine the object of memorial aesthetically, to re-place and re-member the spirit into the social context of the living family and community, or as Ono-san noted, to put the person out into the public life. For the bereaved, who might perform regular memorials for decades after an individual dies, this imaginative practice has a profound effect on perceptions of aging, loss, and care.

As other scholars have pointed out (e.g., Cristofovici 2009; Cruikshank 2009; Goldman 2012), an aesthetic revaluation of old age as a time of both losses and memorials, fragility and beauty, departures and returns, provides an entry point to understanding the sociocultural consequences of "hyper-aging" of contemporary Japanese society (Kojima 2000), also known as the "low-fertility, aging society problem" (*shōshikōreika shakai mondai*). To give a sense of the pace at which the Japanese population aged in the last half of the twentieth century (during the lifetimes of the older men and women I spoke with for this research), from 1970 to 1994, the percentage of the population over sixty-five doubled from 7 percent (the threshold the United Nations set for the category of an "aging society") to 14 percent ("super-aging society")—the fastest increase of any county in history. By 2013, one in four people in Japan were over the age of sixty-five, and it is estimated that by 2050, this number will reach 40 percent, with more than a quarter of the population over seventy-five (Tamiya et al. 2011). In 2013, the birthrate was well below replacement level, at 1.39 children born per woman. People in Japan also lived longer on average than in any other country; the average life expectancy was 80.85 for men and 87.71 for women (CIA 2013). As these trends continue, it becomes more and more difficult to understand Japanese society without first understanding the social and psychological dynamics of aging.

While Japan stands out as the first nation to experience this rapid demographic shift to a "super-aging society," other postindustrial and developing nations around world appear to be following a similar trend of declining birth rates and lengthening life spans. This trend is not limited to places like Northern and Western Europe, but can also be seen in places as diverse as Iran and Brazil. The Asian region is aging particularly quickly, with rates of aging in countries like Singapore, South Korea, and Thailand currently exceeding those of Japan.[3] The situation of an aging Asia is further complicated by the relatively slow adaptation of many institutions, especially those related to kinship and citizenship, such as marriage and elder care, which had developed under very different demographic circumstances. Academics and policy makers are also having to adapt, as they begin to realize that the realities of global population aging have not been fully considered by mainstream political and economic models of globalization, neoliberalism, and governmentality (Curtis 2002; Neilson 2003; 2012; Otto 2013).

One way social and political organization and institutions have begun to acknowledge this new landscape has been to push the horizon of old age further forward, stretching out midlife adult subjectivity through the use of new technologies, activities, and aspirations focused on keeping the body and mind active, healthy, and youthfully beautiful (Cole 1992; Gullette 2004; Jacoby 2011; Katz 2000; Lamb 2014). Brett Neilson has argued that this booming investment in what he calls the "immortalization of the flesh" is accompanied by the "amortization of the body," or the "social disinvestment of forms of care and welfare that address the well-being of the body" (Neilson 2012, 46). In other words, while aging societies like Japan invest a tremendous amount of resources in supporting aspirations of what is generally referred to as "successful aging" of the individual, fewer resources are dedicated to the welfare and well-being of the aging social body. Instead, policies and practices that aim to "disburden dependence" (i.e., reducing the government cost of social welfare) (Mishra 2011) focus on delaying or preventing dependence by encouraging older people to work, stay active, and bear more of the cost of long-term care themselves by choosing from a variety of care options, insurances, investments. However, measures such as these often fail to appreciate the context and conditions of aging.

To most of the older people I spoke with, longevity meant that in spite of the "promise of adulthood" and lifelong self-cultivation (Rohlen 1978), eventually they would become a burden on others. These fears are renewed through the circulation of reports of elder abuse, neglect, and homicide, often perpetrated by family members, and attributed to "caregiver exhaustion" (*kaigo tsukare*). Japan also has one of the highest suicide rates among older adults (Becker 1999; Otani

2010; Traphagan 2010; 2011), which is often tragically related to overwhelming feelings of shame and despair as caregivers feel inadequate in their abilities, and older care recipients feel ashamed of the burden placed on their loved ones. On July 9, 2013, for example, a seventy-nine-year-old man was rescued from the Sumida River in Tokyo, attempting to commit suicide after strangling his seventy-five-year-old wife in their home (MSN Sankei News 2013). The man confessed that he had killed his wife because of kaigo tsukare, and authorities suspect that it was a "double suicide pact" (*murishinchū*). Although such incidences are extreme, their circulation through conversation and gossip indicated that they reflect widely held concerns about maintaining positive relationships in old age. Traphagan, for example, recounts a conversation with an older woman in Akita prefecture who explained that in rural multigenerational households, "even if there is an image of the household as vibrant (*nigiyaka*), there are many who live in solitude (*kodoku*). This kind of solitude or isolation is part of the reason that suicide is common among the elderly" (2011, 97). Since the 1990s, dying in isolation (*kodokushi*) has become part of what David Plath called the "cultural nightmare of old age" in Japan (Plath 1982, 109), which includes increasing rates of dementia, depression, abuse, and neglect.[4]

How can this bleak image of aging exist alongside the admiration and affection toward old age that I saw in the portraits of Ono-san's grandmother? Perhaps the answer lay in the way I related to the painting, as opposed to the way I would relate to other media and statistical data. In each painting, Ono-san's grandmother was alone, her gaze directed at the viewer. The expression invited my recognition, but preserved a distance that could not be breached. She seemed both present and already beyond. These contradictory orientations toward the subject came together so beautifully and harmoniously in part because the portrait was also *memorial,* and like memorial portraits used in traditional Japanese mortuary rituals since medieval times, the image not only represented an actual woman in the world (now gone), but also was *itself* a living manifestation of her spirit (to remain) (Gerhart 2009, 137). In this way, memorial images and displays, which lay at the heart of everyday spiritual life in Japan, draw together seemingly contradictory elements and perspectives; they bridge detachment and closeness, past and future, death and life, the one who leaves and the one who returns (Schattschneider 2003). They might even bridge the beauty of old age and its moments of despair and loneliness.

Just as older adults would look at Ono-san's portraits and be able to see something of themselves in the image of her grandmother, memorials of the spirits provide intimate moments of reflection and identification that extend the self through the other, creating a space of suspense and identification. This book argues that practices of memorialization reveal the conflicts, complexity, and possibilities of aging in Japanese society today. By practicing memorialization, older adults transform experiences of loss into new connections, meanings, and hopes. Memorialization materializes through the aesthetic objects and images, like Ono-san's portrait, as well as through the rituals and practices that display and circulate those objects. In my ethnographic research I found that regardless of sectarian affiliation or formal religious involvement, most older adults performed regular memorial rituals for the spirits of the departed, and even more tellingly, that there was near universal agreement that the feelings motivating these practices were something unique to late adulthood. As older adults come to identify their feelings toward the spirits as signs of old age, they open possibilities for aesthetically restructuring and engaging with their narratives of kinship, care, and loss.

For anthropologists, this book also shows how population aging is transforming cultural meanings and social institutions, and how these transformations produce a staging ground for emergent subjectivities that blend personal narratives, embodied feelings, and aesthetic performances. This book contributes to the field of global aging studies by providing detailed accounts of older individuals' lived experiences and everyday practices, and by situating them within contemporary structural and sociodemographic conditions. Ethnographic and qualitative studies like this one may not lend themselves to broadly generalizable results, but they do aid in development of more nuanced and critical perspectives on models based primarily on data drawn from statistical and quantitative techniques. Finally, while I do delve into theoretical and philosophical discussions throughout this book, my primary goal is to faithfully convey the stories of individuals and families and the ways they adapt to everyday life in an aging Japan. These stories reveal moments of loss and hope, giving and grieving, and like memorial portraits, each one points beyond itself to another imaginative horizon of the aging experience.

PART I

Loss

CHAPTER 1

Loss, Abandonment, and Aesthetics

When I returned to Kyoto in 2013, I stepped into one of the small cafés where I often met with older men and women when I began my research eight years earlier. The proprietress, Tachibana-san, her long silver hair pulled back with a flower patterned bandana, inquired about my research as she prepared a warm cup of tea, and after chatting a bit, I asked her what she thought was most important to include in a book about aging in Japan. She set the teacup on the table in front of me and began, "Being old means first of all that, well, the people around you and that you have lived with over your life, they go away (*inaku naru*). I think that among older people that feeling of loss (*sōshitsukan*) is really important." She returned to the kitchen and changed the CD, and soon the gentle sadness of a popular ballad, "Do Not Stand at My Grave and Weep" ("Sen no Kaze ni Natte"), came drifting from the speakers. Full of loss, yet beautiful and moving, the lyrics of the song, sung from the point of view of the spirit of the deceased, comforted us with images of nature, repeating "do not stand at my grave and weep, I am not there, I have not died."

Aging and loss are not newly emergent twenty-first-century phenomena. Japanese people have been performing the stories of aging, loss, and the world beyond for centuries. In these stories, old age is not only a time of grief, mutability, and renunciation (Washburn 2011), but also a time when one may feel estranged from one's family and community, and must learn to find solace among the spirits of the dead. Phrases such as "old soul" (*oi no tamashi*; Kurihara 1986) and "at 60, one returns to the ancestors" (*rokuju de senzo ni kaeru*; Formanek 1988, 13, quoted in Young and Ikeuchi 1997, 233) suggest both a "return" to and "changing into" a spirit. Perhaps that is why Tachibana-san thought of loss and mourning as such an important part of aging, and why the song "Do Not Stand at My Grave and Weep" was so meaningful. Grave visits and other rituals of memorialization were among the most intimate ways Japanese older adults offer and express care in late life, placing a small bowl of rice on family altar (butsudan), affectionately imagining the faces of the departed, gently pouring water over their graves. This mourning that links memorial to maturity is the topic of this book.

Even these simple acts, however, were complicated by the aging of Japan's population, by political and economic changes, by new technologies and options for dying and for being remembered. Japanese social welfare policies and programs of care remain unevenly apportioned for the growing need, and while some bring their concerns to the spirits and Buddhas, others find themselves removed from an economy of care and support, feeling alone or abandoned. In Japanese stories of old age, the older person is left behind not only by those who have died, but also by the living.

While policies and demographics have changed, the ambivalence between care and abandonment of the old is not new. These stories of abandonment and loss in old age are known as *obasuteyama*, or "The Mountain of the Deserted Crone." Even today, one can go almost anywhere in Japan and find that people are familiar with the story and the central event in its plot: a son carrying his aged mother into the mountains, where he abandons her to die. Before delving into the stories of mourning and maturity in contemporary Japan, I think it is worth briefly examining obasuteyama here.

In obasuteyama, the details leading up to the old woman's abandonment, the events that transpire after she is left behind, and even the nature of the journey up the mountain can be radically different depending on the iteration. The prototypical version of obasuteyama takes place in a rural village, in the mountainous Japanese countryside. Due to ecological, sociopolitical, personal, or generational pressures (or a combination these), a family makes the decision to abandon the old woman of the house high up in the mountains.[1]

The task of delivering the woman to the mountain falls on the woman's son (sometimes at the encouragement of his wife). While many of the details in the story vary, every version includes the middle-aged son carrying his old mother on his back as he ascends a steep, thickly wooded path, the moonlight filtering through the trees. What's even more remarkable is that the old woman does not protest her abandonment. In some versions, she even breaks off small branches as they ascend, so that her son can find his way back safely. In other cases, the son's actions are socially sanctioned, but sometimes this is less clear. In many versions of the story, the old woman is able to return from the mountain, but more often she remains deserted, transforming into a stone, a mountain witch (*yamauba*), a ghostly spirit lingering forlorn in the melancholy moonlight, or perhaps an honored ancestor (Reider 2011).

What can a story like obasuteyama, and all of its iterations and reconstructions over the centuries, tell us about aging and loss in the lives of older adults in twenty-first-century Japan? Do older Japanese adults perceive themselves as "abandoned," like the woman in the story, and if so, what does abandonment mean in the context of current discourses on aging, welfare, care, and the family?

How do older adults shape their own personal experiences of loss through everyday practices such as rituals of mourning and memorialization?

First, it should be mentioned that obasuteyama is not meant as a historical record of actual practices, though abandonment or other forms of selective neglect of older adult dependents has been well documented in anthropological studies of many societies across the world (Glascock and Feinman 1981; Willerslev 2009). Obasuteyama may have come to incorporate themes from local practices of separation of older age grades to the periphery or beliefs in the mountains as places where the dead reside, but the actual situation described in obasuteyama does not to appear to have ever been historically verified for Japan (Yoshikawa 1998), nor does it fit with any patterns of gender dependence and mortality recorded during the premodern period (Cornell 1991). The story has nonetheless remained popular, acted out in numerous stage dramas and films, as well as short stories and even graphic novels (*manga*). Part of the continued interest in obasuteyama is no doubt due to this malleability and reiterability, its constant renewal and reinvention. It also continues to speak to the deep ambivalence regarding old age (Huang 2011; Kurihara 1986; Reider 2011; Skord 1989; Tsuji 1997; Washburn 2011) and the complex emotions that arise (for both the old woman and her son) when weighing the burden of care, the obligations and debts to family, the spiritual value of sacrifice (*gisei*) and yielding (*yuzuri*).

Let us consider stories of abandonment from a cultural and psychodynamic perspective. Several scholars who have looked at the genre of obasuteyama folktales, most notably Nishizawa Shigejiro's *Obasuteyama Shinkō* (1936) and Yanagita Kunio's *Obasuteyama* ([1945] 1979), suggest that obasuteyama resonates with deeply felt orientations toward aging, death, and the family in Japanese society. Evelyn Huang (2011), in an exhaustive review of research on obasuteyama stories across Asia, concludes that although many aspects of the tale may have originated outside of Japan (versions have been traced to India, China, and Korea), Japanese versions tend to concentrate on the emotional weight of the parent-child bond and the deep emotional pain of the son. From this observation, Huang wonders, "Does the tale of Obasuteyama serve as a relief tool when one faces the burden of elderly care?" In other words, the feelings generated from abandonment (including guilt and shame) may actually preserve a bond based in care, while keeping other, more destructive feelings, wishes, and fantasies (that would transform the mother into an object of hate) from erupting from the stress of continued care. The ambiguity in the fate of the abandoned mother in many Japanese versions of the story and the sense of relief felt by the son (physically and emotionally) after abandoning his mother seem to support Huang's interpretation, and yet such a conclusion remains difficult to comprehend in the contemporary context without a clearer understanding of Japanese attitudes toward aging, loss, care, and the family.

Anthropologist John W. Traphagan's (2013) interpretation of obasuteyama in Japan concentrates less on emotions and more on philosophical and ethical dimensions of elder abandonment. Traphagan's view is consistent with Huang's conclusions in that it places the act of abandonment within a Japanese aesthetic framework that values collectivity and interdependence above the desires of an autonomous individual (2013, 130–134). The care of the kin group as a whole overtakes the obligation to care for the very old. While a Western observer might be appalled at what *New York Times* film critic A. H. Weiler (1961) called "the custom, harshly implacable to Occidental eyes" of taking the old to the mountain, a Japanese audience might empathize with the pathos (*aware*) of self-sacrifice for a greater good. Traphagan's aesthetic reframing of the story echoes Ruth Benedict's ([1946] 1974, 193) observation of Japanese dramatic sensibility: "There need be no happy ending. Pity and sympathy for the self-sacrificing hero and heroine has full right of way. Their suffering is no judgment of God upon them. It shows that they have fulfilled their duty at all costs and allowed nothing—not abandonment or sickness or death—to divert them from the true path."

The "true path" comes at the cost of personal suffering; in the case of obasuteyama, the son's path to authority as household head and the responsibility for provisioning descendants comes at the cost of abandoning the elders. The old woman herself must also feel some emotional conflict, and yet she yields to her son, as if to ease his shame, or to transmit the message that her old body no longer has a place among the living. Emotional conflicts as well as connections between the aged parent and her successors emerged in my conversations with older Japanese adults; I came to see obasuteyama as a window into the thoughts and feelings of older adults still face today: fear of being a burden, wishing to yield, yet dreading abandonment, shame, hope. These thoughts and feelings, while evident among older adults across the world, are also shaped by and internalized as a unique array of cultural images, practices, and discourses with a particular social and historical heritage. The most prominent way in which Japanese culture shapes and is shaped by the experiences of older adults is through images and ritual practices for the ancestors and spirits of the family dead, which I group together as *memorialization.*

Memorialization alleviates and reconfigures the emotional costs of upholding social institutions of kinship and succession, and is worth examining in greater depth, especially as it helps us to understand the emotions and subjectivities of older Japanese adults today. The emotional tension depicted in obasuteyama bears a close resemblance to Meyer Fortes's (1967; 1976) descriptions of family relationships among the Tallensi of West Africa. Fortes observed that old age among the Tallensi generated anxiety, especially among male heirs, since in order to keep an ordered tradition of succession, "parents must die, though they cannot but resist and fear this fate, so that children may continue the life they owe to their parents, and children must replace parents though they dare not consciously wish them out of the way" (1976, 14). Fortes saw rituals and taboos associated with the ancestors as cultural mechanisms for easing this tension between generations by "submitting to the reality of the death of the parents which removes them physically, and keeping them symbolically alive and at home among the displacing offspring" (1976, 14). While there are numerous differences in social structure and ritual observance between the Tallensi and the Japanese, the general observation that underlying tensions generated by kinship structures can be symbolically reworked though memorialization offers a fruitful starting point from which to engage the perspectives and practices of older adults.

The approaches of Traphagan and Fortes underline the need to examine older adult subjectivity as a process of psychological self-formation embedded within and inseperable from social practices and political structures. Building on this approach, I argue that ritual practices for the spirits of the dead cultivate an aesthetic discernment and subjectivity that can transform abandonment, estrangement, and loss into narratives of meaning, purpose, and connection in old age. As old age increasingly becomes an object of political and cultural significance, the locus of obasuteyama expands from kin and community to the larger political-economic structures and to the representations of aging and family that they produce. Aesthetic discernment is applied here as well, as older adults find spaces of hope within uncertainty, extending the self into the past (in mourning) and the future (in memorial) (see Lambek 1996). Looking at the experience of aging in this way allows us to situate the work of the self within a social and political world, and to see how the imagination of the "other world" constitutes the lived reality of this world.

SITUATING THIS STUDY

Kyoto City, where I conducted most of my research, is located in the Kinki region of western Honshū, which includes the major urban centers of Osaka and Kobe (Figure 1). It rests in the Kyoto Basin, surrounded on the north, west, and east sides by high mountains. Locals often referred back to the tree-covered mountainsides when making conversations about the timing of the changing seasons, heaving sighs in the humid air that becomes trapped there after the rainy season has ended, or when the cold air would blow in from Mt. Hiei during the winter. The proximity of mountains also provides the city with numerous fresh waterways, including the Katsura, Kamo, and Takano rivers. On nighttime walks to the convenience store near the house I rented in northeast Kyoto, I would be serenaded by frogs (which, I was instructed, say "kero-kero" in Japanese) against a gentle, faint underfoot burbling. Little wonder, I thought, that Kyoto's inauguration as the capital of Japan began the "Period of Tranquility" (Heian Period 794–1185 CE).

Kyoto remained the official capital city of Japan until the late nineteenth century, and over its long history those same mountains and rivers that I became so fondly attached to have served as a backdrop to much of Japan's cultural and artistic life, as well as history books full of religious uprisings, civil wars, and

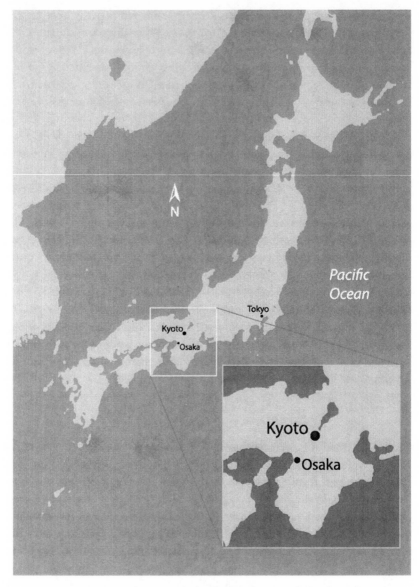

Figure 1. Map of Japan with detail of Kyoto. Image by Paul Stoub.

imperial intrigue (Dougill 2006). Kyoto was formally established as a municipality in 1898, and since then has been gradually expanding in area, incorporating more and more of the outlying towns and villages. When I began my fieldwork, the municipal boundaries stretched twenty-nine kilometers from east to west and forty-nine kilometers from north to south, encompassing an area of 827.9 square kilometers (City Planning for Kyoto City 2005, 2) that was home to

piety and respect for one's elders account for this situation (Sung 2001; Wada 1995); multigenerational coresidence becomes one kind of evidence of this value placed on old age. Of course, popular animated television programs and beloved serial comics like Sazae-san often feature these sorts of families (see Hashimoto 2009), but even influential scholars have reinforced the idea that Japanese families expect to care for the old (Benedict [1946] 1974, 254; Palmore and Maeda 1975).

This picture of aging in Japan, however, overlooks the strong role of instrumental variables such as the health status of the older person, state-sponsored financial incentives, proximity of residence, and the like, which have been found to be more predictive of residence patterns than cultural values alone (Jenike 1997; Takagi and Silverstein 2006). The relative weakness of the cultural explanation may be due in part to the fact that the popular adoption of the Japanese family ideology originates in early twentieth-century Japanese state formation, when the family registry systems and other forms of bureaucratic surveillance monitored compliance with legally mandated responsibilities including providing kin-provisioned elder care (Fridell 1973; Garon 1998; Hardacre 1989). Finally, several scholars have critically examined influential accounts of Japanese culture and the family, including the stereotype of intergenerational cohesion and respect for the elders, pointing out their alluring yet empirically weak or Orientalist biases (Koyano 1989; Kuwayama 2004; Ryang 2002). I think it would be a mistake, therefore, to assume that commonly used measures of care, such as frequency of coresidence, reflect unique or deeply internalized cultural or spiritual beliefs organically emerging from a uniform set of folk-based "traditions."

A related assumption about the place of elders in Japanese society that I sometimes hear is that forces of modernization and Westernization (such as smaller, more dispersed families, greater participation of women in the workforce, neoliberal notions of individualism, and so on) have corrupted "authentic" Japanese views of old age and once cherished household ideals. In this deculturation narrative, it is assumed that elder care in Japan will follow a trajectory similar to other postindustrial states, abandoning its multigenerational ideals and expanding institutional care for the elderly (albeit staffed by futuristic robotic helpers; see Shibata and Wada 2011; Fitzpatrick 2011).

Again, while this assumption does acknowledge the presence of cultural change, it remains predicated on an essentializing picture of Japanese culture "as it was," and overlooks the complexity of contemporary Japanese culture and globalization. Again, it is unclear how changing generational values have affected attitudes toward caring for older family members, but there are copious examples of intergenerational tension and even neglect and abuse going much farther back than the modern era, and it was only with the institution of social welfare services and other modern bureaucratic procedures that family-based elder care became a norm despite the emotional and financial cost to families. If Japan was never a genuine geriatric utopia, then it is not currently a paradise lost. Of course narratives of cultural decline do still persist, especially among older Japanese people themselves as emic means of explaining social change. They should not be ignored completely, but should be tempered by a critical examination of their underlying assumptions.

This book is not only descriptive; it also takes up some broader theoretical concepts in anthropology and social gerontology. In the remainder of this chapter I briefly introduce these concepts as guideposts for engaging with the ethnographic stories and observations that make up the bulk of the book. These concepts are (1) narrative and subjectivity, (2) cultural aesthetics, (3) loss, grief, and mourning, and (4) the economy of care. Each of these themes is elaborated on in more detail throughout the book, producing ethnographic portraits that expose overlaps, articulations, and contradictions in the lived experience of aging. After introducing these themes, I describe the context of this particular study and introduce the chapters that follow.

NARRATIVE AND SUBJECTIVITY

For social gerontologist Dan McAdams, older adults' life narratives represented "the creative, contested, and constantly evolving interplay between a storytelling agent and a complexly structured and storied world" (2005, 253). Subjectivity, then, might be described as the way agents get into the story, both by tailoring it and by becoming the subject of it. Anthropologists use the concept of subjectivity to get at the interpenetration of the psychological and the political (Biehl, Good, and Kleinman 2007; Good et al. 2008; Luhrman 2006), and narratives provide a means to examine this through ethnographic research (Mattingly 2010; 2014). Narratives represent subjectivities as interpersonal, intersubjective processes that strive to shape meanings of personal significance within a temporal framework of possible pasts, presents, and futures. This process takes time and practice, safety and support, and changes over the life course as the significance of relationships, places, and memories are reevaluated.[2]

Who (or what) is the subject in narratives of an aging Japan? In Japan, being a person means "being a nexus in a series of human interrelationships" (Becker 1999, 70). For older adults in particular, it is considered natural that over the course of their life, they would have established and cultivated relational ties (*en*) with many different people, some of whom may have passed away but remain connected as spirits (*hotoke*). Of course debts owed to the spirits of the departed and the ancestors can never be fully acknowledged, and therefore represent a perpetual process of self/other-reflection that I refer to as "memorialization." One man I met in Kyoto told me, for example, that if I was interested in the ancestors, I needed to know that the most fundamental feeling Japanese people have toward the ancestors is *mōshiwake nai*—literally, "I have no excuse." This expression is closely related with *sumanai*, usually glossed as "excuse me," but literally meaning "It never ends" (Wierzbicka 1996, 534). Indeed, for older adults, this never-ending process is a way of cultivating a subjectivity based in humility, deference, and yielding even as they reach a point in the life course where they ought to be afforded the greatest respect.

Examining aging in Japan from the perspective of narrative subjectivity allows us to see how multiple representations of the relational self-nexus, from the face in the mirror to the family gravestone, weave together and adapt to situations of loss and bereavement. Japanese customs of memorializing the spirits materialize the perpetuation of relational ties, telling a story through offerings and embodied practices, so that loss need not in itself constitute a weakening or dissolution of the self. When this narrative is disrupted, incomplete, and under-resourced, or when aging necessitates a change or transformation of former subjectivities, such as in cases of trauma or bereavement, the approach helps us to identify the ways in which actors try to restitch life's remnants and put the story together again. The process of creating a life narrative might seem artless in the sense that it does not seem to require self-conscious intention or skill, and yet I also found that older Japanese adults were constantly producing novel, artful expressions of their experience by engaging with cultural tropes such as connection and loss.

CULTURAL AESTHETICS OF AGING NARRATIVES

Socioeconomic and demographic changes especially since the 1990s have heightened anxieties about the inability to maintain ties, about becoming separated from or abandoned by others (*muen*), or about losing a sense of home or belonging (Allison 2013; Rowe 2011). Growing older in this context means facing an indeterminate but ever-approaching future as part of Japan's most vulnerable demographic, a fate of abandonment and loss that many dread.

If developing an aging self in Japan means developing a mature narrative of past and future possible selves as well as reflecting on relational bonds with both the living and the deceased, then it may appear that we've set the bar fairly high. Perhaps, for those who have lived a long and full life, there is also room for losses, separations, and grief in narratives as well. For many older Japanese adults, this feeling of abandonment and loss tied together personal narratives of aging with the larger social and political world. Hasegawa-san, a seventy-five-year-old retired civil servant whom I frequently met at the Takara Senior Community Center, for example, would often alternate back and forth between passionate critiques of the government pension system and low-key vignettes about taking his wife to a rehabilitation center or his own nerve-related health problems. For Hasegawa-san, loss of health, money, and a sense of agency were directly tied to much larger social and political losses, and confronting these losses became a source of life meaning, or what the Japanese call *ikigai*.

No matter what time of year it was, Hasegawa-san would always meet me in the same ash-gray fedora with a matching gray sport coat hanging off of his slim frame. Because he worked for the city government for most of his life,

Hasegawa-san's pension was among the best. Even still, the medical and rehabilitation bills, which have gradually risen with the increase in the older population, consume most of his income by the end of the month. Although he usually appeared anxious, his eyes darting behind tinted gold-rimmed bifocals, when he spoke, he seemed to let loose when it came to the Japanese government and its neglect of older people like him. "[Japanese] politicians always say, 'No use in watering a dead tree!'" he told me one day, spitting out the words in a hushed but rapid string and taking another quick drag on a Mild Seven cigarette. Hasegawa-san sometimes brought several copies of the pensioners association newsletter to our meetings, excitedly passing them across the table for me to read. On the back page of a one newsletter were several haiku poems written by association members including Hasegawa-san, who would usually compose these late at night when his nerves made it difficult to sleep.[3] I read one of the poems out loud:

> A lonely old man,
> The pitiless bureaucrat
> Tells me "go to hell"[4]

In its few words, it was full of atmosphere, the last line falling abruptly like the thunk of a guillotine's blade.

If understanding the experience of the aging self begins with listening to narratives, then unraveling those narratives, like haiku, depends on a sensitivity to the curve and sway of their arcs, structures, and aesthetics. Narratives and the sense of self they represent reflect cultural conventions and aesthetic modes of storytelling (Jackson 2002; McAdams 2005; Plath 1980; Traphagan 2013). The mini-narrative of the "lonely old man" in Hasegawa's poem, for example, conveys not only an ordinary act of rejection (a kind of abandonment), but also the "ugly feelings" that generate it (Ngai 2005). By conveying these in the form of a poem, however, his careful and deliberate composition creatively transforms the experience into a way to show concern and empathy (*omoiyari*) with the reader. Japanese philosopher Yuriko Saito calls this "everyday aesthetics" based chiefly on morals such as "respect, care and consideration for others, human and nonhuman" (2007, 85). Saito goes on to claim that these values are "rendered invisible" because they are so deeply integrated into daily life (2007, 85). This is as true of rituals and elders' life stories as it is for the appreciation of poetry, pottery, or the weather. Like other older Japanese people, Hasegawa-san found a way to turn his feelings of abandonment into a way to cultivate bonds (en) with fellow pensioners, and he achieved this moral aim through creative means. The poem became a means of producing an expression of care and respect, even inviting us to play with images in our mind, contemplating what will happen next.

Japanese culture has long delighted in the construction of forms and etiquette of aesthetic delicacy, based on an assumption that the natural beauty of things (people included) was revealed only through a process of cultivation and discipline, the way the meticulous snips of the bonsai artist reveal the beauty of a tree. Japanese Buddhists would assert that the tree has no permanent essence, it's "true" nature or optimal "treeness" is also artifice—it is, however, something that reveals the heart of the artist, their caring attention, their ontological interdependence with the objects and others. It takes time to master an attitude of caring attention and to be able to express that through an artistic object, ceremony, or performance.

Memorialization is another aesthetic practice that can lift individual narratives into this realm of the social, intersubjective, and interactive, relieving the seriousness behind tears in the fabric of experience—despair, dependence, abandonment—and making these feelings comforting, even beautiful. Two aesthetic qualities emerged most strongly in my interviews and observations of older adults: transience and open space (*ma*). Both are qualities of everyday aesthetics and the creative arts of personhood in Japan, and both transience and open space point to both the beauty and sadness and creativity of loss.

Transience

One way to understand what aging subjectivity means aesthetically is to look at other ways Japanese people appreciate old objects, or objects that appear old. One of my informants, a seventy-seven-year-old man who made traditional Noh theater masks explained this aesthetic as he appraised a rather cheaply made mask of an old man (*okina*) (Figure 2) that I brought to one of our interviews:

> If you put too much color on it, the age (*furusa*) will go away. You want it to look a little worn, as if you had just found it somewhere in some trunk, maybe you just opened an old trunk that belonged to your grandfather or great-grandfather and you found this old mask. If that's the kind of feeling you get from it, it's good.
>
> The masks we create today are made to look as if they are one hundred or two hundred years old, as if the darkness in the wrinkles here had been exposed to the smoke from the hearth of an old home.
>
> That's the way we have to make it—well, saying we have to makes it is a little, funny. Making it look old brings out its value.

In making his masks and training his students, this artist was not only following a pattern or form, but also creating an ambiance and intimacy that recalled a sense of something that lasts, though not as it once was, something that shows the marks of use that suggest the object was kept because it was cared for. Despite (or as a result of) the care it received, time left its marks—the deepened wrinkles, the worn tip of the nose, the faded edges. The mask maker carefully embellished each mask with these kinds of marks, and yet (in the style that recalls the Japanese sense of self-cultivation) these "lies" imbued the object with a valuable narrative of beautiful transience.

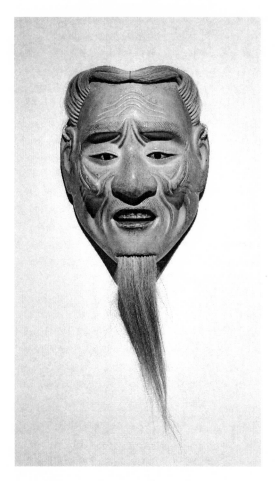

Figure 2. Noh mask of old
man (*okina*). Wikimedia
Commons, March 2011.

For Japanese people, transience, ephemerality (*hakanai*), impermanence
(*mujō*), and the beautiful fleeting nature of reality are best symbolized by the
cherry tree, which loses its blossoms quickly at the peak of their beauty. Ohnuki-
Tierney (2002) has written extensively on the ways this natural symbol of the
interdependence of life and death was incorporated in ancient Shinto and
Buddhist rituals and festivals, eventually becoming a symbol of Japanese
national identity and military sacrifice. Despite its adoption for the purposes of
the state, the cherry blossom maintained alternate and transgressive readings.
Japanese appreciation of time's passing continues to influence art and architecture (Baek 2006; Tanizaki 1977), but it can also be seen in the most causal observations of the weather and the obligatory opening remarks of friendly letters.
Saito explains, "Recognizing and appreciating the impermanent, evanescent
aspects of nature would gently assure us that nothing that exists can escape this
condition of transience" (2005, 170). How does thinking about the body, the self,

and human bonds as changing or impermanent affect the way one approaches the experience of aging?

This sense of transience, combined with the fatalistic attitude hinted at by notions such as en (destined connections) and often expressed in the phrase *shikata ga nai* ("it can't be helped" or "that's just how it is"), meant that many older people seemed well equipped to contend with the changes and transitions of old age. Although most reminisced fondly of younger days, there was typically no sense of debilitating longing, nor did there appear to be spite directed at younger generations. Instead, many older people found it meaningful to culti-vate a sense of "yielding" (yuzuri) to this passage of time, not through passive resignation, but through actions that emphasized passing on traditions and values they felt deeply identified with. Transience of the individual, then, does not disrupt the overall cultural system, but motivates its narrative continuity.

Empty Space (ma)

Despite the value given to transience, many older people did struggle with giving things up. There was a need to balance a sense of care and connection with distance and loss. This struggle, depicted in the plight of the old woman of obasuteyama and ritually embodied through acts of memorialization for the spirits of the departed, created a space of narrative suspense, placing subjectiv-ity between imagined states of abandonment and hope.

This space-time of suspense is given aesthetic meaning through the *ma* (Barthes 1982, 26; Pilgrim 1986; Vartanian and Wada 2011).[5] Ma is an empty, "neg-ative space," a pause or interstice, that accents the "positive" space of an artistic composition like a poem. It marks the beauty of incompleteness, ambiguity, and interdependence. It represents potential, anticipation, and tense waiting (Crapanzano 2004, 51–52). Religious narratives employ ma as a "way of seeing" (Pilgrim 1986, 276) that deconstructs boundaries and allows a transcendent awareness to emerge from the ordinary. One older man described this feeling of openness as the clear water when the silt has settled, in contrast to the murky water in the turbulent waters of one's youth. This man explained that he used that image because for him, aging brought a sense of distinction between the vis-ible and the invisible that had always been present, but which was impossible to discern when he was still restless earlier in his life. Another woman, in her late eighties, told me that as she became older, and the friends she grew up with died, she felt that she needed to get rid of things (*danshari*), even sentimental objects that were difficult to part with, and that by doing so, she was creating a "blue sky" (*aozora*) within herself. Emptying, giving, losing, and being among others— these were the ways ma was enacted and embodied.

It is also important to note that the Japanese word for "person" (*ningen*) is composed of the characters for "human" (*nin*) and "ma" (*gen*). Twentieth-century Japanese philosopher Watsuji Tetsuro popularized the idea that the "ma" refers not only to the spaces between people, or "being among," but also to the space within a single person existing somewhere between the individual and the social (Kalmanson 2010, 197; Pilgrim 1986, 256; Plath 1982, 118). To be human, one must learn to appreciate above all else, this empty space between and among, one's connection to others, to nature, and to the invisible world of the spirits. Ma gives meaning and value to spaces of reflection, possibility, and hope of the everyday. It was more than a metaphor for loss, but a convention that arose repeatedly during observations of rituals and in conversations with older people.

How do we recognize cultural aesthetics such as transience and openness in the everyday narratives of older Japanese adults? What can this tell us about their feelings and experiences of old age? This book takes up these questions, arguing that beauty and ugliness can be means of expressing moral values and subjectivities that might otherwise be unarticulated or unspoken. Instead, they are expressed in works of art, in popular stories like obasuteyama, in rituals of memorialization, and in other formal symbolic exchanges. The cultural aesthetics of these objects and performances preserve a sense of concern and care while acknowledging and yielding to loss.

THE CREATIVITY OF LOSS

When I began my fieldwork in 2005, I wanted to know how Japanese cultural understandings of old age, death, and the afterlife shaped the emotional and somatic experiences of grief and bereavement. As an anthropological puzzle, this would open up questions that intrigued me: What was the relationship between adult developmental psychology and cultural differences in practices and attitudes toward death and the spirits? Did Buddhism or other traditions propose a different model of the self and influence the grieving process for older adults? Do Japanese kinship and religious structures give rise to different psychological experiences of aging and loss than those found elsewhere?[6]

I soon realized, however, that if I was to tell a story about what it was like to mourn the loss of loved ones in old age, I would also have to somehow address all other losses that accompanied advanced maturity. Hasegawa-san would want to me to write about the loss of political voice he feels as a pensioner, his loss of sleep and eyesight, and the stress that came with the loss of his wife's health and mobility. Saito-san would want me to write about the loss of traditional cultural values and of community support, and the ways youth used to respect adults. Shinagawa-san would talk of being tired, of spending his days wanting to die, of his life measured in the steps back and forth to the corner store where he had nothing to buy. These stories filled my field notes, crossing over each other in ways that made it difficult to distinguish between the spiritual and the profane, the mourning for others and for the self. The losses of old age were intensified by the loss of children in the population, which left haunting traces like vacant school buildings and quiet streets. As a result of this decline in fertility, Japan's overall population is expected to decrease from 128 million in 2010 to only 87 million by 2060 (National Institute of Population and Social Security Research in Japan 2012).

Loss is certainly not the defining characteristic of aging in Japan or elsewhere (Graham and Stephenson 2010), but as the previously mentioned examples indicate, it did emerge as a frequent concern in older adults narratives about aging. Even so, it is worth taking a moment to explain why I have chosen to focus on loss in the first place.

This book approaches loss as something that is meaningful for older adults, even if those meanings might be construed as "negative" in some instances and "positive" or adaptive in others. To use a visual illustration, someone who has only ever known the daylight might view the sun's decline with fear and sadness, failing to notice the beautiful vista created by the transition into night. On the other hand, those who have some experience, who have heard the stories and who know that night becomes day once again, may view the sunset with a sense of melancholic loss and hope that can make those colors all the more vibrant. The affective and existential experience of loss is shaped by the experiential context.

Here is another example of how loss might be framed. During my research I got to know a young Japanese acupuncturist who treats many older clients living with chronic and incurable (sometimes fatal) conditions. When I asked him if treating these people was any different from treating his relatively young and healthy clients, he took out a pen and began drawing on a nearby notepad. First, he drew a large yin-yang symbol, the ubiquitous circle divided into two contrasting sectors, each with a dot of the opposite color in each sector. This represented the ideally balanced energies of the body, he explained, proceeding to draw a straight line intersecting a small portion of the circle, making it look deflated, like a flat tire. Finally, he drew an arrow pointing out from the flattened side and explained that his work was to find that spot of imbalance and to restore the wholeness of the person.

He then drew a much smaller yin-yang circle underneath and told me that it was an older person. He repeated his conceptual technique, which was exactly the same as for the younger person. He then pointed to the larger circle, saying, "The goal is not to make the older person like that." Rather, the goal was to work within the boundaries of the body's diminished state. Pain and illness would persist, but as a healer his goal was to "restore that person to *their* optimal condition." This example shows how losses *and* well-being might exist simultaneously in folk models of the "mindful body" (Lock 1982; Scheper-Hughes and Lock 1987).

While these metaphors interfere with the idea that loss in old age can mean only negative decline, I do think it important to acknowledge that loss and abandonment are not all about beautiful sunsets either. Many respondents expressed anxiety and stress from feeling like a burden on others and experiencing loss of independence in old age. In some cases, dependence was at the root of serious tensions in the family. Also troubling was the way Japanese government rhetoric of the indomitable "Japanese spirit" of filial piety or community aid was used to justify inadequate support and resources for older people, perpetuating conditions of loss. This rhetoric shifts of the burden of care away from the state, and onto families, local communities, and older individuals themselves (as if there was not already enough tension between workers and retirees in Japan's aging society). I will elaborate on this kind of loss later in this book, but for now it is worthy to note that some of the losses being produced or shifted in postindustrial Japan involve power dynamics that call for more than a politics of mourning.

Feelings of loss are expressed and transformed through rituals of memorialization. Survey data and social science research in Japan over the past century have consistently recognized not only that frequency of memorializing the spirits of the dead at graves and altars increases with age (which might be attributed to relational proximity to the deceased), but also, more important, that for older adults memorialization often constitutes a strong sense of purpose in life, or *ikigai* (Inoue 2004; Roemer 2012), and may even mediate many geriatric health risks (Imamura 2009). The primary focus on private, personal connections with the dead may partially account for the fact that older adults participate less frequently in organized religious behavior than younger cohorts (Krause et al. 2010; Imamura 2009, 32–34), though this may also be attributed to a shift in expectations as adult children take on more of these tasks and a decline in mobility that can make it difficult to attend services outside the home.

Memorialization rituals are part of aging narratives, revealing both the structure of loss and its creativity. Adding personal touches and unique twists on traditional rituals is the norm rather than the exception for older people, and shows their creativity, agency, and narrative connection to Japanese cultural aesthetics. These personal touches usually come in the form and frequency of offerings for the spirits of the deceased (hotoke). *Kuyō* (making a symbolic sacrifice) performs loss in order to transform it (into mourning/memorial), and thus follows the logic of exchange. The spirit then gives a sense of confirmation through feelings of peacefulness (*yasuragi*), security (*anshin*), and composure (*ochitsuki*). These exchanges are embedded within and echo through other economies of care that are important to older adults, such as kinship, welfare systems, and community groups.

ECONOMIES OF CARE AND SPIRITS OF THE DEPARTED

Several anthropologists and social gerontologists have found that older adults experience and manage loss within a larger context of cultural practices and institutions of exchange (e.g., Dannefer 2003; Guyer and Salami 2013; Hendricks 2003; O'Rand 1996; Tulle-Winton 1999). The position of aging individuals within the economy and their access to networks of people and resources shift over the life course, expanding or contracting, accumulating or dispersing. The losses and gains, risks and hopes, debts and obligations of aging are not merely discursive metaphors, but also material and affective realities of an "economy of care."

The term "economy of care" has been used to describe informal economies and unpaid work dominated by women who look after children and the elderly and whose labor is often rendered invisible to standard economic analysis (Razavi 2007). Others who have studied caregiving have recognized the ways in which kin-based and other informal, nonrationalized systems of reciprocal care intersect with and confound humanitarian-, market-, or state-based systems (Han 2011; Livingston 2007; Ticktin 2011), giving rise to new possible selves as care is sought via claims to biosocialities and citizenships (Rose 2007; Petryna 2002). Anthropologists are also finding this analysis useful for describing the complexity of increasingly global economies of care, which may involve additional layers of immigration, ethnicity, generational relationships, and interaction with new technologies of care (Drusini 2006; Lamb 2009; Lynch and Danely 2013; Oliver 2008; Pols 2012; Twigg 2000; Wentzell 2013).

In anthropology, informal economies are central to understanding social practices on the ground, since exchange relationships are always loaded with symbolic meanings that cut across social domains. Puzzling out an economic system requires moving across cultural schemas, from basic understandings of space and time to more complex metaphysical meaning systems (Hart, Laville, and Cattani 2010). Gift exchange relationships, a particular favorite among anthropologists, are the aesthetic bread and butter of the Japanese economy of care. Reciprocating a gift in an appropriate way also functions to keep relationships stable and organized, opening up possibilities for deeper investment and interest. The giver's attention to the aesthetic details, expressed in the symbol-rich world of the gift's packaging, the brand logos, and the sensitivity to context (status, season, gender, tastes), allows the recipient to feel a degree of unspoken trust and to reciprocate appropriately (Hendry 1995). Givers and receivers together orchestrate a symphony of sentiments in which the value of the gift is measured in the way it conveys feelings (*kimochi* or *kokoro*) of the giver toward the recipient.

Keeping up with exchange relationships and obligations in an economy of care can be taxing. These rituals inscribe debts and obligations, gratitude and humility, into the ledger of the life course, but they do not end there. Gift exchanges continue with the spirits, who continue to perform their personhood and social presence in the home. Whenever I visited the home of an interviewee, my small gift of sweets would be deftly relieved from my hands, and placed on or near the butsudan. This would announce my arrival, and include the dead in our business. In the context of the home, the spirits and ancestors mediated our transactions in the economy of care, transforming the value of the gift by placing it into a more expansive system of past and future, morals and aesthetics.

I was impressed with the skill with which most older adults I knew were able to keep up with the perpetual work of both gift giving and offerings to the spirits. Different individuals had different skills, but the women were clearly more adept and perhaps took more joy in the act of giving and receiving than did the men. Both women and men expressed a sense of unease, however, about how much longer they would be able to keep this up. They expressed fears of frailty and memory loss that would separate them from the economy of care, making them either a burden to someone else or isolated and alone. Japanese people today who live to sixty-five can expect to live about fifteen to twenty additional years (18.89 for men and 23.82 for women; MHLW 2012), around three of which are likely to involve some chronic physical or cognitive impairment that necessitates care. As one ages into one's eighties and nineties, however, the percentage of active life remaining decreases dramatically. Of course such calculations, sensitive as they are to various health and living conditions, are not able to capture the full breadth of care that older adults, and to some extent Japanese people of any age, need to feel a sense of well-being.

My observations on the importance of economies of care in the domestic sphere are consistent with those of other anthropologists who have written on the subject in recent years (e.g., Hashimoto 1996; Jenike 1997; Jenike and Traphagan 2009; Long and Harris 1997). In short, the various kinds of care that circulate among older adults, their peers, their relatives, and the spirits of the dead creates bonds of debt, gratitude, and trust that follow cultural scripts of interdependence and mutuality, which are often contested, manipulated, or negotiated depending on the context (Jenike and Traphagan 2009, 244). Most of the older people I interviewed had regular contact with adult children and relatives, and for the "young-old" (those sixty-five to eighty-five) participation in leisure groups, volunteer associations, work, and religious organizations all afforded ample opportunities to invest in economies of care. Most of those over eighty-five were in the process of withdrawing from participation in these groups, and were showing signs of greater fatigue or physical frailty. However, even when the body had slowed and public social participation dwindled, the economy of care was maintained through small acts of concern and thoughtfulness and requests for help in fulfilling the footwork of gift obligations. For older adults, the least burdensome and most satisfying form of regular participation in the domestic economy of care was conducting rituals for the spirits of the family dead.

MOURNING AND MEMORIALIZATION: DEBT, CHANGE, AND RETURNS

In 2010, there were nearly 1.2 million deaths in Japan (excluding fetal deaths), the largest number deaths since World War II, and over 113,216 more than the previous year. An average of 23,000 more people have died each year in Japan between 2000 and 2010 (Kelly 2011), and the rate is expected to grow over the first half of the twenty-first century. If shōshikōrei shakai (low fertility aging society) was the key word for the 1990s and 2000s, it is already beginning to be overshadowed by the new problem of the *tashishakai* (mass death society) (*Yomiuri Shinbun* 2014). Billboard advertisements for ceremonial halls and funeral services were common sights on train platforms and shopping areas, and despite some reservations on the part of residents living nearby, modern ceremonial halls meant to accommodate an increasing variety of mortuary options have been cropping up throughout Kyoto. Mail advertisements offer a variety of services for internment and mortuary rites for all tastes and price ranges. The business of death is booming.

While the business side of death is readily visible, the rituals that accompany death tend to be much more reserved, private affairs. Rituals of mourning and commemoration appear in human societies across the world, and constitute, perhaps, one of the first indications of our cognitive capacity for advanced symbolic thinking, intersubjectivity, and imagination of supernatural beings and worlds. But rituals are inevitably bound up in other social structures of kinship, succession, inheritance, religion, and narrative conventions, symbols, and performances. It is not surprising then that an overlap has developed within ritual life that links the inner emotional world of grief, uncertainty, and abandonment with the circulation of loss, renewal, and endurance that binds actors and institutions to a larger meaningful worldview (Battaglia 1990; Conklin 2001; Hertz 1960; Hollan and Wellenkamp 1994; Metcalf and Huntington 1991; Leavitt 1995; Robben 2004; Rosaldo 1983; Scheper-Hughes 1993; Stasch 2009; Straight 2006; Wikan 1990). Looking at rituals of death and memorialization practiced by older adults in Japan reveals some of the ways these links are made in the context of population aging, or how bereaved individuals blend their inner narrative of loss with other social narratives.

Before looking at the particulars of memorial rituals for older adults in contemporary urban Japan, we need some basic scaffolding on which to hang the ethnographic descriptions appearing later in the book.[7] There is considerable household and regional variation in memorialization practices in Japan today, and although this diversity is fascinating and revealing, it cannot be given the space it deserves for a thorough review in this book. Instead, I will focus on the rhythm of rituals used to mark relationships of exchange between the living and the dead most relevant to my informants, and the ways this rhythm developed a sensitivity to qualities of transience, openness, and ongoing connections. Ritual practices for the dead followed an imagined economy of care, in which memories and feelings were aligned with debts, offerings, and the return of protection and care.

Japanese mortuary rituals today are most commonly conducted in a Buddhist fashion, which has adapted and integrated other elements of Japanese culture over the centuries, including local traditions and folk beliefs concerning the fate of the spirit (*tamashi*). Japanese Buddhism, like that found in China and Korea, is Mahayana, emphasizing the role of saint-like bodhisattvas whose compassion and wisdom provide the key to salvation without the necessity of numerous cycles of rebirth and merit accumulation more typical in Theravadan Buddhist cultures such as Sri Lanka or Thailand. The resulting blend of folk beliefs, like ancestor veneration, and Mahayana Buddhism is a system where the spirits of the deceased are referred to as "buddhas" (hotoke), but also depend upon rituals of memorialization performed by the living. Aided and comforted by the intercessory acts of descendants and bodhisattvas, the dead proceed to the status of an honored ancestor, or their spirit may return or be reborn. This seeming contradiction is not troubling to the majority of Japanese people, however, who are content to accept that the world beyond is mysterious but surely works out somehow as long as the living do their part to offer respect and gratitude.

Whether one believes in ascent to ancestorhood or rebirth, no one denies that failure to perform the appropriate mortuary rituals risks dangerous consequences for the family. Mourning families observe taboos associated with Shinto-based beliefs about death pollution, such as covering their household Shinto shrines (kamidana), avoiding passing under Shinto gates, not accepting New Year greetings cards, and so on. A Buddhist priest chants sutras and the body is cleaned, dressed, and prepared for its journey into the other world. After the wake and funeral service are completed, the corpse is usually cremated, and the remains (pieces of remaining bone picked out of the ashes by the family after cremation) are kept on a special temporary altar for the newly departed for a period of at least forty-nine days. These remains are eventually moved to a shared household grave where the remains of others have been interred.

As the taboos related to death suggest, the individual spirits of the departed are considered potentially dangerous and require pacification and consolation (Kalland 1991; Smith 1974). This process begins with funerary ceremonies and continues for forty-nine days (ceremonies held every week for seven weeks). On the occasion of the forty-ninth day, the departed is given a posthumous ordination name (kaimyō) and referred to as a "buddha" or hotoke. The living continue to help the hotoke on its long transition from this world (kono yo) to the next (ano yo), just as a parishioner is expected to make offerings to wandering monks or pilgrims. Offerings are made through regular memorial services for the spirit (hōyō), which are conducted on death anniversaries spaced out in periodic intervals (forty-nine days, and one, three, seven, twenty-two, thirty-three, and sometimes fifty years). In addition, the bereaved make regular offerings (kuyō), either at the family grave or at a Buddhist altar inside the house (butsudan). Aside from the grave, the domestic altar, where memorial tablets (ihai) for the deceased are kept, is considered the best place to see and speak with the hotoke. Many older adults conducted such simple rituals daily, adding special decorations or embellishments when memorial gatherings were made throughout the year on death anniversaries and holidays (spring and autumn equinox, summer Obon holiday, and the New Year holiday) (Hamabata 1990).

Eventually, the hotoke merges with the communal body of ancestors and/or deities and the individual's ihai is sometimes ceremonially discarded or placed farther back in the butsudan. Consistent with the value of transience, the individual identities and memories of the dead are gradually reduced to those who knew the deceased person. Transience of the individual is subsumed by the household group, but until then memorials facilitate ways to keep that person alive in the sense that he or she retains a social function, memories and stories of the bereaved are circulated. When I asked one couple I often visited why they observed memorial services at the home or altar, they replied,

NAKAMURA: Well, that's—
EMIKO: [calling from the other room] THE ANCESTORS!
NAKAMURA: —Well, the ancestors, paying respects to the ancestors is, how can I say, it's like a requiem (ekō).[8] Well I guess then what is a requiem? [wife laughs]
DANELY: Requiem?
NAKAMURA: It's called a requiem, it's written [in Japanese characters] like "time"—one time, two times like that. Then "to face" It's read together as "ekō." Well, I guess you might say that it's turning back to face the ancestors (furikaeru).
EMIKO: REMEMBERING THEM!
NAKAMURA: Remembering them.
EMIKO: [entering the room and coming up to the table] It's like all kinds of things—
NAKAMURA: All kinds of things.
EMIKO: Sentimental stories of the two of you, things like that.

Circulating sentiments perpetuates the bond of memory between the living and the dead, and with each turning back to face the departed, there is a sense of seeing one's own future as well, and the Nakamuras and others often wondered about what would happen to them after they died. Would they be remembered or cared for? Would they have a place at the altar and in the household grave? Ideally, the economy of care would perpetuate this flow of memory and affect, but for older adults who are concerned about weakening family bonds, those feelings and values of debt and reciprocity are more uncertain.

Repaying debts through memorials and offerings was a chance to be creative with care, to lighten the burden and seriousness through rituals. While the individuals in this book sometimes referred to their "ancestors" or "generations stretching back," the economy of care that required the most investment and included the deepest feelings of debt was the regular informal practices of connecting with the hotoke. The most common response to the question "Why do you take care of the spirits?" was simply "If it wasn't for them, I wouldn't be here!" Through petitions, prayers, and "conversations" with the hotoke, the spirit was invited to remain socially engaged in household affairs and asked to watch

over (*mimamoru*) the living individuals. Memorial offerings were usually simple
and small: tea or water and cooked rice, set beside candles, flowers, and incense.
One female informant described setting out these small offerings as "similar to
playing house," mostly since the bowls and cups were like delicate miniatures of
ordinary table settings, but also because it was a chance to play at caring, imagining the invisible guests enjoying the beauty of the arrangements. During holidays and memorial anniversaries or when the hotoke was recently departed, the
offerings were more personalized (one altar I saw included the deceased man's
glasses and daily newspaper) or elaborate, with special seasonal or ceremonial
offerings (Hamabata 1990; Rowe 2011; Smith 1974; Traphagan 2004).

Given the linked economies of the old and the dead in Japan, it is not
surprising to see considerable transformations in attitudes and observances of
Japanese mortuary customs and rituals of care over the past century. These
changes reflect the influence of both political policies and ideological discourses as well as sociodemographics, cultural diversity, and ongoing idiosyn-
cratic and creative innovations and adaptations. The case studies I present in
this book offer a sense of the symbols, beliefs, and traditions that older adults
reflect on as they bring their personal circumstances and experiences to their
rituals.

This Book

Like the obasuteyama story, rituals and images of memorialization are meaningful to older adults because they resonate with fears and hopes of growing
older, providing a sense of narrative coherence amid a background of intergenerational discord and alarmist public discourse. Obasuteyama places feelings
and tensions still present today into a narrative and aesthetic context of Japanese
cultural conventions, yet appreciating this depends on understanding some
basic conceptual frameworks around themes such as loss, dependence,
abandonment, and hope. I have argued that these themes, like recurring motifs
in a musical score, weave through each other in the experience of feelings and
practices, such as memorialization, creating narratives and rituals that are
personally and socially meaningful to older adults.

Having briefly introduced the key concepts, chapters 2 to 8 focus on
ethnographic observations and interviews I conducted during my fieldwork on
several occasions in Kyoto, Japan, most recently in 2013–2014. Brief returns to
Mt. Obasute will be interspersed within the ethnographic accounts of individuals'
narratives, comprising life histories, ethnographic interviews, and observations
of rituals. Chapter 2 presents some of the ways grief and loss manifests in the
lives of older adults in Japan. These include experiences of bereavement;
estrangement and dependence in the family; declining health, independence,
and mobility; weakening bonds of community and tradition; and anticipatory

losses of frailty, senility, and death. This chapter also introduces the ways older adults inhabit these losses in personally meaningful ways, through activities, social engagement, rituals, and holding on to cherished objects. These narratives of loss and creativity are placed in the context of the Japanese social welfare and insurance system for older adults.

Chapters 3 and 4 introduce the 1983 Toei Films production of obasuteyama, *The Ballad of Narayama* (*Narayama Bushikō*), which raises questions about the connections among old age, kinship dynamics, and the cultural significance of natural and spiritual worldviews. These chapters describe the spatial and temporal landscapes of older adult narratives. Everyday sites of mourning and memorial, such as the butsudan, the graves, and the mountains, also have their own time, marked by transience, openness, and cyclicality. By attending to the natural rhythms of the body, the environment, and the ritual calendar, older individuals develop a new aesthetic discernment and narrative subjectivity. This sense of aging subjectivity shapes interactions within the family and in other economies of care, sometimes coming into conflict with contemporary conditions and chronotopes of the present-day aging society and changing patterns of kinship and care.

Chapter 5 examines the ways older adults' narratives are constructed through intersubjective and intergenerational practices. Here again, the economy of care and the relational bonds that are cultivated through exchange come to the forefront. Older adults' narratives are not only internal, produced in response to experiences of loss, but also expressed and circulated through practices of concern (Traphagan 2004). While this illustrates the ways in which mourning generates opportunities for creativity and agency, competing narratives and unstable bonds sometimes threaten the social meaningfulness of narrative practices.

Chapters 6 and 7 focus on abandonment, which I argue represents the social death that results from estrangement from the economy of care. The graphic short story *Abandon the Old in Tokyo* (1970) is an appropriately bleak and troubled version of obasuteyama to introduce these chapters. Older adults are constantly made aware of the threat of isolation and abandonment through mass media reports and gossip. Chapter 6 shows that the conditions that give rise to a logic of abandonment are tied to cultural attitudes and political structuring of care. Feelings of being discarded and abandoned (by one's family, by society, by the younger generation) are again reproduced in projections of the ancestors. Chapter 7 looks at how the social and political precariousness of the invisible or unrecognized older person is psychodynamically represented in the ways older adults perceive the invisible presence of the spirits and the visual reappearance in dreams, visions, and other communications with the other world.

Anthropologists sometimes examine variations of multiple iterations of a single myth in order to demonstrate both the repetition and creativity of cultural attitudes evident in other forms of social organization and institutions.

In this regard, obasuteyama might be considered a myth, a living piece of the cultural world of older adults in contemporary Japan. This book is about how narratives bring in additional pieces, layering in a collage of meanings, memories, and feelings, in ways that give rise to subjectivity. By focusing on memorialization, it becomes clear that subjectivity is intersubjective, produced through interactions with others and with possible selves, past, present, and future. As narratives about the spirits of the deceased come to resemble the personal narratives of aging, values such as transience and openness become embodied, making it impossible to separate the hopes and fears of the future from the recollections of the past. In the midst of this process, many older adults find themselves in a state of suspense, looking for narrative anchors—kinship, community, religion—many of which can be found in practices of memorialization. By detailing the lived experiences of older adults, this book addresses the need for descriptive, person-centered studies of aging in Japan (Wilińska and Anbäcken 2013) and offers a chance for a critical examination of discourses on the Japanese "aging society crisis" in light of existential and cultural context.

CHAPTER 2

The Weight of Loss

EXPERIENCING AGING AND GRIEF

When I first read Atsumori Zeami's (1363–1443) Noh drama *Obasute* (ca. early fifteenth century), I tried to imagine watching it as it must have been first performed, the ethereal movements of the actors, gliding across the stage silently to the otherworldly intonations of the storyteller musicians. Zeami is considered one of the founders of classic Noh style (Komparu 2005), and his works (including their precise aesthetic details) form a canon respected by artists still today. In the summer, when the spirits of the dead are particularly near and children "keep cool" by listening to ghost stories, Noh performances are held outdoors, the torchlight casting uncanny shadows that give a sensual life to the stiff wooden masks. The stage set, movements, costumes, masks, and music of Noh are all highly stylized to express the height of Japanese aesthetic refinement; it is theater that represents the world but does not imitate it, enveloping the audience in a "dreamlike atmosphere" (*yūgen*) particularly suited for Buddhist exegesis on transcending the illusion of the world.

The structure of the script for *Obasute* as translated by Donald Keene (1970) is as follows:

1. Two travelers arrive at Mt. Obasute, a place famed for its beautiful view of the full moon, and encounter a strange old woman.
2. The travelers meet a villager who confirms that the woman was the ghost of Obasute, abandoned by her son at the demand of his wife. The villager advises the traveler to make an offering for her peace.
3. The traveler returns to the mountain to write poetry with companions, and meets the old woman again (now clearly a ghost). The two greet politely, their stories mingle.
4. The moonlight inspires the old woman to sing of the Buddha's salvation as she dances.

5. Her dance reminds her of her youth, her loss, and the shame of old age.
6. The traveler returns at dawn, the ghost is left on the mountain, dramatically
   frozen.

As is apparent from this outline, Zeami's script focuses not on the bereaved son
of the folktale, but on the abandoned old woman herself—her desires, her suffering, and her hope for salvation. Read from a Buddhist perspective, *Obasute*
represents the perpetual suffering caused by desire in old age, an abandonment
produced by her inability to see the phenomenal world as an illusion and accept
transition to the next world. In a psychoanalytically interesting detail, this desire
is even painful and shameful to speak:

> OLD WOMAN: Obasute Mountain of the Deserted Crone.
> CHORUS: (for the old woman) Even to pronounce the name—How
>   shameful!
>> Long ago I was abandoned here.
>> Alone on this mountainside
>> I dwell, and every year
>> In the bright full mid-autumn moon
>> I try to clear away
>> The dark confusion of my heart's attachment
>
> (Keene 1970, 121)

When the young traveler and old woman/ghost meet each other again she
appears to merge her story to his, her shame giving way to nostalgic reminiscence about reveling with friends:

> GHOST: Why do you speak of dreams?
>   That aged figure who came to you by twilight
>   In shame has come again.
> TRAVELLER: What need have you for apologies?
>   This place, as everybody knows is called
>   Obasute—
> GHOST: Mountain where an old had dwells.
> TRAVELLER: The past returns,
>   An autumn night . . .
> GHOST: Friends had gathered
>   To share the moon together
>   Grass on the ground was our cushion
> TRAVELLER: Waking, sleeping, among flowers,
>   The dew clinging to our sleeves.
> TOGETHER: So many varied friends
>   **Reveling in the moonlight . . .**
>   **When did we first come together?**
>   **Unreal—like a dream.**
>
> (Keene 1970, 124)

The vocal merger of protagonist with the old woman blends their desires, but while she suffers in the visible yet intangible presence as an old woman/ghost, the traveler appears still lost in the dream. Does he not realize that he too will face old age? Just as the old woman cannot speak the name of her abandonment without shame, she cannot bear the autumn moonlight that exposes her. In shame, she tries to find solace in memories of the past:

> GHOST: Best I speak not, think not,
>   But in these grasses of remembrance
>   Delight in flowers, steep my heart in the moon.
>
>   (Keene 1970, 125)

Her dance and her memories crescendo, becoming more bizarre and dreamlike, her voice alternating with the chorus:

> CHORUS: Fleeting as the dew indeed . . .
>   Why should I have come here?
>   A butterfly at play . . .
> GHOST: Fluttering . . .
>   Dancing sleeves . . .
> CHORUS: Over and return, over and . . .
> GHOST: . . . Return, return
>   Autumn of long ago.
> CHORUS: My heart is bound by memories,
>   Unshakable delusions.
>
>   . . .
>
>   [the traveler leaves]
>   Abandoned again as long ago
>   And once again all that remains—
>   Desolate forsaken crag,
>   Mountain of the Deserted Crone.
>
>   (Keene 1970, 126–127)

At the finale of Zeami's drama, the ghost of the old woman raises her arms and freezes, quiet as a stone. This is the *ma*, or "the stillness that anticipates" (Crapanzano 2004, 52). In this space, we are asked to reflect, to let the story impress upon our hearts. How do we "ache with longing for the past" (2004, 126)? Is there an end to the endless cycle of memory's fade and return? An end to desire, or only repetition? Is there hope in old age?

The beauty in the narrative is in its open-endedness that leads to other iterations and to a more intimate subjective engagement. This is not to say, however, that we are unable to bring in some interpretive tools to begin to understand the tale's thematic significance. Abandonment of the mother, for example, is critical to this story, as are themes of dark and light, and visibility and invisibility. The old woman's transformation into a ghost and her doubled voice in the chorus makes her presence strange and unstable, fading in and out of the world. This instability of the self is rooted in her longing and youthful desires that keep her suspended between worlds, abandoned, yet with a glimpse of fleeting hope. Zeami's script does not dwell on the sins of the family that abandoned the old woman, but points instead to the failures of the old woman's aged subjectivity, a failure to mourn what has been lost.

The lives and experiences of older adults in contemporary Japan continue to reflect the themes of Zeami's play six centuries later. Themes of loss, shame, dependence, fear of abandonment, and hope for transcendence continue to shape the everyday lives of Japan's older adults. These themes intertwine and erupt in families, peer groups, and interactions with health and welfare institutions. They also shape the ways older adults experience grief and practice memorialization. Like the old woman of Obasute, all of the men and women I introduce in this chapter face challenges because of their age and because they live in a certain time and cultural milieu. All of them attend to these obstacles with a certain aesthetic touch, creating spaces for hope in the narrative of aging through everyday practices of care.

Out with the Old: Mori Kyoko

"There's no way that the kami are going to come to *this* house because it is so dirty!"

Haruka-san glared, indicating her mother's small dusty kamidana, the wooden household shrine dedicated to the Shinto deities (*kami*). The shrine sat sadly neglected on top of an old china cabinet bursting with dust-covered bowls, teacups, and saucers of all sizes.

Haruka-san, who lived with her husband in a town close to Osaka, was forty-two and the eldest of Mori Kimiko's three daughters. She had come to help her mother with the move, and when I arrived at Mori-san's house that morning she and her younger sister, Naoko-san, were busy maneuvering several heavy wooden bureaus through narrow paths cleared between heaping piles of half-packed belongings. As the two sisters worked, Mori-san paced the tatami floor restlessly, moving small objects from one pile to another and mumbling half to herself.

Seeing her mother pace this way annoyed Haruka-san, who again dropped the cabinet she was carrying with a thud, and began shouting again: "I don't know why you have to keep all this garbage!" she called out, exasperated. "You can't take it with you when you die! A person should have fewer things so that they can appreciate them more!"

Mori-san walked away and began preparing some tea for me in the adjacent kitchen, and when she returned to the room, she looked to me, saying, "Young people think that everything they say is right. But it isn't all the time." At this, Haruka-san rolled her eyes, responding coolly, "The only suitcase you take with you when you die is your body! Oh I don't want to become a filthy old lady like

YOU!" She lifted the cabinet again, signaling to her sister to keep moving it out-side, and the two left.

Mori-san set out a cup of tea for me, looking down at the table while trying to laugh at the scene that just occurred in front of us. Mori-san was seventy-nine years old, demure and polite, but often appearing nervous or uneasy. Her speech was often peppered with a kind of soft girlish giggling, often followed by a long flow of questions and commentaries, as if she was afraid to pause. Although her hair and clothes were usually quite composed, on this cool day in October she looked worn down; the barrage of abuse from her daughter seemed to diminish her composure even more. As I drank my tea, Mori-san sat across the table from me, stooped over, and pulled her sweater tighter around herself. When I asked about her health, she just replied "I'm an old woman (*obā-san*) now," sounding quietly resigned, as if there was little more to say.

From early spring of 2005 through the winter months, Mori-san was busy with the process of moving from her old townhouse, or *machiya*,[1] to a newer and larger house owned by her son-in-law. Mori-san had told me that she had considered living separately from her daughter, but she quickly dismissed the possibility, mainly because she had few financial and practical resources to make such an arrangement feasible. Tensions between Mori-san and her daughters were amplified by Mori-san's reluctance to dispose of her numerous belongings accumulated throughout the sixty years she had lived there.

Despite the tremendous amount of things that she had collected, and the con-stant fights with her daughters, Mori-san staunchly refused to hire a moving com-pany. Her reason for this was that she believed that strangers would throw away things that were important to her, thinking that it was all garbage. Sentimental objects were difficult for many older adults to discard, recalling the animistic world-view reflected in everything from Shinto ceremonies for discarded sewing needles (Kamiya 2006) to the intimate virtuality of popular toys (Allison 2006). Undertak-ing this move as an older woman seemed to destabilize not only Mori-san's rela-tionship with her daughters, but also the relationship to her belongings, the ways in which she relied on their material and emotional presence to ground her nar-rative identity. While many older people keep a few treasured heirlooms as tokens of the economy of care, Mori-san saved everything as a vital part of her story.

I spent several weeks with Mori-san and the various friends, neighbors, and relatives who offered to lend her a hand. The task was indeed exhausting. Dur-ing the moving process, Mori-san insisted on personally examining each object herself before it was boxed, and even then would repeatedly insist that boxes be reopened and reexamined. Several times I was left speechless as I watched her unceremoniously dumping out plastic trash bags that had been filled over the course of hours in the middle of the floor with an almost frantic need to recon-firm their contents. This kind of behavior made the move a long and tedious process for everyone, and Mori-san herself would often stay awake packing well past midnight, resuming again at dawn.

As the months wore on, I began to worry, and started tracking Mori-san's complaints about her health. On several different occasions she expressed symptoms of anxiety, insomnia, colds, swelling around her face and limbs, joint and muscle pain, chronic cough, and fatigue. She also seemed depressed. She complained of lack of appetite, weight loss, and being in constant pain throughout her body. As she drifted through the house in this weakened state, I could see how the move was aging her. The floors of the house became covered with bags and boxes overflowing with various remnants, unclear what was to be kept and what was to be discarded. A pile of dirty dishes filled the sink and spilled out onto the floor. When I visited Mori-san's house, in the winter, it was dark and drafty, but the blanket of objects, more haphazard than ever, seemed to guard against any open space, as if guarding against loss itself.

This was the house where Mori-san raised her daughters, and where her second daughter, Naoko-san, lived together with her. Naoko-san's reactions to her mother's behavior were only slightly more subdued than her older sister's (the neighbors' nickname for Haruka-san was *kii kii nē-san*, or "shrieking elder sister"). Arguments were still a daily occurrence. Naoko-san told me that she looked forward to moving away from the small, cramped home in Kyoto to a larger house where she would finally be able to keep things neat and comfortable and have more privacy for herself.

For Mori-san, however, the old house was more than just a home. It was what gerontologist Phillip Stafford called a "crucible for meaning" (2009, 447), a place where memories were embodied and where she sheltered her conspicuous hoard and now attempted to mourn its loss on each day of her move. Like the old woman of Obasute, however, Mori-san's nostalgic attachments seemed to deny the transience that could allow her to move forward. When Mori-san and I sat at her dining table, anticipating these difficulties as the move began, she expressed the feeling of abandonment and neglect that came from her daughters' repeated attempts to help:

> I still have things left to do. Even when I look around here, there's the organizing, putting things in order. [My daughter is] starting to say, "Mom, what are you going to do with so much stuff?" She asks me to simply throw it out—throw it out like regular trash. That's why things right now are so terrible . . . .
>
> My own daughter would just throw out her own parents' things, *her parents—simply throw them out.* . . . Well I don't know what to say about all that. I'm in trouble! [laughs] Well it's not like any of this stuff is really worth anything, is just that, well, they hold memories [for me] . . .

Mori-san was in a perpetual state of reminiscence and mourning over the loss of her sentimental objects, and the fact that this sentiment found no sympathy from her children only added to her emotional turmoil. For Mori-san, there was little difference between throwing away someone's possessions and throwing away that person: "Simply throw them out."

THE WEIGHT OF LOSS

The mountain of belongings may have been Mori-san's obasuteyama, a place that held beauty for her, but that drew disgust and pity from her children. Mori-san's narrative of abandonment could not be understood by her daughter, who saw this move as an opportunity to leave the mountain behind, to reinvest in their relationship, and to continue to care for her mother by giving her a better life. But for Mori-san, this move was a pivotal moment; it was the moment when grief and loss became integrated into her story of aging.

JOHN WAYNE AT THE COMMUNITY CENTER: SATO MASAHIRO

The kind of intergenerational disharmony that Mori-san experienced is not uncommon in Japan, especially in situations of coresidence (Lebra 1979; Long 2009; 2012a; 2012b). It may be one reason why many older adults choose to spend their postretirement days in an attached, but semi-independent residence (what Westerners might think of as a "granny-flat") (Brown 2003). Many new homes are built with this type of arrangement in mind. Sato Masahiro, a seventy-year-old widower and retired salaryman, lived in one of these arrangements, occupying the second floor of a small divided house, while his son, daughter-in-law, and granddaughter lived on the first.

Although they lived in the same building, Sato-san rarely saw the rest of his family, and when he did, it was not uncommon for arguments to erupt. Sato-san often complained that his opinions were ignored by his son's family, and that his daughter-in-law was particularly stubborn and bossy. On one occasion, when the discussion again drifted to these frequent conflicts in the home, Sato-san, his voice raised and his body becoming visibly aggravated, suddenly exploded, "They'll only understand what I'm saying after I DIE!" For the time being, an unspoken policy of mutual avoidance kept the situation livable for both parties.

When Sato-san invited me up to his flat for the first time, climbing the outdoor metal staircase that led to the second floor, he took the opportunity to show off some of his many souvenirs collected from different trips he had taken since retirement: masks from Bali, a snow globe from San Francisco, a small totem pole from Canada, a decorative plate from Paris. Aside from these decorations, the small, Western-style rooms were simple and sparsely furnished, lacking the wood and paper patina of Mori-san's machiya. There were dishes in the sink and small barbells next to the sofa, making it seem more like a college dorm room than the home of an older person.

On the wall above Sato-san's dining table was large poster of John Wayne dressed as a cowboy striking a rugged pose. When I mentioned the poster, Sato-san chuckled mischievously and reached behind his couch, proudly producing, to my surprise, a replica of a Winchester rifle. "Just like John Wayne!" he told me, proceeding to explain how John Wayne, because he was so tall, could cock the long rifle by flipping it around in one hand (a maneuver that he did not try himself). On one occasion many years ago, Sato-san had seen John Wayne in person, when the actor visited Kyoto. "He was so *tall!*" Sato-san recalled, opening his eyes wide in awe and admiration and gripping the rifle enthusiastically.

Sato-san's age and short stature may make him an unlikely John Wayne, but his idols and the persona he exudes are consistent with his love of classic icons of strong masculine independence. This was so not only for actors like John Wayne, but also for General Douglas MacArthur, the corn-cob-pipe-puffing director of the Allied occupation of Japan following World War II (1945–1952) and Japanese historical figures like the military commander Kondo Isami (1834–1868), whose memorial monument Sato-san insisted I visit. When Sato-san and I went out to sing karaoke for the first time, he proudly treated me to a well-rehearsed version of one of his favorite songs: Frank Sinatra's "My Way." Among his many treasured items in his flat were several models of sailing ships, themselves potent icons of masculinity, discipline, and perseverance. "They conquer the rain—they just sail!" he told me as he laughed. "I like that about them—against the rain, storm, wind! That's *my life!*"

I often met Sato-san at a large senior welfare center, where I conducted participant observation and volunteered giving English-language lessons to the "English Appreciation Club" organized by Sato-san. Each of the eleven wards of Kyoto City supports a free senior welfare center that hosts various clubs, activities, and social spaces for persons over sixty free of charge. Sato-san visited the center in his ward at least three days each week, and participated in everything from table tennis to poetry recitation to ballroom dancing. While residential nursing homes are sometimes referred to disparagingly as "obasuteyama," or places to dump your aging parents (Bethel 1992; Ozawa 2010; Tomita 1994), welfare centers were places (*ba*) where older people like Sato-san often came to get away from their children and to engage activities meant to support independent living and prevent physical and mental declines associated with isolation in old age (Moore and Campbell 2009; Traphagan 2000).

I enjoyed visiting several of these centers throughout my fieldwork, not only because it afforded me a chance to meet and casually converse with older people, but also because my presence there was not seen as particularly disruptive. After I explained my research interests and affiliation, the staff felt comfortable allowing me to stay and speak with the center's visitors. Most of the visitors themselves showed little concern about my presence at first, but as I got to know the more extroverted, regular attendees, and concerns about my ability to speak Japanese were alleviated, I began to receive frequent invitations to act as an audience or to join group activities. As my research sites moved to other venues, I made fewer visits to the center, but continued to drop in and volunteer, mainly to stay in touch with people like Sato-san.

When I asked him if he socialized with many center people outside of the center, Sato-san quickly told me that maintaining harmony at the center meant withholding a lot. He invoked the Japanese social code, and the importance of protecting one's "true feelings" (*honne*) by observing the division between obligation (*giri*) and the expression of human feeling (*ninjō*) (Bachnik 1994; Benedict [1946] 1974). To underline his point, Sato-san told me, "I have been going to the senior center for ten years, but I don't know anything about those people's lives before they started coming. We don't talk about that. About what kind of job you had before or what university your son goes to or anything— that doesn't matter." In an effort to maintain a sense of solidarity or "horizontal relationships" (*yokō kankei*), friendly interactions necessitated protecting boundaries between the past and present concerns (Nakane 1970). Institutions like the center produced a kind of subjectivity that was individuated from the pasts and futures associated with generations and lineage, situating older adults into a social community of either nostalgic leisure (singing songs or playing games enjoyed as children), or a future of active and stimulating "successful aging" by learning something new, like English.

My first impression of Sato-san when I met him at the center was that of a popular, good-natured, and gregarious fixture among the regulars (he was one of the first regular attendees who helped facilitate my entree into the group), but after several months, and many interviews with him outside of the center, I began to understand more clearly the abrupt change in his personality that occurred when he entered the center. Sato-san was conscious of this change and aware that there was a difference between aging outside the center and aging inside. As we sat on a bench in the foyer watching people change in and out of street shoes as they passed in and out of the open doors, Sato-san began to explain the way he saw the center; to my surprise, he took a small piece of paper from the breast pocket of his golf shirt and wrote the phrase "way of the samurai" (*bushidō*).

For Sato-san maintaining a strict code of separating his social obligations and human feelings defined the aesthetics of his public self. Because of this, he said, it was better not to have many intimate friendships, and certainly not at the center. As we continued the conversation, and the scrap filled up, Sato-san reached for my notebook and wrote out the phrase "A warrior will die for the person who knows his self."[2] As I read it, he explained that he himself is willing to die for someone who knows him, and then asked if I would die for him. I hesitated for a moment, a little shocked by the question. Sato-san began chuckling at my silence, saying, "Of course not! If you said yes, I'd be scared! Wait a second!"

In this way our relationship, and indeed most of his relationships at the center and in his family, was not worthy of dying for. We were not in the trenches together, but met on the playing field of a tenuous gift economy of ethnographic research. Our connection was fated, or *en*, as he would often remind me, but our reciprocity also depended on preserving a certain professional distance. For Sato-san, relationships at the center functioned in a similar way, as a means to fulfill a social duty, of being a "good *rōjin*" (Traphagan 2006) by doing his part in keeping up a healthy mind and body. Visits to the center had little to do with

developing friendships, romances, or other attachments, but much more important, it was about the work of maintaining autonomy and independence in old
age. This work of becoming John Wayne could also be seen as his response to the
institutions like the center, and the expectations and anxieties it generated about
longevity in Japan's aging society. For Sato-san and for many other older adults
I spoke with, the activities and classes of the center kept one from "being out of
it," or *boke* (Traphagan 2000), a concern that Sato-san relates directly to his
social relations at the center and at home:

> Most people that come here, come here to avoid senility. There are a lot of
> motivations, but really, in the end, it's so that they won't become senile—*boke.*
> The reason is that when people become *boke,* they're a burden on other
> people, and particularly to strangers (*tanin*). People that don't know them. My
> son's wife is a stranger to me! [laughs]
>
> But really. Sometimes people die around here. These folks, some of them
> don't have a lot longer to live. Sometimes you have folks that don't come
> around for a while and then people ask "where's so-and-so?" and it turns out
> they're dead.
>
> But that's a good thing! If you die like that, without being a burden on
> someone, that's good! That's what I want! I want it!
>
> Some people wish that I was dead too . . . like my son's wife! [laughs]

Talking and joking about forgetfulness and other mental slips of old age (*mono
wasure*), considered warning signs of boke, were frequently exchanged at the
center, and confirmed Sato-san's perception of the role of the center in people's
experience of aging. Being burdensome to "strangers" or "outsiders," such as
nurses, social workers, and home helpers, was of particular concern to Sato-san,
and the side comments about his daughter-in-law lent an especially chilling echo
of obasuteyama.

Boke is a corporeal idiom of dependence and its consequence of exclusion, or
abandonment—literally being "out of" the economy of care (Traphagan 2000,
135; 2004, 64; 2006, 273). To older adults, boke is much more than a medical condition, or symptom of an aging mind. Traphagan writes that boke "indexes a
state of being characterized by the disembodiment of basic normative values
that operate in Japanese society" (2000, 10). Preventing boke means making
efforts through centers, clubs, and other social and cognitively stimulating activities to intentionally avoid dependence on others and remain embedded in an
economy of care.

If boke signified exclusion, isolation, and abandonment, cultivating the
kokoro was a means of remaining connected, open, and present, not only physically, but socially and emotionally as well. Cultivating the kokoro, however,
meant more than simply attending the center. After one English lesson, as Sato-
san and I left the center and walked to a nearby Buddhist temple and sat near a
group of middle-aged women engaged in a boisterous session of gossip and light

talk, Sato-san turned his back to them and spoke to me in a low, conspiratorial tone:

> You know, women live to about ninety, and men live to about seventy-seven or eighty or something like that? On average. For women it is eighty-seven. Mothers live ten years more. Why is that? How can that be? It's not just a matter of nutrition, so it must be something else. An issue of the heart (*kokoro no mondai*). It's not just that [men's and women's] jobs are different. I've been thinking about this lately, and women are so incredibly positive, right? No matter what happens, they are just so positive. So I'm not really keen on it myself, but you see this kind of, what you might call "chattering" [laughs] all this chattering with other women, it's really great for relieving stress. Men just don't have enough of that. Yak, yak, yak, yak! [laughs] Sure men talk, but they might talk all at once instead of just taking it easy. Well, I guess this just can't be helped, but ... [women nearby begin talking louder] yak, yak, yak. . . . Wherever you go! Men would just be quiet. . . .

EXERCISE FOR THE MOUTH: NISHIDA KAORI

At eighty-five years old, Kaori Nishida-san stayed active by taking regular strolls around her neighborhood. Nishida-san playfully called these strolls "exercise for the mouth" (*kuchi no undō*) since they were organized around dropping in on neighborhood friends, and involved more sitting and chatting than actual locomotion. On the occasions that I accompanied Nishida-san on walks, keeping step with her as she bent over a flower-patterned cane, she was always cheerfully greeted by the neighbors wherever we went. These strolls were easier when she had some help of her eldest son or daughter-in-law, both of whom lived with her. Nishida-san retired and turned over the family business when she reached seventy, but she has not stopped working, telling me with the now familiar expression, "I'll keep helping out as long as I can. As long as I don't become boke." Her long-standing relationships with clients and other weavers gave her an essential role in the business, of which she was very proud.

The first time I met Nishida-san, it was in the early summer of 2005, just before the long drizzle of the rainy season had begun. When I asked about her age, she replied, "I'm eighty-two years old, and I still have all of my teeth!" She smiled wide revealing a couple of silver teeth (she explained that a dentist had removed these without her permission), but indeed, there were no gaps or partials. Nishida-san's complexion was smooth and unblemished for a woman her age, gracefully lined with thin, delicate creases. Her thick silver hair was cut short with a modest well-groomed wave. Nishida-san almost always appeared to be in good spirits, and during our interviews she would alternate between grandmotherly spoiling and flirtatious teasing. On one occasion, when her daughter-in-law was passing through the room from her adjacent office, Nishida-san joked, "Oh, isn't this nice that I get to spend my days with a young handsome guy!" giggling at the embarrassment on our faces.

Nishida-san found ways to combine her daily activities of work, strolls, and housework to support physical, mental, and social health all at once, the last two being most important to her. She did not attend a community center like Sato-san, and told me that although there are social gatherings for older people held at a local elementary school, they are really intended for people either living alone or over age eighty-five. Every couple of months she attended a meeting of the women's temple group, which would invite priests to speak about topics pertaining Buddhist history, philosophy, and art. Aside from this, she looked forward to annual gatherings with her graduating class from the girls' school she had attended over sixty years ago, despite the fact that so many in her cohort were now passing away or were too frail to show up each year.

Unlike some of her neighbors, Nishida-san does not have the least hesitation when it comes to taking advantage of health care benefits of being old, though she has been generally healthy in her old age. Under the Japanese national health insurance older adults are eligible for free or mostly subsidized standard health services, and while many do take advantage of this, there is also variation in quality of services and doctor-patient openness. Older adults who have been socialized to defer to figures of authority, such as doctors, are often at a particular disadvantage in a consumer-based medical system, relying strongly on the assessment and suggestions of health professionals without voicing their own concerns or researching possible alternatives. Medical decisions, especially those occurring near the end of life, often involve families and consensus, resulting many times in decisions that conflict with the desires of the older patients themselves (Becker 1999; Long 2005). Nishida-san was aware of this reluctance to seek out health care services, and often encouraged her older friends to be more active in getting health care, getting regular flu shots, and taking preventative measures such as attending senior community programs. Sometimes she would even try shaming them by saying things like "The community has put so much effort into creating these services for you!"

Nishida-san visited her physician nearly every week, as much for chatting with the other patients and enjoying the serene waiting room as for medical attention ("They play classical music. Sometimes in the morning I'll fall asleep there!"). Nishida-san has been going to the same clinic for over forty years, and since her original doctor has long since passed away, she saw the grandson who succeeded him. She also made regular visits to her massage therapist twice a week, which, with her insurance, costs only a few hundred yen (a few U.S. dollars) each visit. Inexpensive massages and socializing with friends were two of the "the benefits of being old," she told me, shooting a sly wink.

For Nishida-san, physical and social care of the self blended easily with care of the kokoro, or the emotional and spiritual comfort. The spirits of the dead were frequently on her mind. Compared to the sociality of welfare centers and leisure clubs, social ties with the hotoke and ancestors were not seen as a means of preventing dependence, but integrating it. Since the hotoke need to be cared for as well, the dependence is mutual, circulating through memorial practices that direct the past toward the future. Not only did she make daily offerings of rice and tea at her household butsudan, but she visited the household graves several times a month to commemorate the death anniversaries of her other relatives:

> There is the monthly anniversary of the hotoke, right? *Meinichi* is the day that
> the ancestor died. So in my case, my husband died on July 6. Then grandfather
> is March 24. Then grandma is October 9. So on these days I try to offer things
> that they liked. Then every month—it is hard on the priest, of course to come
> so much—so every month on the ninth, the newest *hotoke*-san, grandma
> [death] was October 9. Every month on the ninth [the priest] comes to do a
> service for us. Then when he comes he reads all the others' death names.
> Then we celebrate the *shoutsukimeinichi*. On March 24 we light a
> candle and say "Good morning. May we live one more day in happiness." Well,
> [I have] the feeling (*kimochi*) that the ancestors are over there you know?
> [Danely: Over there?] The feeling that the ancestors are always staying close by
> me, you know? Even if, say, my granddaughter, if she's late coming home, then
> I'll pray "With your permission I'm going to rest, but my granddaughter
> hasn't come back. May she come home safely." And that's the end.
>
> Nowadays, you could say the ancestors are the closest people to me (*jibun
> no ichiban techikana hito*) . . .
>
> I guess you could say that they are what let me live most peacefully.

Nishida-san had a highly detailed mental calendar of particular death days of her relatives, as well as an understanding of the appropriate ritual observances due on each of these days. She described her practice in terms of feelings (kimochi), intimacy, and affection, or "closeness," that gave her a sense of "peace." The term that I have translated here as a sensation of "closeness" (*techikana*) literally means "close at hand," as if she saw them as being reliable or dependable at attending to her needs, even those as simple as watching out for her granddaughter who had gone out for the night. As she listed her many visits and consultations with the hotoke, I had to remind myself that she was speaking not of the living, but of the spirits of the dead. These were the people who really knew her, or in Sato-san's opinion, the ones whom a person of integrity would die for. The affective labor of remembering the dead initiates the hope for "one more day of happiness," and defers to a spiritual agency.

It was easy to become charmed by Nishida-san, whose demeanor did not clearly reveal the same kinds of struggles I could see in households like those of Mori-san or Sato-san. There were no bickering children or in-laws, no concerns about succession and the loss of tradition, no anger of resentment against the government. In contrast to Mori-san's family, there seemed to be a genuine bond of warmth and respect among Nishida-san, her son and successor, and even her daughter-in-law. They not only lived together, but also worked together and helped each other constantly. Nishida-san was not only able to pass her business on to her son, but she has also been able to instill the respect for tradition, from the loud silk looms to the quiet butsudan.

FROM THE GOLD PLAN TO "HURRY UP AND DIE" INSURANCE

Not all of the older adults I spoke with were as sharp and contented in their seventies and eighties as Nishida-san, and as the other examples I have described so far attest, most do not have the best relationships with family whom they currently or in the near future will depend on for care. Belief in the hotoke and ancestors might add an additional moral dimension to family-provisioned care, but it is also clear that coresidence and shared burden of care is a matter of necessity as well. Given the unprecedented numbers of older adults in the Japanese population, how is the state providing the care and resources to achieve not only health, but also a sense of security and safety in later life? How satisfied are older adults with the health and long-term care systems, and how are they implicated in the discourses that form these systems?

With the transition of the baby boom generation (*dankai no sedai*, born between 1945 and 1950) into retirement, more and more Japanese people are eligible for the benefits of being old, yet those benefits are becoming more limited. From a national welfare perspective, there are just too few working age adults (fifteen to sixty-four years old) to keep government expenditure on elder care (including pensions and health benefits) at current rates (Tamiya et al. 2011). The number of working adults supporting one elderly person in Japan has dropped from 11.2 in 1960 to only 2.9 in 2009 (Muramatsu and Akiyama 2011, 426) and is predicted to fall even further to only 2.0 by 2025. On one occasion a presenter I saw speak about this growing dependence illustrated the change by first showing the audience a photo of an old man atop a Shinto shrine palaquin hoisted by several young men (the 1960s). This was followed by a slide of Japan's future, where the same old man was now being carried in the classic obasuteyama pose, on the back of just one adult child.

There is accumulating evidence that the Japanese national health care system is feeling the strain of providing care for its aging population. Japan has had a universal health care system since 1961, and can provide relatively inexpensive and sufficient care for the majority of the population with some of the lowest cost per patient ratios of any other industrialized countries (Campbell 2008). However, for older persons themselves, it is all too easy to find the weaknesses in state-based elder care provisioning, since many kinds of health care commonly needed in old age may be limited or expensive, and residential institutional care lags far behind demand. Cancer treatment, for example, is covered by national health insurance program, but options are limited and benefits are capped (Hiratate 2008). One fourth of Japanese people, for example, own some kind of cancer insurance, available through private companies such as AFLAC and American Home Direct. Given such limitations, health and long-term care expenditures, especially for low-income older adults, can come at a heavy cost, resulting in reliance on family-provisioned care.

There is also a shortage of qualified geriatric medical staff and nurses and high burnout and turnover rates of certified care workers. This is in part due to institutional disincentives such as low pay, expectations of overtime, and stressful working conditions (Yajima 2009). Care workers in many places in Japan earn and hourly rate about equal to that of a convenience store clerk, and because the training required for certification is minimal and offset or entirely subsidized by government incentive programs, it has become an easy way for unemployed workers from the industrial sector to find work, not to mention women looking for part-time work (Shirasaki 2009). The cost of providing training is more than made up for by the tens of thousands of low-wage workers who help keep long-term care affordable and institutional care limited.

Geriatric nurses are also in high demand, yet the state is yet to take serious steps toward providing incentives to meet the need. Nurses in Japan make about 70 percent of the average wages of all industries, and small increases in insurance premiums meant to improve wages for medical professionals as recent as 2012 will not directly affect nurses. Japan also currently has one of the most conservative immigration policies of any industrialized country. Foreign nurses who migrate to Japan to find work in elder care are faced with heavy limitations and an arduous examination process, which, even if applicants do pass (a record high 11.3 percent pass rate in 2012 among non-Japanese testers according to the *Japan Times* 2012), grants only limited stay, not to mention other challenges of ethnic or linguistic discrimination (Inoue 2010, 14–16; Takenaka 2012).

The biggest change in the Japanese health care system affecting older adults since becoming an "aging society" was the 1989 "Gold Plan," which promised a shift "from care by families to care by society" (Campbell 2000), and created a universal entitlement for every adult sixty-five and older for a variety of institutional programs regardless of family support. However, while the Gold Plan seems to shift biopolitics toward the more centralized institutions of the state, implementation has resulted in an increased burden on family caregivers. Prior to the Gold Plan, bedridden older adults accounted for over one-third of the institutionalized adult population, compared to 6.5 percent in the United States and only 4.2 percent in Sweden (Ushikubo 1998, 128). With the introduction of the Gold Plan, the demand for institutional care increased, and insufficient affordable nursing care institutions were made up for by an increase in long-term beds in hospitals or family-provisioned care at home (Long 2009).

Since most families with frail older adults, even under the Gold Plan, still had to rely on family-provided care, either because of a shortage of hospital beds or because of insufficient coverage, the Japanese Ministry of Health, Labor and Welfare introduced a new policy of mandatory long-term care insurance (LTCI) in

1998 (Ogawa and Retherford 1997; Olivares-Tirado and Tamiya 2014; Traphagan
and Knight 2003, 16). Enrollment in the LTCI plan is mandatory for those over
forty, with some benefits becoming available at sixty-five based on a classification
of care needs (*yōkaigo*). Given the extension of average number of dependent
years an older person faces at the end of life in Japan, long-term health care is
essential, but the cost of providing this care is tremendous (Ikegami et al. 2011),
and Japan's LTCI funding structure is reviewed and revised to try to account for
this every year, a process anxiously perceived by many older adults as a way to cut
benefits and raise premiums. Indeed, in April 2014 major changes in LTCI not
only decreased benefits (insured would pay twice current rates for services such
as adult day care or short stay) but also constrained eligibility to those who had a
greater need for care (*Asahi Shinbun* 2013). As a result, many care prevention programs, which have yielded mixed results on health and decreasing need for care
later in life, will no longer be covered directly by LTCI insurance.

The biggest difference between LTCI and the Gold Plan is that while the latter was funded entirely by taxes, the LTCI is paid for though a combination of
insurance premiums and taxes. In Kyoto, for example, about 50 percent is
funded through the social insurance program premiums, 25 percent by municipal and prefectural taxes, and 25 percent by national taxes. The expansion of universal coverage and options for services has brought on a proliferation of
programs and facilities administered not only by local municipalities, but also by
nonprofit organizations, volunteer organizations, and private interests (Long
2009, 141). The diversification of services and sources of care is reflected in more
flexible roles for caregivers in the household, both kin and professional home
help. Partial reliance on family-provisioned care is still high even when home
helpers are employed, as the family of an older or bed-ridden adult must be
involved in sharing and coordinating information with care managers and aides,
paying for medications and services, and providing social support and emotional care (Yasuhiro 2012). For those who cannot afford in-home care, there are
often few alternatives to family-provisioned care. The mission of the Gold Plan
to replace care by the family with care by community has not come to pass, but
the relationship between family and state has changed as a result of a host of new
mediating entities that sometimes help and at other time complicate or obstruct
access to care.

During my fieldwork, when the Japanese government again increased the
cost-sharing burden for health care and LTCI for older adults, it was immediately publicly criticized by many elder advocacy groups as overly costly and
insufficient (one of the only times I saw older adult leafleters on the streets). In
an effort to educate and gain support, health policy experts were dispatched to
local school-district-based social welfare associations. In one presentation I
observed, a man in a doctor's white lab coat first extolled to the group the ways
Japan's health care was better and cheaper than that available elsewhere in the
world, before moving on to ways the audience of older people could maintain

Japan's prominence by engaging in various preventative measures and "maintaining independence." Prevention of health problems (from strokes to depression to traffic accidents) was compared to "watching out for fires" and quickly extinguishing them. "Rebuilding one's house" was then compared to various ways to avoid the need for long-term care, such as avoiding falls and isolation. Nursing homes or long-term hospital care was not mentioned, and the polite audience did not ask any questions about these institutions, although it was widely understood they were costly and there were extremely long waiting lists (over 520,000 older adults estimated to be on waiting lists nationally as of 2014; *Yomiuri Shinbun* 2014, 1).

While Japan's health care system for older adults is still impressive from the point of view of economic efficiency given the enormity and speed of Japan's aging society, it is increasingly following a trend toward a more neoliberal model of biopolitical governance that relies on a diverse array of mediating institutions, and places responsibility for care on individuals assumed to be self-reliant actors. In 2008, a new health care system for those in advanced old age (*Kōki Kōreisha Iryō Seido*) was introduced that removed an estimated thirteen million people over seventy-five from the National Health Insurance system and placed them on a plan funded from a wide array of sources administered on a local level. Fees vary widely, but Kyotoites and other city-dwelling older adults were likely to have higher fees than rural residents. Fees are deducted from pensions, and the inability to pay results in the removal of benefits previously guaranteed under the LTCI regardless of ability to pay (Hiratate 2008). Because of this insecurity, and the distrust in the political maneuvering of the government, the new system has earned the nickname *hayoshine hōken*, or "hurry up and die insurance" (Campbell 2008).

While this might seem a little extreme or jaded, five years later (2013), finance minister and member of the dominant Liberal Democratic Party Taro Aso said almost exactly that. During a meeting of the National Council on Social Security Reforms, Aso was quoted as saying that the elderly should "hurry up and die" (Associated Press 2013) as a solution to the cost of end of life care. While Aso attempted to explain his comments as merely personal opinions about his own end-of-life wishes, it did little to reassure citizens who already feel a strong dissatisfaction with the government on the issue of care.

How do older adults who heard these things from politicians and who experience firsthand the strain and stress of making health care decisions in later life build them into their narratives of aging? Reactions varied, but in general people did their best to find the advantages they could and accept losses elsewhere. There was widespread distrust of the government policies and a sense of passive resignation.

The Hasegawas, a married couple, both in their mid-eighties, summed up several of these views as we sat down one afternoon in their small, rented house. Mrs. Hasegawa began, saying, "You have to think of something that you want, and then even if you can't make it happen (*jitusgen dekinai*), at least you're moving in that direction. You're facing forward (*mae muki ni*). Of course when you get to be over eighty, every year feels like you've aged five years. It is really hard to get through even one year without some incident (*buji ni*)." Her husband, who had been sitting stone quiet in the chair next to her suddenly jutted forward and spoke up: "This country's policies have gotten so much worse! The long-term insurance plan gets more expensive and the pension system keeps going down! Most people just mumble to themselves but don't do anything about it so it just keeps happening this way. It's a huge problem!" Together, the Hasegawas voiced feelings of both hope and defeat, aging subjectivities haunted by abandonment, but still moving forward.

TRADITIONS AND TRANSITIONS: NAKAMURA ICHIRO

Whenever we visited temples together, Sato-san seemed uninterested in religious activities, and would usually mill about in the rear of the hall, far away from the reverent visitors kneeling in prayer or dropping coins in the offering box placed directly in front of a central Buddhist statue. Sato-san, like many other Japanese I people I spoke with, called himself *mushukyō* or "un-religious" (Reader and Tanabe 1998). Many Japanese people distinguish between being "un-religious" and being "atheist" (*mushinkō*), the latter case indicating a purposeful avoidance of all religious practice. In contrast, to be "un-religious" means that although one observes some religious practices, these practices are based on circumstances particular to one's life, rather than a universalistic and absolute faith that requires personal experience of the supernatural. The word "religion" (*shukyō*), itself is a relatively recent addition to the Japanese lexicon, coming into popular use only in the early modern period in response to Western Christianity and debates among Shinto and Buddhist supporters on the role of religion in national politics (Josephson 2012; Krämer 2013). For most Japanese people, religion connotes a kind of exclusive devotion to some faith community such that it defines one's complete personality. However, affiliation (a matter of individual or household relationships over time with temples and shrines), praxis, and faith are not necessarily linked, and need not follow each other or be exclusive to one doctrine but are dependent on situational practices and pragmatic concerns (Reader and Tanabe 1998). Survey data on Japanese lifestyles indicate that although over 80 percent of Japanese people affiliate with either Shinto or Buddhism, or both, and observe most of the lay customs associated with these traditions, such as memorialization, around 80 percent of respondents also indicate that they are "unreligious" (Krause et al. 2010; Reader and Tanabe 1998).

In Japan, rituals for the spirits of the dead, like festivals and other traditional social customs, are not seen as "religious," despite their implication of superhuman agency and the assumption of at least partial efficacy of things such as offerings, prayers, and petitions. In practice, the boundary between something that can be rationally explained and something that requires a more mysterious or supernatural explanation is quite blurred. While Sato-san at first dismissed my research topic, claiming that religion isn't important in Japan, he was just as quick to point out that traditions of caring for the spirits did become more important for older people than they were for younger people and that he has felt this transition personally.

When Japanese people like Sato-san spoke of the ancestors, buddhas, and dieties, they usually preferred to use the term "tradition" (*dentō*). These are traditions in a Durkheimian sense, as emanations of a social reality refracted through and circulated via individuals' practices (Durkheim 1996). Traditions constituted a moral community around sacred things, shared rituals, and symbols. They connected him to generations past and future, and to the self-satisfaction of having fulfilled his role in this chain of obligation and love. Tradition is, at its core, the repetition of cultural practices, the ritualization of the world that continues beyond the individual, even as it is up to each individual to enact it (Danely 2012b).

During the two years of research that I conducted in Kyoto, I not only observed individual rituals at household graves and butsudan, but I also participated in a number of local festivals, events where men appeared to have more involvement and investment as the women in constructing aesthetic narratives around an economy of care (Ivy 1995; Kawano 2005; Traphagan 2000; 2004). In these narratives, tradition functioned as an authoritative metaphor for embodying a past that extended the self into the future, and older adults still held an important role as links between these two temporal worlds. Shinto festivals, which recruit local men to lift enormous palanquins of the gods (*mikoshi*) through the streets, are a source for creatively linking the imagined landscape of community to the labor of young male bodies, but their work was always supervised and guided by a cohort of senior men, often easy to miss on the periphery of the impressive dramatic displays of strength and spirit that enlivened the festival atmosphere.

It was during one of these festivals that I met Nakamura Ichiro, a married man of sixty-seven, similar in stature to Sato-san, but with a thinning head of gray hair and an impish grin that rippled in laugh lines across his face, making him look both older and more amiable. In fact, it was a rare occasion when Nakamura-san was not smiling, even when discussing less than cheery news about family deaths or declining health. Only his wife, Emiko-san, seemed to smile more than her husband, and it was a smile that was much more prone to burst open into laughter. Emiko-san rarely sat in the same room as Nakamura-san and me, but preferred instead to observe the etiquette she was brought up with, where women would sit just on the other side of the threshold ready to hop up at any moment to fetch something as the men conversed. Even so, Emiko-san was far from invisible at her post, and she felt free to interject her own thoughts from time to time, many of which were loud and lighthearted zingers aimed at her husband.

Together, this husband and wife lived in a two-hundred-year-old traditional-style wooden machiya in the center of the city, just blocks from the busiest downtown intersections. They were charming, generous, and truly part of the fabric of the city. Nakamura-san's grandfather came to Kyoto as a young man just prior to the beginning of the Meiji Period (1868–1912), and both Nakamura-san and his father were born and raised in the same neighborhood where Nakamura-san still resides. As the eldest son in the Nakamura household's main patriline, Nakamura-san's identity was strongly invested in a sense of place and the continuity of traditions that he inherited with it, such as festivals.

Although Nakamura-san told me that when he was younger he had once thought about going to a university and working for a bank, he ended up, instead, starting a small wholesale stationary and school supplies business, which he continues to run out of a home office overlooking his narrow residential street. While Sato-san, a youngest son, had struck out on his own at an early age, throwing his energy into work and play before settling down, Nakamura-san chose to stay close to home, and while he is a hardworking and capable businessman, his real passion was his devotion to maintaining community traditions and particularly his family's rituals for the gods, buddhas, and ancestors.

No object in Nakamura-san's house linked tradition to concepts of the aging self as clearly as his elaborate butsudan. Since butsudan are embedded in the architecture of the living space, they offer a window into everyday private practices that connect the self and family to interiority, exchange, and mourning. Gilded in gold and painted with black lacquer, Nakamura-san's butsudan resembled a miniature temple, or a portal to Amida Buddha's "western paradise."[3] It was similar in structure to others that I had seen in almost every home I visited, consisting mainly of a large wooden cabinet embellished with carved transoms and set atop a pedestal with drawers for storing important items and ritual implements. Butsudans like these evolved from structures originally set on the periphery of the house used for making offerings to the unclean spirits of the unconnected dead (*muenbotoke*) (Bokhoven 2005, 196–197). Now they house the inscribed memorial tablets for hotoke and the honored ancestors (the connected dead), and are usually located in the intimate and honored space of one of the innermost rooms of the house, next to the central pillar.

Inside the butsudan were several layers of step-like platforms on which various statues, memorial tablets (ihai), offerings, and other ceremonial objects had been placed. On one of my morning visits, there were two plump yellow grapefruits resting on decorative offering dishes and a fresh flower arrangement of seasonal and subdued coloring set in a vase next to them. The Nakamuras have these flowers delivered each month, replacing them temporarily with cloth flowers if they wilt. Another small platform had been placed at the base of the butsudan, and next to it was an incense burner and a gong used to call the ancestors. On top of this platform was a booklet, no larger than a checkbook, filled with the names of the household's ancestors and the dates of each of their deaths. For

Nakamura-san, the butsudan was more than a personal possession; it might be more accurate to say that he was possessed by the butsudan, which required him to fulfill obligations to the hotoke and the ancestors of his household. It provided an aesthetic link between his investment of care and traditions and transience in the household life cycle:

NAKAMURA: It's a really *o–ld* [drawing out the word] butsudan. It's really hurting though. I really have to get it fixed. It's really banged up. Well, it's an old butsudan, you know? So, I can't really make it like new again. Of course, [whispered] it would be much better just to dispose of it but, well, up till now, I've been allowed to use it [by the ancestors].

DANELY: This was your father's?

NAKAMURA: Oh, it's from the second-generation grandfather [Nakamura's grandfather].

DANELY: Oh, then it must be quite old!

NAKAMURA: Yes it's quite old. Going to be about one hundred years old in a little bit if I'm not mistaken. If I could repair it that would be nice. Make it clean—it's called *arai*—from the arai they take off all the stains and I think that they could make it look nice, but. . . . [trails off]

DANELY: And the [Amida] Buddha statue?

NAKAMURA: The Buddha statue is, something like, well, I don't really know for sure. But, something like [sucks in breath], from what I've heard, they say that it's quite an old Buddha. That's why I don't have the heart to dispose of it. Because it's the ancestors' Buddha, you know?

DANELY: The ancestors?

NAKAMURA: Because this Buddha has been passed down from the ancestors. That's what they say. And changing this butsudan is really—well, you know? I can't give it up [laughing] even if it gets old! [laughing]

Nakamura-san belongs to the Jōdo (Pure Land) sect, which historically has been known to have many wealthy supporters, but this was not the only reason that his butsudan was so old and important to him. As the fourth-generation heir to his household, Nakamura-san's butsudan not only contained the memorial tablets of several generations, but the butsudan was itself a testament to his household's tradition of the continuity of ancestor memorial over these generations. For objects like these, being old granted them a greater connection with the ancestors, deepening rather than diminishing their worth. Repairing or replacing the butsudan might make a strong (and expensive) statement about his desires to have the traditions carried on for several future generations, and Nakamura-san's hesitation to do away with the old might be due to a lack of trust in this continuity.

Just as the memorial rituals conducted at the butsudan aid the spirits' transition to the other world, caring for the butsudan was itself a reminder of one's position in the household, and of the transitions of the life cycle that all must eventually pass through. It was touching to see Nakamura-san's face light up as he spoke of the butsudan and easy to see how transitions, transience, and transformation represented by the aging butsudan became the emotional and aesthetic stuff of memorial. Japanese ancestor memorialization, as practiced and embodied in offerings and words, is part of the work of self in mourning, recruiting, and reintegrating memories, impressions, and feelings of oneself and others, into a narrative of meaningful change. Changes can happen, as people grow old and pass on, but this need not rend the fabric of life.

Grief: Weightiness and Light

In the summer months, the sliding paper doors between rooms of Nishida-san's machiya were left open, allowing a faint breeze to enter from the small rear courtyard. In the very back of the house, down a narrow corridor past the stone-floored kitchen, is a room housing a small factory that has been producing silk neckties since 1916. The rhythmic clanging of the seven heavy cast iron power looms and other machinery in the factory room was so loud that it was a wonder to me that Nishida-san and I could hear each other from where we usually sat to talk. Only a gentle rumbling hum could be heard from behind the rooms full of tall stacks of boxed orders and shelves shimmering with wooden bobbins of silk thread. The house itself was a work of art, with beautifully preserved carpentry and a kitchen still outfitted with a well and a wood-burning stove.

During our talks, Nishida-san and I usually sat around a low wooden table hiding a recessed floor for lowering tired legs. She leaned over and pushed a button on the hot water dispenser that sat on the floor next to her, and fixed two small cups of green tea, setting them down next to small plate of cookies. I asked after her health, noting that she appeared in especially good spirits that day. Nishida-san smiled and told me that she had been to the doctor that morning and everything was in order, adding half jokingly that the reason she has had such good health over her lifetime is that she got all of her serious health problems out of the way in one go when she was younger: "After that, my illness was cleared out, I haven't gotten sick since!"

The illness that Nishida-san was referring to occurred in 1944, one year after she was married in a Shinto ceremony in Kyoto. It was autumn, and the mountainside was transforming into its palette of red and gold as Japan was plunging into an even more desperate and tragic phase of World War II. While Kyoto was spared the devastating fire bombing attacks that leveled much of the nearby coastal cities like Kobe and Osaka, the evidence of Japan's total war was everywhere. Women and children were enrolled in mandatory labor (kinrōhōshi), and most of the men were pressed into military service; vital supplies, such as food and medication, were rationed. Nishida-san remembered her iron looms, pots and pans, and other metal items being collected to melt down, and making long trips to farming relatives in the countryside, exchanging kimono for food and hiding as they returned home. Pamphlets rained down from U.S. planes, warning that "The flower capital will be come a capital of ashes" (*Hana no miyako ha hai no miyako ni naru*). There was a strong chance that Nishida-san's husband would soon be called to service, despite still suffering health problems from previous service in Korea, at the time a Japanese colony. Fortunately, the war ended before her husband was called, and the couple had a chance to begin a family.

It was against this background that Nishida-san gave birth to her first child, a girl. Complications during delivery rendered her in a comatose state for nearly two months. The situation was so bleak that after she finally regained consciousness, she found out that her relatives had already begun making funeral arrangements for her.

During her stay at the hospital, Nishida-san recalled having a vision. She was in a wide, expansive field, high with waving grass and beautiful flowers, and she had such a wonderful feeling there that she wanted to continue moving through it, passing over the next hill. Her eyes lit up and she smiled as she told me the story of this vision. In a twist on the "white light" of many near-death experiences, Nishida-san recalled that moving through the field, her spirits "felt light" as if she was floating through the landscape. At this point in the story, however, Nishida-san paused pensively and leaned back against the cabinet that served as her backrest.

"Just as I was going to go further, I heard faint voices calling my name. They said 'Kaori, come home!'" Nishida-san wanted to continue—to depart—but was compelled to return.

Eventually, Nishida-san's health recovered and she was allowed to return home, but her infant daughter, who was also affected by the difficult birth process, remained in the hospital. Eight months after Nishida-san recovered from her illness, she was told that her daughter had died.

In most cases, when a person dies at the hospital, the body is removed from the rear door, but the hospital staff, out of sympathy (omoiyari), allowed Nishida-san to exit through the front doors, carrying her daughter wrapped in a blanket, as if she were alive:[4]

> It was during the war, and then it was only a ten-month-old child too . . . But anyway, we had a proper funeral. They didn't just dump her into a coffin and send me home, but they told me to hold her and take her home. Usually you can't go out the north entrance to a hospital with a coffin, but if you go out as if you have a living baby, you can go out of the usual gate.
>
> But still, even a baby, even a baby is *heavy*. So *heavy*. [Danely: Ten months old?] Ten months. So very heavy.
>
> Well, when she died, I couldn't even move, I just thought that she was so heavy and I returned like that in the taxi. She was so heavy.
>
> Really the wisdom that I got from that was, I wanted to hold her, always, I wanted to be this way with her, I wanted to play with her but, I couldn't do it, I just had her weight on my knees, I felt her weight on my knees.

Recalling this episode, Nishida-san repeatedly emphasized the *weight* of her daughter, whose body rested on her knees as the taxi took them home. As Nishida-san realized that she could not hold or play with her child, she was left only with the heavy weight of grief, and the heavy thoughts of the child whom she would not raise.[5]

There was a tangible contrast between the lightness of the field Nishida-san envisioned as she lay in the hospital and the weightiness of the child's body. The weight of a small, frail child, like the death of a child, presents something painfully counterintuitive, something that calls into question one's assumptions about the world—something that isn't as it is supposed to be. As Japanese tradition held that it is taboo for parents to bury their young children, Nishida-san and her husband did not attend the funerary ceremonies. "If the child dies before the parents," she explained, "it is opposite, so the parents cannot send the child off."

Nishida-san's brush with death followed quickly by her daughter's death amid the backdrop of the last years of World War II must have produced an incredible amount of strain on her. Certainly the trauma of war could not be the best environment in which to build a family, let alone nurse one's grief over a lost child. When Nishida-san spoke about this period during the war, however, her stories all seemed to revolve around survival, and more specifically a narrative of survival as a result of exchange and cooperation.

The community- and kin-based economy of care was Nishida-san's means of not only surviving, but also mourning in the years following her daughter's death. Although she received significant financial help from her siblings and affinal relatives, she also worked hard to give something back, lightening her spirits and giving her a new confidence to continue on. As Steven Parish (2008) noticed in the midst of his own suffering during treatment for cancer, "giving empties and lightens; it is easier to float away; one is buoyant with the lightness of being; one is good, a moral self, as much an agent as one can be" (Parish 2008, 113). In the economy of care, grief also empties and lightens as an open gateway (ma) inviting in others, restoring the sense of agency and morality. Nishida-san continues to give in this way, calling it "distributing the kokoro" (*kokoro no kubari*), a phrase that poetically uses the charcters in the word "worry" (*shinpai*) into an act of sharing the self.

Memorialization is also a way to continue giving over or distributing the kokoro. Nishida-san's daughter received a small, simple memorial tablet and was included in the prayers for all of the household ancestors during services. For Nishida-san, the flowering field and the calling voices were not merely hallucinations brought on by her illness, but an entry point to a much larger and meaningful cultural world of giving and grieving. Entanglements of giving and grieving remind us of how the phenomenology of loss in old age is embodied in ways of thinking or seeing the world into being, of imbuing experience with a sense of the real (Csordas 1994; Woodward 1991). Loss is dimensional; it has a weight. For Nishida-san, the grief work of memorialization also provided a means for the weightiness of loss to be filled with the "lightness of being not" (Taylor 2009).[6]

"THE BUDDHA'S BIRTHDAY"

The responsibility to care for the spirits of the departed weighed heavily on Nakamura-san, who has devoted so much of his own life to maintain face in his role as an eldest son of his lineage. But like the lightness that characterized Nishida-san's mourning, Nakamura-san's narrative also found ways to incorporate acts of giving and grieving that seemed to place his own concerns about the demise of tradition temporarily aside. The day Nakamura-san showed me his butsudan was what he called "the buddha's birthday," or *shotsukimeinichi*, a monthly memorial day for the household ancestors and spirits of the dead performed by a priest. Since it is believed that mortuary rituals transform the spirit of the dead into a buddha, the conceptual analogy of birth anniversary and death anniversary does follow a sort of logic, even if the atmosphere of the ritual is meditative and solemn.

When the priest finally arrived to conduct the service, he was quickly ushered toward the butsudan. The priest was relatively young (perhaps in his midforties), and wore a formal black robe with a gold embroidered sash. The Pure Land sect of Buddhism does not require clergy to shave their heads, and the priest's hair was neat and businesslike. Later I learned from Nakamura-san that the priest joined the clergy only after marrying the daughter of an heirless temple abbot, a reminder that older people were not the only ones affected by an aging society. As an adopted successor, he enrolled in a Buddhist university in order to join the clergy. Given that Buddhist priesthood is typically neither as lucrative nor as easy as popular stereotypes paint it, this young priest's willingness to take tonsure earned praise from the Nakamuras.

Emiko-san had prepared three cushions at the back of the room where the butsudan was kept, and another directly in front of the butsudan for the priest. When Nakamura-san and I entered the room, she casually retreated to the dining area, and sat near the threshold. I sat to the right of Nakamura-san during the ceremony, as the priest began chanting, drumming like a metronome on a small wooden gong set on the floor close by at his feet. Nakamura-san sat on the cushion, his legs tucked underneath him, his palms pressed together, his eyes closed and his head bowed in reverence.

The chanting for the most part was low, nasal, droning, and monotonous. Occasionally the priest launched into quick passages, the mysterious syllables coming out in sharp staccato matching the wooden gong at his side. At other points, the gong slowed, sounding much like the drips of an old water spigot that had just been turned off, then resuming, steadying the humming flow to more moderate pace. When the priest chanted "Namu Amida Butsu," the praise of Amida Buddha whose statue occupied the uppermost shelf of the butsudan, both Nakamura-san and his wife joined in with low whispers. Apart from this, they did not seem familiar with the words being recited, nor did they join the priest to chant the posthumous names of the deceased (kaimyō), which he read from the small record book at the altar. Each name was punctuated with the clear, high-pitched ring of the altar's bell. I glanced over at the Nakamuras during the priest's recitation, then I looked toward the ceiling and noticed the black-and-white portraits of Nakamura-san's parents and other relatives peering down at us, unsmiling from the their frames.

The entire shotsukimeinichi ceremony took slightly more than ten minutes, and concluded with a few more rounds of "Namu Amida Butsu" while the priest massaged his wooden prayer beads in his palms. When he stopped abruptly, there was a brief moment of silence, that ma that always seemed to punctuate memorial occasions, during which Nakamura-san and Emiko-san both bowed deeply, almost touching their foreheads on the tatami floor. The priest then swiveled around on his cushion to face us, and breathed out a sigh as if coming out of deep concentration.

The shotsukimeinichi memorial service was neither as formal as nor as publicly visible as periodic Buddhist memorial ceremonies (hōyō) conducted at temples or graves (Smith 1974, 95). On the other hand, because shot-sukimeinichi did require a visit from a religious specialist and a formal sequence of ritual procedures, it was also of a different order than everyday petitions, prayers, and offerings made privately by individuals at the butsudan. It was less visible than grave visits to community surveillance. For Nakamura-san, holding the ceremony meant honoring the hotoke, whose faces looked down on us during the priest's chanting. As the eldest son, he was to carry on the narrative as he had learned them and how he would like them performed for himself.

The service was also a way for him to maintain a relationship with the temple. He explained on another occasion not only that was the priest from the same temple his father patronized, but also that he himself hoped to have his own mortuary arrangements conducted by that temple. Emiko-san joked that he wouldn't have as nice of a ceremony or as long of a kaimyō as his own father (longer posthumus names associated with parishioners of high prestige who have made generous donations). When I asked why, she replied that they were expensive, and doubted their sons would be willing to pay up. "Your father would make a lot of donations to the temple," she told her husband. "Do you think your sons will be like that?"

The seemingly simple ceremony of mourning refracted loss through the prism of an aging Japan. The hotoke, whose portraits hung overhead were deceased, but the traditions that memorialized them were fading away as well. The priest performing the ceremony was adopted into his job in part because of smaller families and weakened ties of succession. The Nakamuras held to their ceremonies but anticipated their end. Nakamura-san worried that ending these ceremonies would mean that he had not held up his obligations to the ancestors.

As the priest was leaving Nakamura-san's home, we exchanged business cards and agreed to meet again in a couple of weeks. Nakamura-san and his wife both seemed relieved and pleased that they were able to make the introduction, excitedly talking about the opportunity and praising the priest as the three of us sat down to a lunch of take-out sushi. When I met with the priest again, he told me that people like Nakamura-san and his wife are indeed rare. Conducting shotsukimeinichi ceremonies is common just after someone in the family died, and most people stop the practice after about three years. Nakamura-san, however, had continued this practice for his father every month for ten years. The priest guessed that only one or two other households in his parish were as dedicated to keeping this custom going for so long.

Anniversaries, whether memorializing a death or a birth, are occasions to reimagine moments that have passed. They acknowledge both transience and repetition that characterize Japanese narratives of loss, like the haunting "over and return" of the old woman in Zeami's *Obasute*. Rituals of memorialization provide symbolic resources to give meaning to these feelings of transience and repetition, placing them within a creative aesthetic value system. This value system was what people like Nakamura-san referred to as "tradition," but what was also referred to as *kokoro*, as in Nishida-san's use of kokoro no kubari. Giving or circulating the heart, offering, or passing it on reflected an openness, a sense of agency and worth. Other people, such as Mori-san, struggled with finding such openings. Instead, her narrative of loss was one of retention, holding in and holding firm. These lives and stories do not allow us to easily separate personal thoughts and emotions of grief and mourning from the larger political and symbolic realm of interactions. Changes in long-term care policies, religious participation, and family expectations all contribute to the narrative of aging in Japan, but so do more subtle and intimate feelings of loss and mourning. Extending the self through grieving and giving allows one to remain suspended between abandonment and hope, between open spaces of meaning and possible selves.

PART II

Mourning

CHAPTER 3

Landscapes of Mourning

CONSTRUCTING NATURE AND KINSHIP

Loss always seems to haunt narratives of care. Obasuteyama brought my attention to not only the ways feelings of loss in old age motivate religious behaviors, but also how these religious behaviors could then feedback into how loss was experienced. In the landscape of these circulating aesthetic images, objects, and practices, natural features, such as mountains, rivers, and the moon, symbolized the temporal flow of aging, generations, and the spirits of the deceased. In the fifteenth century, Japanese Buddhist Bikkhuni (female mendicants) would proselytize by sitting on the roadside and unrolling a large hanging scroll known as the Kumano Mandala, which represented the many realms of existence, including various forms of fiery hell and the peaceful realms of the buddhas. Along the top of the Kumano Mandala was the "hill of aging" (*oi no saka*), depicting the ascent and decline of the person over the life course, recalling of nineteenth-century American stair-step images of the life course (Cole 1992). The Kumano Mandala, however, contains some interesting details. As the person pictured ages, the trees and flowers surrounding the person turn from spring to winter. Not only this, but all of the images revolved around the somewhat mystically suspended character "kokoro," or heart consciousness. The seasons of life and death are ultimately emanations of the kokoro; death and birth were only open gates through which spirits passed between realms (Hosoda 2012). The map-like mandala shows only the constant change unfolding around us, which from the perspective of the everyday appears full of loss. Yet the bent form of the old woman at the last approach to death is drawn seated, wearing a nun's robes. She does not suffer, but waits at the interstice. It is a picture not of decline at all, but of completion, perfection.

From the hill of aging, I return once more to obasuteyama. Perhaps the most popular iteration of obasuteyama in postwar Japan has been Fukuzawa Shichihiro's *Narayama Bushikō*, or *The Ballad of Narayama* ([1956] 1981). The novel won its first-time author literary acclaim and the prestigious Chuo Koron Prize for literature, leading to the production of two domestically popular and internationally recognized films, one in 1958, the other twenty-five years later, in 1983 (Imamura 1983). The novel and the first film appeared during a time of transition from the U.S. occupation to a new modern Japan including the rapid decline in fertility rate and lengthening of older adult life spans. In the 1950s, older adults were about 70 percent likely to spend their old age in the home of an adult child, and one intention of the original 1958 film was to raise awareness and improve conditions for older adults. By the time Imamura Shohei directed the second adaptation in 1983, the social and cultural context was dramatically different.

By the early 1980s, Japan's aging population was beginning to face greater social and political changes, even as the children of the baby boom generation were redefining the Japanese family in a time of greater material abundance and internationalization (Hashimoto 2009). Other stories that took care and abandonment in old age as a theme in the years between the two versions of the film included Niwa Fumio's *Iyagarase no Nenrei* (The hateful age, 1962), Inoue Yasushi's "Obasute" (1965), Ohta Tenrei's *Rōjin-tō* (Island of the old, [1970] 1984), Tatsumi Yoshihiro's *Abandon the Old in Tokyo* ([1970] 2006), Ariyoshi Sawako's *The Twilight Years* (*Kōkotsu no Hito*, 1972). These stories had already brought issues of modern obasuteyama into public consciousness, but Imamura Shohei's 1983 version of *The Ballad of Narayama* (Figure 3) could be considered the culmination of this expanding aesthetic genre.

Why would a story like obasuteyama, a story of poverty and kinship in a rural village, seem relevant in a time of Japan's 1980s economic ascendance? The portrait of village life is far from sentimental or nostalgic; it is not a call to return

Figure 3. Tatsuhei (Ogata Ken) carries his mother Orin (Sakamoto Sumiko) on his back as he walks up to the place of abandonment. Film still from *The Ballad of Narayama*, directed by Imamura, Shohei Toei Films, 1983. Permission by Toei Film Company.

to simpler times or core Japanese values espoused in the popular genre *nihonjinron* ("Manifestos on Japanism"), which supported a tone of cultural nationalism (Befu 1991). The power of *The Ballad of Narayama* resulted from a story about not only Japanese ethics but also aesthetics, not the present abundance but the losses obscured or misrecognized by that abundance.

The Ballad of Narayama is different than the versiou by Zeami discussed in the previous chapter. Imamura's film tells the tale of the old matriarch named Orin, who, on the eve of her seventieth birthday, is preparing to follow her village's tradition of abandoning the old on the eponymous mountain. With this abandonment at the forefront of her thoughts, Orin spends most of the film caring for others, including caregiving for her grandchild, comforting aging friends, and matchmaking for her moping, widowed son (Tatsuhei) and her young, cocky grandson (Kesa). Orin even goes so far as to arrange a tryst for her youngest outcast son. Throughout these episodes, Orin remains fixed on her own fate, determined to follow tradition despite her vitality and the worries of her son. The journey up the mountain is full of tense emotion and the quiet stillness that anticipates—the interstice of suspended meaning, the ma. Orin is left on the mountain, the snow falling on her silver hair, and Tatsuhei descends back to the village, a new inner landscape of loss stretched out before him.

The film, which spans a single year in the life of Orin's family, depicts moments both tragic and humorous that ring true to the everyday lives of older people even today. The filmmakers also retained a bit of the dreaminess of Noh, especially when depicting the fundamental nature and kinship: sex, aging, and death. Many scenes are interspliced with close-up footage of animals such as snakes, insects, or mice, eating, copulating, and dying, as if to show age choreographed to the changing tune of each season.[1] Nature, both vital and wild, stands in for man's basic desires and drives against which cultured struggled, but could never quite master.

What distinguishes this tale most from Zeami's is that Orin does not resist or even simply accept her abandonment on Narayama stoically; she demands it. There is no cruel daughter-in-law that we can hold responsible for the abandonment. In fact, Orin's widowed son Tatsuhei has little interest in remarrying and longs to keep his mother close to facilitate his own narcissistic desire to prolong the period of mourning for his deceased wife. Orin will have none of this. Though she is both strong minded and able-bodied, she knows that staying in the village will bring shame on the family. She attempts to rationalize with Tatsuhei, explaining that delaying the trip to Mt. Narayama would only lead to a greater burden on resources, further delaying the birth of new children and disrupting the orderly process of succession necessary for the survival of the household. Tatsuhei in particular, however, is reluctant to give up his attachments and recognize her humble yielding.

Orin takes responsibility for her aging, but it is Tatsuhei whom she must rely on to abandon her. Tatsuhei's father, Rihei, deserted his wife and family, troubled by the grief of his own aging mother on Mt. Narayama and his guilt for selling his young daughter to avoid poverty and starvation. At several points in the film, Rihei returns, mysteriously, as either a gust of wind in the trees or a ghostly figure in the mountains. His unsettled ghost lurks in the shadows and blows dreamlike through the trees. Tatsuhei is haunted by the memory of his father, evidence of the intergenerational transfer of suffering produced by abandonment (Pollock 1989, 137–144).

Orin, again, shows little sympathy for her husband's actions or her son's hesitation. "The law is the law," she sternly rebukes as the two pick wild herbs in the thick grass on the slope of a mountain.

> ORIN: Pity gets you nowhere. [Rihei] acted like he was the only one suffering, and he ran away. He shamed us in front of the entire village. [turning to Tatsuhei] You'll probably. . . .
> TATSUHEI: [forcefully interrupting] I'm different! I'm not like my dad!
> ORIN: I wonder. . . .

Orin fears that Tatsuhei, grieving for his wife and unwilling to take his mother to the mountains, will follow a similar shameful fate. Her only insurance against this is to transform herself into a suitable object of abandonment, to dissemble or deface her own image in such a way that Tatsuhei is forced to carry out his obligation and let her yield.

Orin embodied old age through spiritual, social, and somatic practices of kinship, practices that demanded a mortification of the youthful body. In one particularly uncomfortable scene, Orin knocks out her own teeth on a grindstone in order to appear older and more feeble, returning to the house and encouraging her soon-to-be daughter-in-law to eat heartily. The violent removal of the teeth mutilated not only her means to consumption (teeth and mouth), but also her means of production, a fact foreshadowed in an earlier scene of the film where she is shown using what her grandson calls "demon teeth" (*oni no ha*) to rip plant fibers for weaving. Orin's bloody self-defacement is paradoxically what makes her self-sacrifice so noble, and therefore restorative to the "face" of the household. She is not truly frail and decrepit, but has made herself a resemblance of old age through an extreme case of creativity of loss. This creativity allows old age and death to flow through kinship. Kinship, in this obasuteyama tale, is not antithetical to loss or transcendence; it does not bind the body or spirit to the world. Rather, kinship is an idiom of exchange, succession, losses, and recoveries; kinship is the means to transcendence and a good old age.

Orin follows the village laws and requests to be taken to Mt. Narayama and abandoned there. Tatsuhei reluctantly, but dutifully, complies, like Abraham's sacrifice of Isaac (Kierkegaard [1843] 2013); there is a dramatic yet hopeful tension that demands an otherworldly solution, a meaning to the abandonment for both mother and son. The film ends with Tatsuhei's return to his house, where the rest of the family has already divided up the old woman's belongings.

One of the more touching, quiet scenes in Imamura's film is a conversation, not between family, but between Orin and an old and ailing friend, Okane. It is one of the few scenes where Orin offers a glimpse of her own thoughts on old age. As Orin gently massages her old friend's back, the two discuss their fears of death and abandonment, and their hopes of return:

OKANE: I envy you Orin.

ORIN: Why?

OKANE: I wish that I could live longer.

ORIN: But being as healthy as I am is embarrassing. I eat a full portion.

OKANE: I want to go to the mountain . . . I don't want to die of sickness. They'll just bury me here.

ORIN: It's all the same. Either way, our spirits go to the mountain. We will all meet again on the mountain.

OKANE: Will we all meet again?

ORIN: We will all meet again. Your husband is waiting for you . . . I don't know about my husband though. . . .

In this scene, the mountain is a place of both redemption and reunion for the old and for the spirits of the departed. *The Ballad of Narayama*, like other obasuteyama tales, locates this hope in the mountains. As both womb and tomb, the mountains are reservoirs of the symbolic (Hori 1959; 1968; Ivy 1995; Schnell 2007; Schattschneider 2003), whose power is indexed through the monolithic aesthetic of objects such as the Japanese gravestone and the memorial tablet. As places for memorial and communion with the spirits of the departed, they are highly charged sites for constructing narrative subjectivities, blending the aesthetic motifs of nature and kinship, loss and care. In cultivating this narrative landscape, older adults form personal meanings that are also, importantly, tied to aesthetics and ideologies of the family and belonging in an aging Japan. This chapter explores this idea of landscapes—inner and outer, psychological and political, natural and built—examining the spaces older adults occupy and open up to as they age and, like Orin, come to embody a new sense of kinship and loss.

RIVERS AND MOUNTAINS OF KYOTO

From almost anywhere in Kyoto, it seems that one can hear rivers or see mountains. The city streets flow down from the mountains, pooling thickly in the busy basin below. I often walked upstream to find the source of these flows, past the 7-Eleven and the pachinko game parlors, past the tightly packed farm houses with their clay-tiled gables, even past the tree-shaded shrines, temples, and cemeteries that marked gateways into other worlds. A walk of only a few minutes from my home in Kyoto's northeast periphery would bring me to a cathedral of cypress and cedar. The mountain forests of Kyoto City shelter their own highways of trails, some in use for thousands of years. Even though I knew this, I still found myself thrilled by the fantasy of hiddenness, of being so quickly spirited out of the urban and into the cooling and quiet wild. There was something dreamlike about this sudden transformation from city to mountain, the ghostly wisteria growing wild through the treetops, or the traces of wild pigs digging up bamboo shoots in the spring. Across the ranges, worn stone markers, some recognizable as statues or graves, blended with landscape.

Walking back home from a day at one of the senior community centers, I was joined by an energetic white-haired woman who told me that she too loved mountain hikes around Kyoto, and that she usually climbs Mt. Daimonji (466 meters) twice a week, starting up the mountain early in the morning and descending around midmorning. This mountain, located on the city's eastern edge, was a popular climb for both residents and tourists, with most of the paths up through the forest well cleared and maintained, eventually opening up to a large viewing platform overlooking the city. As we walked and talked, the woman from the center emphasized how these climbs provided an excellent opportunity for physical exercise, enjoying nature, and cultivating self-discipline. I thought of Orin, and the ways in which this mountain routine produced and cultivated aesthetic values that allowed her to reach a good old age. Mountains help us to embody the good; they are a fitting place for the spirits.

Mt. Daimonji is known by most Japanese people as the site of one of Kyoto's iconic images of ancestral veneration: a series of seventy-five bonfires forming the Chinese character for "great" lit on the eve of the late summer holiday of *Obon*. In obasuteyama legends like *The Ballad of Narayama*, mountains are widely associated with the ancestors and the spirits of the dead, not only in Kyoto, but throughout Japan. They are metonymic symbols of the city, tradition, history, as well as religious syncretism (sacred sites in folk, Shinto, Taoist, and Buddhist traditions). For Kyotoites, Mt. Daimonji was considered so close to the other world that on one occasion, after a visit, a friend of mine refused to allow me into her apartment until I had first purified myself with sea salt, a ritual typically associated with postfunerary customs (Kenny and Gilday 2000, 172). Luckily the convenience store across the street sold small bags of salt, and I was liberally brushed down as I stood outside on her second-story landing.

This kind of everyday precaution against tracking in spirits from the mountains revealed the invisible boundaries implied in the pattern of departure and return, or ascent and descent (spatial and generational), that marked the narrative of *The Ballad of Narayama*. Navigating these boundaries through practices formed a different way of mapping the city, one that relied on an imaginative ontology of the unseen whose power, nonetheless, worked through people, practices, and objects. As if to underline this sentiment, one Shinto poster I saw showed a simple wooden shrine floating amid rays of sunlight shining through tall cedars with the tagline: "It is what you can see when you close your eyes." The awe and power of nature could be found at the border of the senses, within oneself.

Another example of the imaginative stitching together of past and future in the landscape is the frequently reproduced image of the map of current-day Kyoto overlaid with a sort of thickly lined grid of the original eighth-century city plan. This map, bordered by mountains on the west, north, and east sides, depicts the continuous structure and sensibility of the past, even as it has reinvented itself as a modern city. Looking at a map like this, one might feel compelled, as I was myself, to try to line up recognizable landmarks, such as streets or shrines, with the important intersections and interstices of the original city plan.

On one occasion, I was doing just that at the Kyoto National Museum when I was approached by an older Japanese man wearing thick glasses, a weathered baseball cap, and a green vest with multiple small pockets like those worn by photographers and fishermen. After chatting for a bit about the city design and history, the man asked if I had seen the Hollyhock Procession (Aoi Matsuri) at Shimogamo Shrine, pointing to the shrine's location at the triangular delta where the Kamo River and Takano River meet and flow south toward Osaka. He then paused, smiling, before saying, "That is the story of my life."

He gestured again, using the word *mata*, which means both the joining of rivers as well as the crotch of a person. I had heard in other casual conversations that Kyoto was female, but this landscape of resemblance drove the point home. The man elaborated, telling me that the procession to Shimogamo Shrine at the mata of the rivers was a "return to the womb" and a kind of "rebirth" (*umare-kawaru*). While I could see how such a ritual brings together the realms of life and death through the metaphors of geographic resemblance and memorial offerings (Schattschneider 2003, 58–60), what struck me the most was the enthusiasm with which this man spoke to us about its personal meaning for him. His earnestness left me with a humbled feeling of an outsider rather than a participant observer; I still had not learned to see the landscape like this man and other older Kyoto residents saw it. After talking a bit more, the man handed me his business card and wished me a pleasant stay. The card identified him as a former member of the self-defense forces, but said nothing of him being a volunteer tour guide for English speakers, as he had claimed.

Like other large Japanese cities, Kyoto had undergone tremendous changes during the lifetimes of my informants. For older residents of Kyoto, the city and geographic landmarks evoked both personal recollections and collective loss; it was a site of repetitive memories that inscribed the landscape and the story its maps. But what happens when the memories of a place and the selves bound up in those places haunt its lived presence? To understand the way a place like Kyoto is experienced by older adults who have spent their entire lives there, we need what Byron Good, after Jacques Derrida, called a more robust "hauntology" (2012, 32), a way to listen to what haunts the ordinary, whether that ordinary is the experience of growing old or the ground beneath one's feet.

"I Don't Need Anything Anymore"

Historically, death had been located on the periphery of Kyoto City, tucked into hillside cemeteries and even climbing several stories up the steep mountainsides (Figure 4). At the base of many of these cemeteries are Buddhist temples, so that between mountain and city, there is a ring of sacred sites. These temples are often associated with not only the spirits of the dead, but also the deities of the mountains and streams, and the various gateways of good and bad fortune, blessings or contamination, that flow into the city from the outside.

Cemeteries are familiar places, open, often wedged between residences, shops, schools, and other places with frequent pedestrian traffic. During the four principal memorial holidays that punctuate the annual cycle at seasonal interludes (New Year, spring and autumn equinoxes [*higan*], and summer [*Obon*]), the cemeteries and temples of Kyoto become busy hives of visitors carrying their long-handled ladles, blue or red plastic buckets of water to wash the grave stone, and bags of offerings: flowers, packaged food, and drinks the dead would enjoy (beer, soda, sake, juice, tea). The thick fog of incense and spent matches give the air its own otherworldly perfume. Although crowded, the atmosphere at the cemetery would be quiet and respectful, the aesthetically precise ritual care of the dead creating a peaceful feeling of the spirits and their watchfulness.

A cemetery plot, like any home, is sometimes chosen on the basis of its peacefulness and view of the surrounding scenery. I often found myself drawn to these

Figure 4. Gravestones in a temple cemetery on a hillside in Kyoto. Photo by author.

cemeteries, wandering through the rows of gravestones, admiring the different styles and shapes of the monuments, and reading their carved inscriptions, which gave clues about the age, family composition, and even sectarian affiliation of the members of the household whose remains were interred below. Most visitors came in the early morning, and most were older people. For them, the grave was not merely a monument to the deceased, but also the place where they would soon rest and be memorialized themselves, the place where they leave old age behind and reunite with the lost loved one, not unlike the mountain Orin imagines in *The Ballad of Narayama.*

One woman I met at a small cemetery at the base of a mountain in northern Kyoto was typical of these daily visitors. She was dressed modestly for the warm fall weather in a long cardigan sweater, and her thin frame bent gently over her brown metal cane. Japanese people sometimes refer to this posture as that of a ripe stalk of rice, or the elegant curve of shrimp. She was the only visitor I saw that afternoon, and came alone and on foot. She did not bring offerings, but stopped at the water pump at the cemetery entrance to fetch water and hefted the bucket to her gravestone. I watched as she slowly extended her arm with what seemed like great effort to pour water on the top of the gravestone, bathing its sun-bleached surface. It was not dirty per se, but the act of carrying the water to the grave and letting it flow down the surface of the stone until it glistened a deep, dark gray was an aesthetic performance, a re-creation of the flow of water down from the mountain peak to its base. After this act of purification was performed, she bowed quietly, having prepared a reflective space for sensing the presence of the spirit.

After a moment, the woman placed the ladle back into the bucket, and without straightening posture, put her palms together and paused quietly for several seconds. When she was done, she gathered her things and tottered cautiously back though the aisle of graves with aid of her cane. I greeted her, reassuring her that I spoke Japanese, and then struck up a conversation about her visit:

WOMAN: I thought I just come over and put a little water on [the grave]. Of course I'm getting up in years, y'know. If I was younger I wouldn't be doing this, right? I'm ninety years old ... I don't need anything anymore. [motioning toward the grave] One more person is going there [soon].

DANELY: Whose grave did you visit today?

WOMAN: My husband's. And the ancestors from all the way back (*senzo daidai*).

DANELY: Do you come to this grave often?

WOMAN: I come every day. Usually in the morning. Today I was at lunch and then I thought I should go and look at the grave. Once you get old, you don't need anything anymore!

With this, she smiled and began walking home, carefully holding her cane as she cautiously made her way down the steep stone steps. For older adults like this

woman, the grave may be a place to go when "you don't need anything anymore," but it is precisely this function that makes the grave and loss so meaningful in old age—memorialization provided an alternate set of aesthetic tools
for experiencing loss and solitude, an alternate position in the economy of care,
a way to live and to give, a space to imagine the next life.

Perhaps it was this social imaginary that Orin demanded, but which her son
did not understand until he had descended Narayama. No longer a burden, and
no longer bound to the home, abandonment and loss may have an alluring sense
of freedom if they also entail hope of reunion with loved ones. Everyday rituals
like visiting the grave create aging subjectivities suspended between the weight
of being burdensome and the lightness and hope of returning to the other
world. Their performances are critical material anchors for this cyclical narrative
of life and death and its embodiment of feelings and affects of caring and
being cared for in old age. This is the old age that Orin was to achieve in her
abandonment—old age as oiru—a narrative of old age that can incorporate a
space for a "heroics of waiting" to be brought to the other world.[2]

CEMETERY AS LANDSCAPE OF MEMORY

Memorialization at cemeteries are what Michel de Certeau terms "spatial practices" (1984, 93), activities that exist in relation to structured spaces and landscapes but that are not fully determined by them. While cemeteries in Japan, like
those elsewhere in the world, are culturally constituted spaces that organize the
process of mourning according to principles, rights, and obligations of kinship
and spiritual worldview, they are also constituted by the personal memories of
visitors and the felt presence of the spirits that extend beyond the parameters of
their material architecture (Francis, Kellaher, and Neophytou 2005). In other
words, spatial practices, like visiting a grave, are aesthetic expressions of both
cultural institutions and individuals who interpret them through subjective
experiences.

For most people, the grave is the "home" of the family spirits, where their
presence is especially strong. It also serves as what Jean Langford called a
"communicative interface between the living and the dead" (2009, 685). As one
widow put it,

> Well, sure we have the butsudan but, it's set up in the house but it's like deco-
> ration. Because he's at the grave. Father is. Well, I mean the ancestors. So I'll
> go there and say things like "Things are like this these days. . . ." And then I
> myself will feel something like relieved (ochitsuku, literally falling away). It
> feels like that. Well you know how they're always saying that the hotoke comes
> home on Obon? Well they say it returns home. So if you just have a butsudan,
> he can't return from anywhere. So when I go to the grave I feel kind of like I've
> come close to [my husband]. So I feel at ease (ochitsuku).

Between these comings and goings is the inescapable space of the *ma*—all those moments of suspense in which desire, memory, grief, and love pool up, where abandonment and hope are both possibilities. The "ease," "relief," and "solace" reported by older people after visiting the graves was not very different than the comfort of finding something momentarily lost, right where you remember seeing it last. One of anthropologist Ronald Dore's informants explained that easing sense of closeness another way: "For us old people, visiting the graves is like going to the pictures and so on for the youngsters. You go to meet your dead: you can see their faces in your mind's eye and you can talk to them—you don't get any reply, of course, but it feels good" (1958, 323). Spatial practices like these engage memories, images, and most of all feelings within a symbolically rich landscape.

Sato-san brusquely dismissed funerals as frivolous expenses for corrupt Buddhist institutions, but after his wife died at the age of thirty-four, he chose a grave plot in a Zen Buddhist temple cemetery about a mile from his house rather than at a newer, secular "memorial park." As the youngest son, Sato-san has only this one grave that he visited regularly, and the only remains buried there are those of his wife, whom he often spoke of joining in the other world. He has already arranged with the temple to have his own remains interred in this grave after he dies.

Sato-san first mentioned his wife's grave as we walked around downtown Kyoto one summer morning, casually mentioning that it was only a few blocks away from where we were talking. When I expressed interest in seeing it, he abruptly turned around and started quickly down one of the narrow side streets, leaving me fumbling with my notepad as I began to frantically jot notes and keep up.

As we approached the temple where the grave was located, we passed the kindergarten his granddaughter attended, and Sato-san stopped to peek through the slats of a wooden fence to see if he could spot her playing among the other children noisily clambering around the playground. He could not find her, looking in through several different places in the fence before giving up, a little disappointed. We kept walking without speaking, but soon reached the gate of a modest wooden temple structure that would have been easy to miss amid the shops and houses that vied for space along the street. As we entered the cemetery grounds, crunching along the gravel pathway, we could still hear the sound of the children playing at the kindergarten less than a block away.

The transition into the space of the cemetery was marked in this case by a seated statue of the Bodhisattva Jizō, guide and guardian in the other worlds, covered with decorative offerings.[3] Past this were the neat, uniform rows of granite pillars set atop their pedestals, standing just below eye level. Each was fitted with surfaces or impressions for placing small offerings or incense, vases for flowers, and racks for large and small wooden memorial slats, or "stupas" (*sotōba*), purchased from temples that were inscribed at different memorial occasions with names and dates of the purchaser (Smith 1974, 42–43). At a distance, the larger boards almost resembled tall picket fences between rows of homes.

Japanese graves are highly communicative objects. As we crunched down the gravel paths, dotted with green accents of moss and lichen, I thought about how the rows of names etched into the pillars reminded me of the name placards posted outside each home in lieu of a building number. Like a model of the temple parish, I could quickly and easily assess new and old residents, wealthy and poor, devout and abandoned. Sato-san's wife's plot was located in the very back of the cemetery, against a dark gray cinder block wall that surrounded the temple grounds. Six tall sotōba had been lined up behind the gravestone, and the wood was worn and discolored from the weather but still clearly marked in dark india ink with the date of each memorial.

Sato-san stood in front of the grave for a moment and then picked up a half stick of incense and a candle that had been lying on the pedestal and asked me for a match in a hurried but hushed voice. I handed him a lighter and he attempted to light the incense and candle. Both crackled from the dampness and quickly blew out in the slight breeze. Sato-san tried once again, turning and hunching his body in an effort to block the wind, but eventually gave up, erecting the unlit incense and candle in their places on the stone as we stood in the narrow pathway between plots, facing the grave.

"Hi! Jason has come! Jason has come!" he announced, in a soft, affectionate voice, as if to gently wake someone from a midday nap. Sato-san always took a softer tone when he spoke of his wife, and it was softer still when we visited her grave. Still standing, he bowed his head and raised his hands, palms together. After a short, silent pause, he chanted "Namu Amida Butsu" several times in a hushed voice.[4] I watched Sato-san, copying his movements, waiting for his cue before raising my own head. He stepped back and resumed his usual speaking tone. "I'll bring the flowers a little later," he apologized, still looking at the stone.

As if to assure me that he has not been neglecting his wife, Sato-san pointed out the memorial slats: "They cost thirty-five hundred yen [about thirty-five U.S. dollars at the time]. Really expensive! Everyone has the temple inscribe theirs for them but I write it myself. It's fine if you don't write it yourself but. . . . Well, it's a sort of, a sort of record. [pointing to a memorial slat] See, over here it says twenty-three years, right? That means that twenty-three years had passed [since the death] when it was made." Actions like writing out his own sotōba and making the small annual grave upkeep donations were hardly forms of resistance to Buddhist orthodoxy, but they did constitute a small way for Sato-san to exercise creativity though the labor of caring for the grave. Being financially responsible, even thrifty, was an important value for Sato-san's sense of independence, responsibility, and masculinity; therefore the extra care invested in writing the memorial also supported his sense of agency and sufficiency. Managing the grave also echoed his attitudes toward the senior welfare center (chapter 2), which helped stave off homebound dependence in old age while at the same time offered opportunities to express interdependence, care, and concern for his peers at no direct financial cost.

Curious about how his relationship with his wife and the way her memorial changed his views on aging, I asked Sato-san how often he visited his wife's grave. To my surprise, he answered, "Only four times a year: Obon, New Year, spring and autumn equinox." While it had been over thirty years since her death, this seemed a bit infrequent given the amount that she came up in our conversations. After a moment, however, he added, "and on her birthday. Well, if I go to the supermarket, I'll also look at the flowers and if there are some inexpensive ones, I'll get them and come here to give them to her too."[5] The affectionate tone of Sato-san's voice, his casual but thoughtful gestures of buying flowers from the supermarket, and his sweet yet clumsy attempts to make offerings were not simply idiosyncrasies or failures to enact a proper ritual form. If we forgot, for a moment, that his wife was no longer alive, we might see these as the little affections of any "old married couple," still keeping things alive not through words, or grand sacrifices, but through the kind of simple intimate care and remembrance that most people would hardly notice.

While the butsudan and memorial tablets (themselves similar in shape to gravestones) generate spatial practices for ritual interaction with the dead, the movement of departure and return is inverse: the living go to and return home from the graves, while the dead come from and return to the grave from the butsudan. This pattern mimics the cyclical movement of the deified ancestral spirits from the fields to the mountains in Japanese folk belief (Tanaka and Yamaori 2005), and the double-grave system once widespread (Yanagita [1946] 1970). Both reconstitute the separation and transversability of "this world" and the "other world" by means of ascending and descending. Thinking back to *The Ballad of Narayama*, we might think of each memorial ascent to the mountain/grave as carrying the weight of grief and the burden of age, while practices of careful offering allowed this burden to be relieved by the spirits, and the descent back to the mundane world lighter.

Changing Myself into the Buddha

Joining a lost loved one in the other world involves becoming a "buddha." This is not as daunting a task as it may sound; while in some Buddhist traditions, this would involve countless rebirths and eventually complete release from the karmic cycle, Japanese lay Buddhists tend to embrace the view that salvation from suffering can be attained through the compassion of those who have achieved enlightenment, such as Amida Buddha, the numerous bodhisattvas (Kannon, Jizō, e.g.), and other superhuman entities.

Of course, even with the help of these powerful beings, lay people have little hope for freedom from suffering in this world, and concentrate primarily on saving the spirits of the departed, who become hotoke (a term that glosses as "buddha") after the first forty-nine days of pacification/memorialization rituals. If memorialization practices avoid easy categorization as "worship" or even "religious"

(Plath 1964), a point made clear by the confusing survey data using religiosity scales developed in Western contexts, the spirits generally avoid easy categorization as well. In practice, the spirits of the departed who have been placated through memorial rituals and have received a posthumous name are considered hotoke until they have faded from the memories of the living or upon the thirty-third death anniversary when they are considered an ancestor.

In many ways, formal religious language can be imprecise or misleading, and the simple, intimate, and animistic depiction of memorialization in *The Ballad of Narayama* appeared closer to the actual feelings people spoke of when referring to their families. Most people made little distinction between the practical ways of relating to the hotoke, the Buddhas, or the Shinto kami, all of whom, as we've seen in the history of Kyoto, are intimately genealogically entangled, "as waves to the ocean." Even Nakamura-san, who cared for ten different graves and gave daily offerings to many different kami in his home, struggled to explain any substantial ontological difference among the hotoke, Buddhas, bodhisattvas, or kami.

Although Nakamura-san seemed happy to have been able to show me memorial services, he also found himself tongue-tied when trying to explain the purpose of the monthly service, or why he continued to observe it for so long at such a cost. In fact, one reason Nakamura-san continued to work, even into his mid-seventies, was serious financial concerns about living off of his pension allowance of about seventy thousand yen (about seven hundred dollars) per month (each service would cost about a hundred dollars). Instead of answering why he continued the services, he rose from the table and went to the butsudan, where he retrieved the registry booklet of death anniversaries and posthumous names, a little bigger than a checkbook, opening up its accordion-folded pages and spreading them over to the dining table. Perching a pair of wire-rimmed glasses on the end of his nose, he began flipping through the pages, running his finger over the pages, while his wife looked over his shoulder. Rather than finding answers, the couple found themselves tripping over the pronunciations of the complicated names and wondering who many of the entries referred to (there were many).

The death names of the hotoke signal their otherness, a way of forgetting the living soul by memorializing the new "buddha." At the same time, practices of memorial constantly betray this otherness, as the "buddhas" of recently departed are spoken to as if they were still alive, receiving personal attention and care. The shotsukimeinichi service mediated this suspension through aesthetic practices of ordering and ritualizing transience and loss. After shuffling through the booklet and describing some of the other practices of caring for the hotoke, Nakamura-san still did not feel confident in his explanation and arranged for the priest to answer some of my questions after one of the monthly shotsukimeinichi services I attended at his home.

When we met with the priest again, the three of us sat in front of the butsudan as Emiko-san brought in the tea tray. Nakamura-san explained that I had brought up some questions about "Japanese religious traditions." As if on cue, the priest crossed his arms and leaned back dramatically groaning, "Oh, that's a tough one!" We all let out polite, slightly embarrassed laughter, while I braced myself for the reply.

"It's hard even for Japanese people!" added Emiko-san from the threshold of the next room, quickly breaking the tension. As the priest began to explain, Nakamura-san seemed to hang on each word, interjecting at one point about his own future as a hotoke:

PRIEST: If you think about it, here you have the hotoke-san [points to butsu-dan] and over here you have the kami-san [points to a kamidana near the ceiling of the room].

NAKAMURA: Oh, right, right! [everyone laughs]

PRIEST: It's kind of funny that we have the hotoke-san and the kami-san.

NAKAMURA: The other day Jason and I were talking together [and he asked] "What's the difference between kami-san and hotoke-san?" [Emiko laughs] And I really couldn't explain very well. . . .

PRIEST: Basically, in any kind of Christian or kami-san faith . . . when we die, when we die we go to the place of kami-san, right? With hotoke-san we change. Changing myself into the Buddha . . . it's a [bodily] transformation (*henshin*). But in case of Christianity, whatever we do, we don't change into a God. In the end, that's the most basic difference.

NAKAMURA: [laughing] I wonder if I'll change like that too? Oh, what will become of ME?! [laughing harder]

[After the laughter at Nakamura-san's comment dies down]

EMIKO: We sometimes ask things of the hotoke-san, but most of the time [laughing] we ask more of the kami-san, right?

PRIEST: Well that's because the Japanese government is a system that reveres the emperor, and that's the kami-san. So nowadays, a nation's govern-ments, for example Malaysia, the country is Muslim. It's mandated, right? And if you go to the Philippines, it is more or less Christian. . . . In the case of Japan, we said, well, if you want to choose our national religion it is the shrine [Shinto]. If you think of it as emperor centered, right? [Nakamura: Oh, I see, is that right?] So the essence is the kami-san. But in the end, Prince Shōtoku brought in Buddhism, and our beliefs changed once more.[6] So we started to think like, there are kami-san and hotoke-san and if Christmas comes around, we celebrate Christmas [everyone laughs]! Even I do this! So really, if I was to say that there was any remnant of a *purely* Japanese religious ritual (*junsui na shukyō gishiki*), the only thing left in Japan is . . . well, the funeral is the only one. Look at weddings. There's no sense of religious feeling (*shukyō-kan*), right? [Nakamura: Oh, right!] you have a butsudan in your home and I say "*namu amida butsu, namu amida butsu*" but when I leave, there's a fee, right?

EMIKO: Yes! There are so many things we need to make donations for!

PRIEST: So if you are Jōdo-shu you pay the fee at the temple, or for weddings
   at the [Shinto] Shrine, and it's really no different—
EMIKO: According to your preference, right?
PRIEST: So that is what you might call a kind of "style" (*sutairu*), a kind of
   flow (*nagare*) . . . so it is probably difficult for someone from abroad to
   understand this but—
EMIKO: It's something that even we don't understand! [laughs]

The priest's explanation was unexpected in two ways. The first was the way the
priest distinguished between becoming a buddha and reuniting with the gods,
something that was particularly interesting in light of Nakamura-san's interjec-
tion ("Oh, what will happen to me?"). Older people, like Orin in *The Ballad of
Narayama*, often spoke of the hope of reuniting with lost loved ones in the
"other world," but did not mention becoming a buddha themselves. It is not surprising then that the Nakamuras would also find this difference worth noting.
However, becoming a buddha in no way means that one does not reunite with
other buddhas, and the image of the afterlife as a paradise where one meets one's
family (buddhas as well) is consistent with the sense of close similarity between
the visible and invisible worlds inhabited by spirits. Nakamura-san's comment
also reminds us that for an older person this hopeful transformation of the spirit
depends not only on the compassion of supernatural beings, but on the continued actions of the rituals performed by the living, which are less secure when
traditional bonds of succession are weak. Tradition is more than a symbol of
continuity, but of repetition and reproduction of exchanges that must be anticipated before the event of death. Changing into the buddha depended on securing bonds of kinship and care.

The second related point of interest was that while the priest fully acknowledged Japanese religious syncretism from Christmas to the cult of the emperor,
he explained that only funerals remained something "purely Japanese." He did
not elaborate here, except to contrast it with a consumer model of ritual where
there is little religious "feeling" and where consumption appears to replace
observance as the primary mode of relationality. Given all of the changes in
Japanese mortuary and memorial rites, even over the past century, why would
the priest find it important to call funerals "purely Japanese"?

One possible reason is that mortuary and memorial rites are inseparable
from the idea of "tradition," or the "unconscious tradition," as folklorist Yanagita
Kunio phrases it (Yanagita [1946] 1970, 178–179), in that their perpetuation
depends upon a continuity of generations.[7] By definition, something ceases to
become a tradition when it is not or cannot be passed down from generation to
generation, and because ancestor memorial depends upon succeeding generations to remember the dead (rather than institutions operating peripheral to
kinship such as shrines and temples), abandoning such practices unsettles the
foundation of what it means to mourn, and indeed to be Japanese.

Nakamura-san's concern about the continuity of memorial traditions was not uncommon among older adults. Some have embraced alternate memorial schemes such as *eitai kuyō*, or "perpetual memorial" sites maintained by temples rather than kin (Rowe 2011), but this option meant not only abandoning tradition, but abandoning the graves currently maintained, and was almost unthinkable for someone such as Nakamura-san. Better then to practice hope by continuing an investment in the care of the spirits, however risky the future seemed.

A GRAVE FOR MOTHER

On my way to Mori-san's house to visit and help with the move for the first time since New Year, I decided to stop my bicycle by the temple where she and I had made offerings at the graves for her mother and grandparents a few months earlier. I locked my bicycle on the gravel path just inside the gate and walked to the cemetery grounds at the back of the temple. After wandering through the rows, I came to the place where I thought the grave plot was located, but when I read the stones, none of them were familiar. I circled around, trying to jog my memory, looking for clues, suddenly feeling disoriented.

Finally I decided to leave, still a bit puzzled. When I reached the cemetery gate, however, I caught site of one of Mori-san's family's gravestones, which had been moved to an area reserved for the memorial of abandoned spirits (muen-botoke). Many cemeteries include a space like this, usually near the entrance, and they are easily identified by the tightly arranged grouping of worn and crumbling stones (Rowe 2011, 47). I reread the inscriptions to make sure I was seeing correctly. Had Mori-san abandoned the grave prior to her move? Did the expense of moving force her to sell the plot? Had she fallen behind in her grave upkeep donations?

Certainly placing the gravestones on the *muen* pedestal seemed like a very serious matter, and I began to feel somewhat unnerved by the thought of unconnected ghosts hovering in front of me. Moving the family remains in itself is not uncommon, and may be a means of adjusting the landscape of the past (the place of the departed) as well as that of one's own future (the place of reunion), and its symbolism reverberates throughout the system of care and reciprocity that links kin and congregation alike. However, since Mori-san had not discussed this with me, I decided to approach the subject as delicately as I could.

My concern came from knowing something about Mori-san's position in her kinship network, which developed over the course of her life through family religious affiliation and marriage. The result of these life circumstances meant that Mori-san (and to some extent her daughters as well) was responsible for the graves of two nearly extinguished patrilines: her father's (represented by her mother's grave) and her mother's parents'. While Mori-san was fairly confident that her own daughters would dutifully look after her grave, they would most likely not have their own remains buried there (having married into other households and having children in separate patrilines). It would be difficult and extend well beyond their filial obligation to attend to the graves I was looking for as well as those of their husbands' family and those of their father, whom Mori-san divorced many years ago.

In order to understand this fractured and disrupted landscape of memorial, and the way it might influence Mori-san's experience in old age, we need to know more about Mori-san's life story and bonds of blood and care that structure her position in her kin network.

Mori-san was born in Kyoto, the eldest of two girls. Her father came to Kyoto to start a radio business after his parents had died, and he converted to Christianity before marrying Mori-san mother, a Kyoto native. Although Mori-san and her younger sister both attended Catholic schools, the family was not particularly devout, and they still observed traditions such as visiting with relatives on Obon and on other Buddhist holidays.

During the early years of World War II, Mori-san, like other teenage girls at the time, was enrolled in a variety of compulsory labor jobs to aid the war effort, from potato farming in the countryside to packing mortar shells in a factory. In the later years of the war, however, she contracted tuberculosis, which depressed her chest and made her lungs extremely weak. Her parents did their best to keep her happy and satisfied, but good quality medicine and doctors were in short supply at the time, and the possibility that Mori-san would die was frighteningly high. These fears were not unfounded, since at the time (around 1950) tuberculosis was a leading cause of death in Japan, outranking cancer, heart disease, and strokes. For years, Mori-san was confined to her bed and frequently admitted to the hospital until better medical care became available during the American occupation (1946–1952).

Soon after her recovery, however, Mori-san's mother, who had cared for her throughout her illness, died of acute liver cancer. While Mori-san admits that the direct cause of her mother's death was cancer, she primarily blames "mental strain," which she said affects the liver most of all:

> My mother died of liver cancer, but that's because she pushed her body past its limits. At that time, my father was . . . [inaudible]. It was such a mess . . . since she was suffering mentally, it affected her liver. The way I see it, from long ago in Japan they would say lots of things "get carved into your liver" (*kimo ni meizuru*).[8] It's mental (*shinkei*)—well, *kokoro? Kokoro* means the "heart" but it also means spiritual (*seishin*)—that sort of thing. Well [you get] liver trouble. She really stuck it out for two or three years, working hard! [laughs] you know, that changes a person. It transforms them. And it went to her liver.

Mori-san refused to accept her mother's cancer in strictly biomedical terms, but felt the cause of death must have been something more: a tragic transformation resulting from mental and spiritual self-sacrifice. Mori-san also noted that her mother was the youngest of seven children, and that her own mother (Mori-san's maternal grandmother) had died when her mother was only one year old, as if her own abandonment was linked to a tragic lineage of abandonment.

Understandably, the death of her mother and its premonition embedded in the coincidence of Mori-san's recovery and the genealogical pattern of women in her family, became a pivotal moment in Mori-san's life. It created not only deeply painful feelings of shame and guilt, but also a fixation on the dependence that could not be fulfilled. This is a common source of pain for many people in Japanese society who have been socialized to desire indulgence of dependence and also to be sensitive to excessive dependence (Johnson 1993; Tomita 1994, 41–42). Mori-san's narrative of her mother's decline and death, utilizing Japanese cultural models of the body, and references to ethnomedical folk theories of bodily inscription (things "get carved into the liver"), indicates her desire to find meanings that reach beyond the visible, and that make sense of her lingering attachment, her guilt for being a burden to her mother, and her shame for having been "abandoned" by her mother in death. Mori-san almost seemed to blame her father for causing her mother's stress early in her description, but quietly mumbled this to herself.

Mori-san was already in her mid-twenties when she fully regained her health, and did not marry until her early thirties. The man whom she married was a woodworker and sculptor as well as a friend of her father's from a neighboring city. Mori-san had a son and three daughters with this husband, but even before the last child was born, things in the marriage had already started to take a turn for the worse. Her husband, who had initially been very successful in work, began to see his business decline. He also began to drink heavily and was increasingly violent and abusive toward Mori-san: "He was an alcoholic so, he got violent, you know? He would be violent in the house, when I would make food, I'd make dinner and he would take his cup and say "What is this dinner?" and take the fry pan and BAM! Hit me on the head. He was crazy. But of course from his childhood, he was spoiled, and so he was used to getting his way—those people are all around nowadays!" Eventually, a divorce was obtained and Mori-san returned to Kyoto to live with her father, taking her three daughters with her, the youngest still less than a year old. Mori-san's ex-husband and son stayed in their home, but there was almost no contact between her and her son until the husband passed away, over thirty years after the divorce.

Mori-san raised her three girls by herself, and never remarried. She worked at a number of part-time jobs (teacher, day care for a Catholic church, textile dying, kimono wearing classes) to help support the family and send the girls to school.

As Mori-san's father grew older, she assumed responsibility for his care as well. Like her husband, however, he too became difficult to live with, a fact that may have colored some of her negative feelings toward old age:

> Families have all sorts of problems because they're taking care of [their old parents]. My father, my own father, he has grandchildren, right? Well at first

he spoiled them, but after they got a little older they always argued. For example, they'd want to watch cartoons on television and I would let them watch at six o'clock, and at seven the news would come on and my father would come in and turn the channel to watch the news. Oh, and the kids would have a tantrum and they'd be crying for their cartoons, and well, the news comes on again at nine and so I'd say, why don't you watch the news at nine? But he wouldn't want to wait and just shout "It's seven o'clock and I'm watching the news!" Older people just act like that's natural, they act like it's matter of fact [to get their way].

There was a striking difference between Mori-san's description of her father and that of her mother, and the gendered difference in life trajectories. While her mother died young and was always described in sentimental and flattering terms as caring to the point of the ultimate self-sacrifice, her father was described as a stubborn, self-centered "old person," and not a very pleasant sounding one at that. When I asked Mori-san how long her father lived, she replied curtly, "He lived a long time [drawing out the words]. Until he was eighty-six. But that person was hopeless" (*ano hito ha shikata ga nai*).

Mori-san's life narrative points to the insecurities of old age for women in particular. Her case is complicated by her prolonged illness that kept her from pursuing an education or marrying earlier, and by the early death of her mother, who may have been a source of social support after her divorce. With few means to support herself and her children, Mori-san endured an unhappy relationship with her ex-husband and later with her father. She also bore the weight of blame and resentment from her daughters, as was evident in the tense interactions described in chapter 1.

Mori-san's connections to the spirits have been severed not only by the broken relationship with her husband and son, but also by the fact that her father was not Buddhist, and had his remains interred in a Catholic mausoleum. Mori-san and her daughters still visited and observed memorials there from time to time, but these occasions were far fewer in number than those made at her mother's grave, which is located separately at the Buddhist temple. Mori-san's mother's remains could not be placed in the grave of her family of origin (Mori-san's maternal grandparents), since her surname identified her as a member of her husband's household. As a result, there was a separate gravestone placed next to that of her parents on a small shared plot at the Buddhist temple. That is, until the day I discovered the stones on the altar for abandoned spirits.

Since Mori-san changed her surname back to her maiden name after her divorce, she will be able to place her remains with those of her mother's. Unless Mori-san's youngest daughters retains her name (she was not married at the time), Mori-san and her mother will be the only ones under that stone. Mori-san has no male siblings in the Mori patrilineage, and at the time of my fieldwork, two of Mori-san's daughters had married and taken different surnames, while her son retained his father's surname. Mori-san's death, while reuniting mother and daughter in the spiritual world, would likely mark the end of the household lineage (*zekke*).

With this understanding of Mori-san's life, and the resulting instability of her kin-provisioned support, I could not help but wonder at why the gravestones were moved. Not long after my discovery, I stopped at Mori-san's house to help her with some gardening chores. All afternoon I turned over the question of the gravestones in my mind, and by the time we had finished, I mentioned my interest in seeing the graves again soon and if they were still at the same temple we had visited earlier in the fall. To my relief, Mori-san told me that she had purchased new gravestones to be set at the same location, and when I asked further about what had been done with the old ones, she explained that she didn't feel that it was right to just dispose of them, since the spirits of the dead might still have attachment to them. Instead, they would be entrusted to the temple as a kind of safeguard, and would receive the occasional offerings for the abandoned spirits.

Purchasing new gravestones, which can cost on average ten thousand dollars or more each, was a considerable investment, especially for Mori-san, who received a small fixed pension benefit. And yet, she seemed to casually shrug this off. It was just something that she had been meaning to do for a while, and now that she was moving away, it became another matter of putting things in order, the way Orin made arrangements in her immediate kin network in old age, and perhaps the spirits would help ease the transition to her new home, she added. For Mori-san, it seemed, ordering the graves was a means to ordering her life course narrative and the landscape it inhabited, perhaps even functioning as a gesture directed toward her daughters to maintain the graves (and consequently the memory of this narrative) in the same way Nakamura-san hoped his sons would maintain the family traditions.

As I was leaving Mori-san's home, I noticed several bags of belongings that she had arranged neatly by the entrance in the front room. Surprised again by what seemed like Mori-san's new capacity to put things in order, I asked about the bags, and she explained that these were things that belonged to her mother and father that she had been collecting either to take with her to the new home or to dispose of in a formal religious ceremony. She reached into one bag and pulled out a wooden block beautifully inscribed with calligraphic characters. This was a "certificate" her mother received for *ikebana* (Japanese flower arrangement arts), and Mori-san told me that she could not bear to throw it out. "It has her name on it here [pointing to the block]. So, I'll take it along with some of these other things to a shrine to make an offering."

The stories that Mori-san told me about her mother were always filled with admiration, intimacy, and love—beautiful feelings that contrasted the ugly ones directed at the men in her life. In collecting her mother's old belongings, and especially those that reinforced this recognition like the ikebana certificates, Mori-san constructed a narrative of the past that she could recognize in her own experiences of sacrifice, disappointment, and perseverance. Following Lester's (2005, 236–241) application of the Kohutian framework to describe culturally situated psychodynamics, we might suggest that the traumatic break from her self object (mother) at a crucial point in her own self-formation produced a fissure in her ability to represent herself to herself. Memorial was an attempt to repair this fissure by appearing to her mother and seeking her affirming response. Like the old woman in Zeami's *Obasute* (chapter 1), however, the shame produced by memories, and by her failures to live up to the idealized self of her mother, was, like the moonlight, too much to face, and she retreated, yet again, into other objects.[9]

For Mori-san, memorialization was in part an interpersonal, intersubjective response to the absence of a mother when she was a young woman; the mirror that might have sustained her in old age is now imagined as the face of the hotoke. She had willingly taken on the role of the custodian of these memories and through her efforts at memorialization could generate a new narrative and imagine a new moral relationship with her mother. Transforming the graves by purchasing new stones and aesthetically transforming the discarded objects into ritual offerings could all be seen as the creativity of loss. Mori-san was able to become a caregiver to her mother, and to imagine a care for herself that would extend through old age and past her death, when she would join her mother in the grave and the other world.

As meaningful as these gestures were, there was still much work to be done in the house and a sense of apprehension in following her daughter to the new home. I wondered how the objects we packed up would translate to the new spaces and circumstances of her life. After months of packing and repacking boxes, I began to come across many old photographs in the piles marked to be thrown away. I decided to ask Mori-san if she had any photographs of her mother that she could show me, since there were no funeral portraits like those hanging prominently in Nakamura-san's home. Mori-san shuffled through some stacks of papers and then through a bookshelf that appeared to be overflowing in a slow-motion avalanche of loose leaf onto the ground. Perhaps it was just a matter of things being out of place because of the move, or the fact that there were so few photographs for someone who passed away in the 1950s, but after several minutes, Mori-san gave up. In all of the bags of sentimental objects she had collected from throughout the house, not a single photograph of her mother could be found.

THE PHOTOGRAPH

It was just after New Year, and Sato-san and I sat on the couch in his flat admiring an unframed pocket-sized photo of him and his wife standing side by side. "When I die, I will have this photo in my casket. I told my son this," he said, proudly.

The photograph was taken when they were honeymooning at a beach resort in Atami, and even though it was taken in black and white, I could see the brightness of the sunlight across their young, hopeful faces. Sato-san wore a light-colored suit and stood confidently with his legs apart and hands behind his back. His wife wore a Western-style dress and smiled coyly. The newlyweds appeared to be standing on a hill, a clever use of the landscape, perhaps, to mask their height difference. They seemed happy, but did not embrace or even touch. Satisfied that I had appreciated the photo, Sato-san took one more glance himself before placing it back in the small butsudan in his bedroom.

Sato-san met his wife through an *omiai* (literally, "matching looks"), a formal arranged meeting between two eligible persons meant to encourage their marriage, which was typical for that time, but is less so among younger people in Japan today.[10] After meeting a few other prospective brides, he finally chose her because of what he saw as a simple, conservative, and feminine style that reminded him of his own mother:

> Okay, first, my ideal woman was, I don't know why this is so but, my mother never wore makeup. My mother never wore makeup when I was young. So she didn't wear makeup. For me, I hate makeup . . . makeup is too *dense!* [laughs] No, no, no. She is very simple first. [in English] Supine? She didn't wear makeup so she was more "supine" maybe? [in Japanese] When I first met her, she wore kimono. She fit it perfectly. I don't know why. Besides that I thought she looked clever. [in English] Looks like clever! [in Japanese] And really she was quite smart. That's what I thought. That's what it really was. Three points! So she herself hesitated, but she deferred and I asked for her [to marry me].

The "three points" that attracted Sato-san to his wife (wearing no makeup, looking good in a kimono, and looking clever) were all appearances, aesthetic images, or resemblances to an ideal woman, represented by his mother (see chapter 7). Interestingly Sato-san recalls that his late wife was initially slightly reluctant to marry him since they stood at roughly the same height and if she wanted to wear high heels, she would be taller than him. When he told me this, I couldn't help but think again about the John Wayne poster on the wall, and Sato-san's remark, "He's so TALL!"

The photograph allows these memorable aesthetic qualities to seep into the personal narrative as concrete visual metonyms for underlying values. It holds the vision of the lost other and the lost self into a two-dimensional rendering of the other world. It is an object of both mourning and hope, holding abandonment in abeyance. As seen in the funerary portraits of Nakamura-san (chapter 2), photographs and other mementos can be rich with implications about what it means to be bereaved (see Schattschneider 2004). Sato-san's determination to have the photograph placed in his casket recasts the ordinary object into a ritual one, by means of which he constructs his narrative subjectivity. It is not a photograph of him as an old man, or a representation of aging. If anything, it is a visualization of a past sense of self as seen by the lost loved one, anchoring the desire for continuity with that particular self after old age. As with rituals of memorial, this plan depends upon the action of his descendants, who must follow his instructions ("I told my son this"). Sato-san's ability to imagine his future self does depends on his present authority as an older man in the household.

The aesthetic visual recollections of his late wife also introduce an important structuring element of Sato-san's own self-understanding: the importance of see-ing and being seen by others. As with Mori-san's attempts to be recognized by the spirit of her mother, and thus to reorder the aesthetic landscape of kinship that will lead to her own peaceful ascent to the mountain, Sato-san's desire to appear to the world as tall and confident as John Wayne is part of his own self-construction as he would like to appear to his late wife, and as he appears in the photograph. Buried in the grave where his wife's remains already reside, Sato-san would merge his vision of the couple with the transcendent space of memorial.

This photographic entombment achieves what psychoanalyst Jed Sekoff has called "holding time," in a way that gives a "second look" at what was lost after our initial visual grasp at "wish, phantasy, imagination, and memory" (1999, 109–110). Such holding on to time, however, seems to clash with Japanese Buddhist aesthetics of transience, ephemerality, illusion, and the emptiness of the ma. It appears at first to echo the longing for the past that marked the suf-fering of the old woman in Zeami's *Obasute*. However, this comparison holds only if we see the photograph, the image, as an object, and not as an act or a subjective process as it will be employed in the ritual context. The photograph constitutes memory as an interpersonal and intersubjective act of the relation-ship between Sato-san and his wife—of seeing and being seen—that extends past his own death through the ritual emplacement. It was a means toward tran-scending death and embracing the transience of life by reaffirming the funda-mental interdependence of the self. The photographic memorial brings with it the hope of potential for reunion in the next world. Although there was certainly more to Sato-san's life story than being a widower, his mourning practices and his own reflections on late life and death were tightly focused on his wife's death and the subsequent memorials that he had been observing for her for more than three decades. Gradually, this long mourning process changed his feelings and allowed him to begin accepting the loss. He explained,

> SATO: After my wife died, my older brother's wife said to me, "that was just her destiny (*sadame*) to die now."
> DANELY: How did you feel about that?
> SATO: I was angry! For a long time, I couldn't believe she'd say something like that. I was really angry. But now, well, I'm older, and when I look back on it I think it was destiny. I have to believe that it was her destiny.

Sato-san took out another photograph, a glossy color print clearly taken more recently. A much younger Sato-san, still with a full head of jet-black hair, sat next to an elegant, older looking woman in a dark kimono. "This one is my wife's mother," he said, pointing to the woman in the photo. He explained that after his wife died, his mother-in-law came to help with the children, and when she herself became old, he was one of the few people who took care of her. He was even with her in the hospital the night she died at the age of ninety-three. Although this photograph would not be placed in his casket, it was clear that he felt a deep affection for this older woman as well.

As we talked about this, Sato-san leaned forward in his chair, looking directly in my eyes, saying, "Well you see I'm seventy-two. So, I'm always—well not always—there are times where it is always, but, [switching to English] *death*—I think about death. [Japanese] I think about it [English] I have no fear. [Japanese] None whatsoever. However . . . [trails off searching for the word in English] *regret*. Many regrets." He then turned to me, speaking in English and counting on his fingers, "Now, my parents have gone to heaven. My wife has gone to heaven. My wife's parents have gone to heaven. I am lonely."

CHAPTER 4

Temporalities of Loss

TRANSIENCE AND YIELDING

While there are many studies of global aging have been designed to capture longitudinal changes, few have consisted of sustained ethnographic accounts.[1] Although many anthropologists make a point to return to their field sites over years and decades, having made friendships and even established family ties with the subjects of their research, these returns are rarely part of intentionally designed research agenda on aging.

And yet as Jon Hendricks and Mildred Seltzer observed, "time and temporality are central to the gerontological enterprise: Its very existence is predicated on time-dependent processes" (1986, 653). I agree, and while anthropology has not been as successful as other gerontological disciplines in tracking changes over time in aging populations, it has contributed to our ability to grasp the meanings and values people in different cultural and historical circumstances have attributed to temporal change over the life course.

Anthropological insights into aging and time provide evidence not only that subjective experiences of time do vary according to other social and spatial organizational schemas (Hallowell 1937), but also that perceptions of time, like those formed in practices of memorialization, change as one grows older (Han and Moen 1999; Hazan 1980; McFadden and Atchley 2001; Tsuji 2005). How do subjective perceptions of time impact the experience of the self and the aging process? How do the practices and institutions that bring about these perceptions facilitate or disrupt older adults' efforts to compose an aesthetically harmonious narrative of aging and loss?

In this chapter I examine Japanese temporal aesthetics, and specifically the ways older adults cultivate "yielding," or yuzuri, as a means to position themselves within interdependent relations with others in a continuously transitioning line that extends into both past and future. Practices of memorialization not only represent yielding, but also affect the aesthetic discernment or sensibility of the actor toward feelings of yielding. This discernment is embodied through what some informants have called "real feeling" (*jikkan*), a term meant to describe the limits of rote knowledge and the importance of practice. This jikkan associates aging with other valued expressions of temporal transience (mujō) symbolized in memorial. If aging in Japan entails a narrative reordering of the landscapes of kinship and a repositioning of subjectivity within it (as seen in the last chapter), it also entails new ways of experiencing the passing of time. Temporal aesthetic sensitivity to transience and openness (ma), gives aging a kind of structured indeterminacy that provides opportunities to exercise agency and to participate creatively in the perpetual flows of loss and renewal.

Japanese psychologists Yoko Yamada and Yoshinobu Kato (2006) investigated this dynamic of culture, personhood, and temporality in Japan by conducting experiments using the Image Drawing Method, asking participants to create a visual representation of the life course. Even among younger college undergraduate participants, the results showed strongly shared aesthetic depictions of *both* linear, progressive, ascendant trajectories and cyclical, repetitive versions of time. These two basic orientations toward time and human development (usually echoed in beliefs about the soul or spirit in the afterlife) are stereotypical of "Western," individual-centered, Hellenistic models of the self, and the "eastern," collectivity-based model of the self, respectively. Rather than explain their results as a matter of cultural hybridity, however, Yamada and Kato understand them as reflecting a Japanese orientation toward time that encompasses two seemingly contradictory forms of movement.[2] Life naturally moves forward, but it also moves back to the future: the hotoke move further away from "this world" and closer to ancestor status, just as they become reborn as future children within the household. For the Japanese, such seeming contradiction entails not conflict, but rather an acceptance of duality (analogous to the way a physicist might accept that a photon acts as both a particle and a wave according to one informant). Studies of Japanese end of life reaffirm not only the comforting sense of purpose this orientation provides in late life (Kondo 2012), but also the ways it allows bereaved persons to cope with loss by constructing narratives of a good death (Valentine 2009).

While the experience of linear temporal progression of aging implies a gradual yielding to younger generations, culturally this orientation is secondary to or enfolded within the more cyclical temporal framework that implies reciprocity (the successors as dependent on elders), wisdom, and spiritual ascendance. One common image of the life cycle that Yamada and Kato received from Japanese subjects followed the seed-to-plant cycle of a fruit tree:

> An apple tree never bears exactly the same fruit as other trees, even if it continues to bear many fruit year after year. Each fruit is unique. Nevertheless, if we can change our viewpoint, from looking at its uniqueness to the regularity and reproducibility of the event, or to its similarity with other things, we can say, "Autumn has come and the apples are ripening again!" Both viewpoints

can coexist. The same is true for humans: we can experience multiple perspectives on our life and world simultaneously. Certainly, each individual is
unique and can never be reproduced exactly. Nevertheless, we can say that we
are reproducible in the sense of endless continuity, from generation to generation. It is a kind of repetition, not in the sense of a perfect reproduction of a
unique individual, but in the sense of reproduction with variants. (Yamada
and Kato 2006, 154)

In this example, the notion of repetition and reproduction depends on yielding.
Yielding retains its various meanings here: turning something over (*seki wo
yuzuru*, "give up one's seat"), letting someone else pass (*michi wo yuzuru*, "make
way for others on the street"), and, turning over a responsibility (*sekinin wo
yuzuru*, "hand over responsibility"). While each of these implies loss, we might
also think of yielding as creativity, such as in a yield of wisdom or crops. The
generational regularity and reproducibility found in the family traditions of
memorialization, like the seasonal cycles of fruit-bearing trees, do not eliminate
uncertainty; uncertainty has only temporarily placed it in abeyance, in waiting.

Thinking about the cycle of rituals and generations not as closed systems, but
as dynamic and variable processes, opens up the possibility of the creativity of
loss, and the aesthetics of ephemerality and emptiness. Yamada (2003) locates
Japanese participants' representations of change, interdependence, and transience of life as arising from the Buddhist worldview that everything is in a state
of constant change and movement between appearance and disappearance
(Yamada 2002, 56). Although this worldview provides a philosophical structure
for the value of yielding, Yamada also provides examples from Shinto and popular beliefs about the spirits of the ancestors (2003). The stories in this chapter
explore this Japanese phenomenology of loss and transience in aging through
the narratives of the older adults themselves as they contemplate and creatively
adapt to a self that inhabits a temporality of yielding.

"SHOULD I LIVE THAT LONG?"

Kitano Reina, a bubbly fifty-eight-year-old woman who worked cleaning houses
in Kyoto, told me that she learned about the rituals for the spirits when she was
a young girl. "It wasn't from my parents," she explained. "I used to tag along with
my grandmother and we'd go here and there. I was a real granny's child, going
all the time to where the old people were all gathering, and so we'd go to the
graves too." Kitano-san said that her family was not very devout, but she did
remember visiting temples or celebrating holidays with her father, who worked
as a fireman, and her mother, who tended to the home and raised Kitano-san and
her younger sister. "There was no one to carry on the family line," she explained
to me, "so eventually we turned the butsudan over to a temple. My father died a
long time ago. My mother, she wanted to have a perpetual memorial (eitai kuyō)

arranged for her. You see, she and my father were not really getting along so she told me, when I die, I don't want to be next to that man!" Kitano-san's mother's clever strategy of perpetual memorial was a practicality rather than a sad or desperate measure taken only as a result of neglect. Mark Rowe (2011) describes how Buddhist institutions are slowly adapting to these increasingly popular arrangements, creating new forms of sociality and connection, especially among older women like Kitano-san's late mother, who do not like the thought of lying with their husbands in death and becoming abandoned by descendants at a traditional household-based grave. Kitano-san herself seemed to admire her mother's spirit, and visits her memorial site often.

Kitano-san was still in high school (she held up her hand to her head to portray pigtails) when she was introduced to a young, single architect and the son of a family friend near her home. "I never thought I would marry him at the time since he was eight-years older," she explained, "but we dated for a while. It was right at the time of the World Exposition [in Osaka, 1970]! And he brought me and along to that and lots of other places." After high school, the two continued to date while she attended a two-year vocational school, and they were married not long after she graduated. "I don't remember how he proposed to me," she told me giggling, "but the kids are always asking me!"

Kitano-san and her husband had five children within a span of eight years. Three years after their youngest child was born, Kitano-san's husband died suddenly in an automobile accident. "I thought, what's going to happen to me now that my husband is gone? I thought about how grateful I was that I had so many children. They've helped me so much. When they were young it was terrible, but now they take such good care of me! It is bliss! (*shiawase*)." At first Kitano-san described the shock and pain of her loss, the overwhelming desire to care for her children, and the constant thought of "What was going to happen to me?" running through her mind. She tried to keep her tears hidden from the children, the eldest of whom was ten years old. She described how she would withhold the tears all day long, waiting until night, when she would hide behind a curtain strung up in their small, two-room home and cry alone. Later, the children told her that they remembered her crying, but said nothing at the time. Reflecting on this during one interview, Kitano-san smiled, saying, "[The children] took care of me while I was trying to take care of them!"

As the children grew older, Kitano-san noticed more of her late husband in their features and mannerisms. They too have more moments when they suddenly recall an interaction with their father, going out to buy his cigarettes, and other everyday memories. She was most impressed with the way they would visit his grave, an unusual thing for most younger Japanese people:

> Oh, and grave visits! They're so good at doing them! Alone. The eldest goes quite a lot, he just says "I'm going out" and he'll go. Not even on the death anniversary. Of course on the meinichi you are supposed to go and express

your gratitude and everything, right? But they just go when they get a little feeling inside. And his sister will go too. When I go there are times when we can coordinate, but of course there are times when we can't. So they'll just go off by themselves. It's so unusual that they'll just go by themselves, I thought. It's amazing! [They go] without having to say "Go visit your father!" [pausing, smiling] They'll tell me "I went to the grave today and talked to dad for a long time." They would just talk about whatever was going on with them [long pause]. Going to the grave settles you down (ochitsuku). I feel close to him when I go to the grave.

Although their home was small, with all six of them sleeping together in one room, they did own a butsudan where Kitano-san made daily offerings and performed other acts of memorialization for her husband. As the years passed and she herself grew older, these practices changed, somewhat imperceptibly, as the cognitive and affective dimensions of her grief changed:

You see, at the time of my husband's death, I did a lot of, well, prayers. [pausing as if thinking hard] There's the "Hanyashingyō" [Heart Sutra]. [in a hushed voice] I prayed that but, I came to not do it every day anymore. In the ma,³ I stopped doing it. Hmmm. I said Hanyashingyō but, hmmm . . . [trails off]. Before I knew it I was just praying, or there are times when I just say "See you later!" [as I leave] [laughs]. I did that the whole time, I said the Hanyashingyō and now it is in my head. I can even do it without looking. So wherever I go, I can do it, without a book or anything.

Although the frequency of her chanting and prayers gradually declined, they also became more internal. With time, the emptiness of "ma," her grief, had shifted, strengthening her sense of self. It provided a context of interdependence to heal and to understand her children.

When I asked how she had changed since her husband's death, the first thing she said was that she had become "strong," giggling a bit at her own boast. Kitano-san continues her memorial rituals, but she had recently been doing a little genealogical research looking into her husband's family's names and posthumous names and the locations of their graves. "Since my husband died, I thought, I ought to do something like that," she explained. The mourning continues, but as a method of hope: "So I was thinking, maybe I'll see if I can live until my husband's fiftieth death anniversary ceremony. I'll have to live until I'm eighty-five of course. That's when the fiftieth will be. Fifty years. Oh, I wonder what will happen. I guess I'll have to have a long life [laughs]. [The fiftieth] is pretty much what they say is the last time. The last time you have to go to that kind of yearly anniversary ceremony. Hmmm, I wonder. I wonder should I live that long? [laughs]."

Waiting for her husband's final memorial ceremony has become a way to imagine an old age to look forward to, one where death made possible the reunion with her husband. This long arc of mourning provided a *ma* in her narrative, a space and time where the excess of loss could be slowly, almost imperceptibly absorbed into her subjectivity. Her story was bound not only to the loss of her husband, but also to the future she saw in her children, not in the formal sense of carrying on the family name or tradition, but in the affective economy of care that she would yield to them.

Constructing Communities of Memory

Symbolic performances have the power not only to inscribe the landscape on the body, but also to intertwine the aesthetics of time and extend the aging self beyond the individual and into other social imaginaries. If visits to graves and offerings at the butsudan performed this in the private realm of the domestic economy of care, festivals, like the Hollyhock Procession described by the man in the museum, linked narratives of aging to the social worlds of neighborhood and nation. Indeed, the term *matsuri* is commonly used to refer to private acts of memorialization as well as communal celebrations or commemoration (both explicitly religious or secular, such as school "culture matsuri").

I first met Nakamura-san when I volunteered to participate in the annual Gion Matsuri, one of the largest and grandest festivals in Kyoto, if not all of Japan. The Gion Matsuri has existed since 869 CE, and is named after the Gion district in eastern Kyoto. The patron Shinto shrine (*ujigami jinja*) of Gion is Yasaka Shrine, which enshrines three deities, the most prominent of whom is Susanoo no Mikoto, brother of Amaterasu the Sun Goddess, from whom the Japanese Imperial lineage is said to have originated. Similar to the Hollyhock Festival, the Gion Matsuri is said to have begun as a ritual to dispel the spiritual pollution thought to have caused an epidemic of infectious disease by placating the kami of immunity. The matsuri also functioned as a way to soothe the souls of those who died as a result of the epidemic, with the kami as mediating agents rather than the objects of the festival itself (Tanaka and Yamaori 2005, 61).

The matsuri, and especially the tradition of building "floats" to attract and dispel malicious spirits, gradually evolved from Kyoto's early medieval period to become a way for wealthy merchant families to display their status by making them bigger, and decorating them with exotic treasures such as European or Indian tapestries, and other symbols of foreign trade (Roemer 2007). Each July, the materials for the floats are taken out of storage at Yasaka Shrine and rebuilt downtown by local festival association members at tremendous costs, which are only partially offset by municipal funds, and still depend on generous donations from businesses and wealthy patrons.

The reconstruction of the floats (some as tall as five stories and weighing several tons) and the slow labor of physically pulling these massive, unsteady structures around a circuit in downtown Kyoto are remarkable feats. The procession is not a mere reenactment, staged for the sake of tourists or history buffs. The labor of the festival brings the spectacle of the past into the present, following a temporal cycle of the calendar (many participants considered July as the true "New Year") and the cycle of construction and deconstruction of the floats.

The Gion Matsuri, like most other festivals I encountered in Japan, was not immune from the effects of Japan's aging population. Because of the general residential decline and aging in the Yasaka parish and the immense resources of manpower needed to construct, direct, and pull the floats, organizers have had to call for greater participation from people throughout the city and, in my case, even those from overseas. Most of these details of the festival I learned from a small group of longtime Kyoto residents, foreign visitors, and dedicated, almost obsessive "fans" (otaku) like Nakamura-san. Given the way that much of the heavy labor of care has been outsourced to other areas or institutions, I was impressed by the commitment to somewhat esoteric local details and the general weariness of incorporating outsiders among many of the members of Gion Matsuri groups.[4]

Each float remains managed and funded through the activities of parish representatives, one of whom was Nakamura-san. One of Nakamura-san's constant concerns whenever we spoke about Gion Matsuri was the shortage of money needed to be raised from residents and businesses in his neighborhood for costumes, implements, construction, and other costs. Throughout the year, Nakamura-san was perpetually busy with preparations for the matsuri, and these preparations put him in the role of both leader (teaching others the proper protocol of the festival, including teaching traditional music and dances to the young child performers) and petitioner (soliciting donations and participants to build, pull, and perform with the float). As was typical of most Shinto festivals, leadership was limited to men, many of whom were retired or nearing retirement and were concerned about yielding when there was a lack of experienced successors.[5]

About a week prior to the grand parade of festival floats marking the midway point in the Gion Matsuri festivities, I met Nakamura-san on the street where his neighborhood's float was being constructed. Nakamura-san and I surveyed the construction as we wiped beads of sweat off of our faces. Watching the float being constructed was almost like watching someone build a ship in a bottle, the huge pieces of lumber, lashed together with thick rope and intricate knots (no nails or screws are used in the construction), all swinging dangerously close to the metal and glass façades of storefronts and pedestrian traffic on one of Kyoto's busiest streets. I watched as Nakamura supervised like a parent coaching children on a school playground, clipboard in hand, beaming with pride. As we watched, he told me about how the floats used to be pulled along much narrower streets when he was a child, and not the four-lane thoroughfares that make up the current route. While this made the parade much longer, dangerous, and physically tough, he remembers it fondly, with residents and shop owners extending food from their second-story windows to participants sitting on the floats, and lively interactions between neighbors when floats would pause or get stuck. Children would dash out in front of the floats to try and catch special protective charms (*chimaki*) that were thrown down from the each float, something that would never happen today along the well-policed route. The need to accommodate and maintain tourist interest has changed the traditions, but the nostalgic desire kept the event alive, a fact evident in Nakamura-san's face as he studied the beams and ropes coming together piece by piece.

For Nakamura-san, the festival was undoubtedly the thing that made life worth living, or his ikigai (Mathews 1996). In it was encapsulated all of the key elements of memorialization, those aesthetic conventions of the narrative that situated him into a different order or belonging and created a sense of continuity between past and future selves. Foremost was the fact that the matsuri was an intersubjective act of remembering, a process of creating something new, yet something that bore an aesthetic resemblance to the imagined past. It was a way of materially dreaming up this past, bringing the invisible into form. As a memorialization, it functioned to placate the spirits as well, circulating this memory within the economy of care. As with memorial of the household spirits, Nakamura-san's age lent him a special role as mediator between the ritual performance and its tradition, a kind of wisdom and agency that underlined the work he did to organize year round. Also like traditional memorial, the matsuri faced challenges as a result of the aging community and the privatization and commoditization that displaced spiritual observance with consumption of the spectacle.

In some ways, the matsuri's public performance of "tradition" masks the erasure of "traditional" forms of sociality that should be at its core. As a commodity manufactured for tourists to consume separately from this sociality, it has outsourced both its financial support as well as its labor. Many of the Gion Matsuri floats are now supported by large businesses and services established in the area only recently, and companies that donate from throughout Kyoto send their newest male recruits to pull the floats on the day of the procession as a kind of team-building exercise rooted in the Japanese practice of *shugyō*, or "training." To say that these private companies have displaced the traditional composition of the festival from kin and *chōnai* may not be far from the truth, but without such changes, it is difficult to say if the festival would be able to survive at all. Indeed, many smaller local festivals have died out or gone through cycles of death and reincarnation. Organizers like Nakamura-san are caught between the matsuri as community and commodity, uneasy about the thought of "outsiders" (even the municipal police providing security for the event) participating, and yet bound to meet expectations of a national and even international audience.

As mentioned elsewhere in this book, many longtime downtown residents of Kyoto have had to close businesses in recent decades (often small-scale manufacturing, local arts and crafts producers, and wholesalers like Nakamura-san) and sell their homes due to a lack business or rising property values, or because of the absence of a family successor or skilled apprentice. While Nishida-san's silk-weaving business has been able to adapt to modern customers by producing Western clothing like neckties and marketing internationally, most of the once vibrant kimono trade in downtown Kyoto has shut its doors (Hareven 2002). Rather than refurbish the old machiya homes, developers have taken advantage of the high downtown property value to build modern apartment high-rises (*manshon*), which Nakamura-san and other community members felt attracted people who do not participate in community groups like the block association, or *chōnai*.[6] While the large residential apartment projects (*danchi*) that are emblematic of the dismantling of communal identity and the low fertility/old age trajectory are located on the periphery of the city, manshon appear here and there throughout, usually crammed into lots once occupied by older machiya. If danchi remake the villages surrounding the city, the architecture of the typical manshon implies the demolition of a prior sense of lived aesthetics, including not only the tile-roofed machiya, but the older residents and their businesses.

Occupants are singles, nuclear families with few children, or older people, all groups whose subjectivity is tied to the current demographic crisis. Nakamura-san's neighborhood float had not been active for several decades, as it fell into disrepair and he could not raise the money needed to rebuild it. He and the others involved in other festival matters often talked about fears that with the aging of the festival committee, the float may be forced into storage once again. Nakamura-san often disparaged the social changes affecting the festival, fondly reminiscing about the old days when his neighborhood was a lively place, with children and adults gathering in front of their homes, playing games, and exchanging gossip. This narrative became most evident when discussing the changes in the chōnai:

> NAKAMURA: Well, first of all, the most obvious thing is, um, before the war, there was more of a sense of neighborhood interaction.
> DANELY: But isn't that still the role of the chōnai today?
> NAKAMURA: Well that's, that's—that's something you're *supposed to do*. You're supposed to do it, but lately it's been fading out. It's become so individualistic. People just want their own privacy. It's gotten especially worse since they started building manshon. In those manshon, there's really no greetings at all. There's a manshon close to here, and I'll say "hi" to people I know that live there, but there's absolutely no greeting back!

"Community," to Nakamura-san, depended not only on institutions like the chōnai, but on everyday reciprocal measure of bonding expressed in polite greetings (*aisatsu*), themselves a quintessential form of aesthetic performance that forms the basis of social relationships. As newcomers, the manshon and its inhabitants disrupt the rhythmic cycle of time represented in memorial and matsuri, and create instead a tense uncertainty marked by an inability to communicate, to yield or recognize connectedness (en). In contrast, Nakamura-san's subjectivity was based on his position as a member of the community and his genealogical connection to place over a long time. On the wall above the special alcove of his house, Nakamura-san himself proudly displayed a large certificate he received for living in the same neighborhood for over one hundred years. Even though he moved to the house in which he was currently living in the 1940s, his family had lived in the same district for over 120 years.

Time mattered because community mattered. Now both seemed to be slowly unraveling with the passing of generations.

THE PASSAGE OF TIME

The Gion Matsuri came and went, and Nakamura-san did not rest for long in his satisfaction. The float needed to be deconstructed and stored, the participants' costumes would need washing and mending, thank-you cards needed to be sent, and the retirement of some of the older members of the preservation society needed to be addressed. He was even busy making the rounds to local donors, thanking them and soliciting funds for the next year. Like those of Orin, Nakamura-san's investments of care provided the partial solace of a good narrative, yet he still worried about what would become of these traditions when he was gone.

A few months after the matsuri, Nakamura-san and I sat around his low dining table, talking once again about family. Around the walls were photographs of his grandchildren, and I was interested in knowing more about his sons and their families, both of whom had taken jobs outside of Kyoto. The youngest son's family lived in a neighboring town about a half hour away by train, and they would sometimes call on Nakamura-san and his wife to help with things such as babysitting a sick child sent home from school. When I asked whether Nakamura-san would like his son to come live with him after he himself had grown older, he let out a low groan and rubbed his forehead as he replied,

> NAKAMURA: If something were to happen, will they be able to help me? Of course even if you telephone [trails off, then laughs] I guess you could call that sort of thing the passing of the time (*jidai no nagare*). It's the passing of time. Japan's. [wide smile]
>
> DANELY: Sometimes when one's parents get older, then once more—
>
> NAKAMURA: Well, I guess there's the possibility that they'll come back home but, it's not like, it's not one hundred percent! [laughs loudly]
>
> DANELY: Is that so?
>
> NAKAMURA: [still laughing] Absolutely not! But you can't know until the time comes. There's absolutely, there's no insurance, right? There's no formal agreement that they'll come home.

What does one do "until the time comes"? How do the Nakamuras and those in a similar situation wait and maintain hope and keep abandonment in abeyance?

The remarks on the lack of "insurance" and "formal agreement" reveal the slippery nature of kin-provisioned labor of care. In order to maintain an ethical viability as filial care, the labor should not be rationalized, but should be offered as a gift.[7] On the other hand, such lack of certainty, or more accurately the lack of agency elders have to demand and receive care, generates desire and risk. Rather than a source of support and reliability, as in ancestor-based models of kinship, increased mobility and opportunities for wealth have made family a risk rather than an asset (Yamada 2001).[8]

Clara Han (2011) observed a similar process of indeterminacy, risk, and waiting in her observations of subjectivity and the domestic economy of care in urban Santiago, Chile. Han writes that indebtedness created in this economy presents struggles and symptoms of illness and suffering; it also creates the basis on which people "draw on a wider network of dependencies that provide temporal and material resources" that demonstrate "the shifting forces at work in creating a time for waiting and costs thereby involved" (2011, 9). Much like the seemingly arrested moment of ma in Japanese aesthetic composition, Han's use of the term "waiting" identifies a critical temporal component of hope, care, and the possibilities of relational futures. I find this useful for thinking about Nakamura-san's cyclical and repetitive use of ritual to structure time and social relationships in the space of old age.

While social and emotional support are important for older adults in Japan, it is the dependence enacted through the physical body that most strongly demands bonds of care and tests its possibilities. Although Nakamura-san was one of the younger older adults whom I interviewed, he was also starting to show symptoms of age-related fatigue. When I asked him about his health, he was reserved, mentioning in vague terms that he had been having trouble with his heart. Later he admitted that he had diabetes and needed to watch his diet and visit the physician regularly to monitor its status and adjust medication. He quickly segued to his concerns and expectations about kin-provisioned care, succession, and the continuity of the traditions he held dear. He expected that they would have to sell their home, either before or after he died. Emiko-san said that in that case, she would rather live alone than move in with her son's family.

Who would take care of Nakamura-san, and who would take care of the graves? What would be left behind? Unlike Sato-san, Mori-san, and Nishida-san, Nakamura-san does not coreside with his children, a fact that brings him considerable uncertainty about these questions and his future care in old age. His anxieties each year about the solvency of matsuri and his ability to make it one more year are a microcosm of this time of waiting and return, the withdrawal of care and its subjective act of return, as the spirits and kami descend from the mountains to circulate through the city.

One thing that was certain was that smaller families, greater mobility, and new opportunities to live independently have altered this landscape of kin and external dependencies available for older adults. These changes have attenuated ties of obligation and debt to the household, the importance of place, and the traditions tied to locality, such as ancestor memorial (Rowe 2011). As seen in the case of Mori-san, the household graves and remains are often difficult and costly to move, and children living in distant parts of the country may not feel it necessary to maintain them if they rarely visit. For those like Nakamura-san, whose narrative subjectivity is woven into locality and tradition, dependence on non-kin affinities not only threatens his ideal of a good afterlife for himself and his household, but also threatens the bonds of care that make the aging body and its remains an ethical subject. Abandonment in old age calls into doubt the hope for memorial; in abandonment, one might be forgotten. Not only do older adults resist abandonment of this sort by maintaining ties with family and keeping the traditions of the past in tact, but they are also aware of the passing of time. Like the deserting father Rihei in *The Ballad of Narayama*, who was unable to abandon his own mother or mourn the loss of his daughter, an unwillingness to accept transience and yielding risks throwing the subject into another kind of shameful social abandonment.

The plaintive shrug of the "passing of time" brings up questions of changing perceptions of temporality in old age, and its relationship to the possibility of constructing meaningful narratives of loss and continuity. The spirits of the dead are intimated in these narratives, as the very embodiments of what is lost and what continues. The family of risk, uncertain of reciprocity, seemed to perpetually occupy Nakamura-san, but the idea of living (or dying) spiritual time provided the hope for an alternative, a way of looking toward horizons rather than blocking himself into the past. The memorialization of the spirits, like the shotsukimeinichi death anniversary services described earlier in chapter 2, opens productive space for reframing the ambiguous and paradoxical nature of time's passing, as each death anniversary marks another step further from the memories and social world of the living.

Putting time's passing in order and regaining agency in later life are most noticeable in Nakamura-san's management of his household graves. Whereas families like Nishida-san's erected a single grave dedicated to the "generations" of a household (_ke no senzo daidai), Nakamura-san's household tradition had been to establish separate graves for each married couple. On the annual death anniversary of each one of these relatives, as well as the first and fifteenth day of the month, Nakamura-san and his wife visited the cemetery to change the flowers and clean the stones. This tradition raised the stakes for future generations since it required a special commitment of time and money, and its continuity was directly related to Nakamura-san's own admiration for the family history of devotion and sacrifice that it has required.

Nakamura-san's situation is further complicated by the fact that in addition to his patrilineal ascendants' graves, he had also taken it upon himself to maintain the graves of three generations of his father's mother's terminated patriline, and four other deceased relatives who died without children (two great-aunts

TABLE 1

RELATIVES REPRESENTED BY THE TEN GRAVES
MAINTAINED BY NAKAMURA-SAN (THE EGO).

1. Father and mother

2. Father's father and mother

3. Father's father's father and mother

4. Father's father's eldest sister (died as a child)

5. Father's father's elder sister (died as a child)

6. Younger brother (died unmarried)

7. Father's father's younger sister and her husband

8. Father's mother's parents

9. Father's mother's father's parents

10. Father's mother's father's father's parents

who died in childhood, a younger brother, and a great-aunt and her husband).[9] As a result, Nakamura-san was responsible for the care of a total of ten different grave plots (Table 1), each measuring about the size of half a tatami mat (ninety by ninety centimeters).

This tradition of erecting separate graves, however, made Nakamura-san especially uneasy about his own memorial, and he and his wife coped with humor:

> DANELY: So when you pass away, your son will erect [a new grave] for you and your wife?
> NAKAMURA: Well it would be really nice if my son would erect one for me but . . . [laughs nervously] I'm a little worried about that! [laughs]
> EMIKO: [deadpan] I don't think he's going to set up anything for you! [laughs]

In a later interview, I asked again what plans Nakamura-san or his family had for continuing their pattern of ancestor memorial, considering the fact that it seems so time-consuming and expensive. This time Nakamura-san seemed less able to find humor in the situation. Still smiling, he took off his glasses, hung his head, and rubbed his face again. Emiko-san, still in good humor, decided to answer for him:

> EMIKO: [smiling, but with a raised voice] WE DON'T NEED A STONE!
> NAKAMURA: Because the plot is expensive and our children won't continue the rites!

Nakamura-san's voice was raised, but his tone was not angry, more defeated. He then told me that he had been considering consolidating the graves and replacing them with a single household grave. The relatives whose remains would not be able to be interred in this grave (such those of his grandmother's patriline and his younger brother) would be ritually disposed of, to which Nakamura-san's wife half joked in reply, "We might get some sort of ancestral vengeance (*tatari*) for that!"

Despite their laughter and modesty, Nakamura-san and his wife seemed genuinely concerned with the continuity of their family's traditions, just like Orin in *The Ballad of Narayama*. The passing of time was hard, but it also held a hope. If one considers that old age might generate concern, that oiru might lead to a kind of wisdom and aesthetic discernment, there was still space for imagining the possibility that descendants would continue the memorialization. Aging, in this way, becomes a kind of insurance, if in old age one can cultivate a sense of mature hope and mourning that allows the meanings of memorialization to become part of oneself. Sato-san's remark that his children will understand only after he is dead (chapter 2) holds at least some hope that aging and loss will perpetuate memorial and hope. Only time will tell.

When I asked the Nakamuras if attitudes toward these kinds of family traditions changed with age, they both agreed that it was natural that younger people would have less appreciation for this sort of tradition:

NAKAMURA: So for me—If you were to ask me if I felt like doing this when I was in my thirties, I would probably say I didn't. If I was thirty. Well, but that sort of thing, thinking about looking after [traditions] and that, I'd say it doesn't happen until you get to be fifty or so. . . .

EMIKO: Of course, after your parents die. When you think, "Oh, this happened to my parents," well at least you'll want to remember them. Yes.

DANELY: And so that's why this continues?

EMIKO: Well, if [the descendants] continue this, that's good but . . . [laughs] really!

NAKAMURA: Well that's right. Everyone says "What are we going to do now, blah blah blah blah!" Oh, when I die, I don't know what's going to happen, afterward. I don't know if they'll continue [the practices]. Well, that's like, at that age, if they have the feeling that they want to continue or if they're not at the age when will they want to, that's a hard thing for anyone to answer, isn't it? If they're someone in their thirties that really wants to do all that, that's really a person who has appreciation (*kanshin*). Well, I don't really know but, well that's where I think there's the generation gap, or, different thinking. Well, even now, people in their twenties, teens—probably if you're in your twenties you don't even think about having ozoni (traditional soup) at New Year! Even though you're a Japanese person!

Both of Nakamura-san's parents died, in quick succession, when he was in his fifties. But Nakamura-san and his wife were far from alone among older adults whom I spoke with in relating sentiments about how the significance of tradition and ancestor memorial changes after the age of fifty. One older informant told me in a rather mysterious tone, "When you get to be sixty or seventy, you know a lot. You don't say much, but you know a lot. It is like spiritual sensitivity (*reikan*). Older people understand a lot, but they don't say it. Maybe they know what is to come." Aging in Japan, to the extent that it is constituted through dependency and waiting, also provides a premonition operating without words to signify it, a sense of experience that, while offering a sense of hope, also functions as a subjective estrangement from younger generations.

In the event that Nakamura-san decides to consolidate the remains of his ancestors, the land that the graves currently stand on would be sold, and there would be little need to observe memorial rites on the death anniversaries of individuals, since any visit to the grave would constitute a visit to all of the deceased of the household; individuals will be forgotten, abandoned. The older the Nakamuras became, the closer they felt to having to take this step, but the decision was unlikely to come until they had left their own house, finding some place less expensive and more suitable for an older body. Although traditions would continue in some fashion, something had already been lost. Nakamura-san was ambivalent about consolidating his ancestral graves, evading direct responses when I asked him further about the matter. He has been thinking about it, however, for over a decade and still hasn't made up his mind about what to do. It wasn't long before Nakamura-san's wife chimed in once again, saying to her husband, "You have to decide one way or another before you DIE you know!" Nakamura-san still seemed vexed, rubbing his forehead pensively.

DISAPPEARING ANCESTORS

If the society that values attachment and intimacy generates a fear of loss, one that values interdependence and group cohesion generates the fear of abandonment. Abandonment, like that of the old woman of obasuteyama, is a departure from which there is little hope of return, where loss closes in on the person, depriving him or her of experiencing self-continuity, of a self that links the past and moves toward the future. In my conversations with Japanese people, what they feared most—more than death, frailty, or even dependence—was abandonment: "being left behind" (*hottoarkasu*), "alone" (*kodoku*), "thrown out" (*suteru*), "forgotten" (*wasureru*). While some of these terms might have positive values as well (having "solitude" vs. feeling "lonely," for instance), all were used by informants to express the uncertainty of time's passing.

Japanese ancestor rituals hinge on bonds of exchange and care that keep the spirits of the dead dependent on the living for offerings and other forms of ritual commemoration. Abandoned spirits are typically represented as pitiful, lonely "wandering spirits," "hungry ghosts" (*gaki*) or "buddhas without bonds" (muenbotoke) (Smith 1974, 41–50; Rowe 2011, 46). These spirits are not necessarily harmful (as Emiko-san's joking comment about ancestral vengeance suggested), but they do haunt people, and therefore constitute the threat of transgression for which the living must bear the psychological burden (Kalland 1991; Smith 1974, 212–213; 1999, 262). Yanagita Kunio ([1946] 1970) wrote about his concern of the prevalence of such abandoned spirits in Japan as a direct result of changing families after World War II (anticipating the publishing of his book as he was writing): "Continuance of the family is a big problem now . . . when people lived peacefully and had few changes, they could believe that their descendants would love them and give them *matsuri* with the same feeling and affection as they had had for their forefathers. As relatives who grieved over their death pass away, their souls are ignored and go wandering about to look in on other family altars, an undesirable condition for helping them go peacefully into the other world and to soothe minds disturbed by the war" (1970, 178–179).

Yanagita's depiction of the haunting aftermath of the war is evocative of the way individuals are haunted by their debts and obligations to the departed. In this way it gives a clue to why the thought of consolidating graves was so troubling to Nakamura-san. Graves and butsudan locate the memories of the dead, and therefore hold the possibility of care, remembrance, and pacification. They make the spirits of the dead, their memories, if not the remains of their bodies, aesthetic objects of sociality, transforming the world of the living even as the living transform the very substance of the dead. When memories are used in this way, they have the potential to become what Michael Lambek describes as "a function of social relationships, in part a mutual affirmation of past interaction, in part traces of our introjection of one another" (1996, 239). Memorialization places uncertainty and the threat of abandonment in abeyance by facilitating both the affirmation of the past (linking the significance of the bonds that pre-ceded death) and the introjection of the other (the recognition of the spirit in oneself). Thus, for the bereaved, memorialization becomes a way of relating both to others and to oneself and finding balance between "continuity (caring) and discontinuity (mourning)" (Lambek 1996, 239).

Despite the practice of referring to death as "becoming a buddha" (*jōbutsu*), frequently circulated tales of abandoned spirits underline the tenuous and uncertain nature of the other world as well as the excess of loss (Ivy 1995, 149). At the same time, the living assume responsibility for the care of the spirits, and for the always incomplete process of paying one's debt of gratitude (*on*) to them (*sumanai*). One of the strongest emotions felt toward the ancestors is expressed as *moshiwake nai*, a deferential apology literally meaning "I have no excuse" for my behaviors. Such expressions do not convey deep pain or guilt but, like everyday greetings, expressed humility, respect, and a recognition of one's place in the economy of care. While the pain of grief often overshadows discussions of loss, grief can also constitute ways of relating, of giving, and of receiving.

Resolution to grief is always deferred, even though the ethical demand of sincerity requires that one continue to "act as if," to hope by holding the self suspended in a state of "not yet," until the memory of the dead has faded or has been ritually extinguished through final death anniversary ceremonies. As seen in the example of Kitano-san, the "final" anniversary might be linked to one's own aspirations of living a long life, even if the doubt remains if one should "live that long." Until the final memorial, spirit and mourner are held together and suspended between abandonment and hope, reciprocating affection, care, and offerings in ways that resonate not only with the tales of obasuteyama, but also with the economy of care that underlies intergenerational relationships.

Looking at Nakamura-san's case, it becomes clear that the effectiveness of memorialization relies not only on the cultural symbols and dispositions of individual mourners, but also on kinship and economic concerns used to assess the future. Intimate concerns about the care of the ancestors merge with those about paying for retirement and the decline in participation in local self-governing societies like the chōnai. The weight of this loss, when framed by discourses of the national aging crisis and the uncertainty of care, is internalized as the shameful burden of age. An intergenerational flow of care, where older adults become a bridge between ancestors and descendants or other caregivers, distributes this burden, both materially and emotionally, mobilizing the ugly feelings of grief (guilt, shame, envy, e.g.) into the reproduction of rituals of offering, sacrifice, and linked fates (en). Memorialization liberates not only the aesthetic but the political possibilities of the aging self. How can Nakamura-san be sure that the spirits of the household (including he and his wife) will be accorded care when they die? How can they prepare, like Orin, for aging and a good death? In this context, graves and butsudan might be viewed as forms of material insurance to manage the risk involved in bonds of kinship; thus, we might look to them for actuarial signs of how hope is calculated and maintained.

Most temple cemeteries and temple graveyards like the one where the Nakamuras had their graves require regular donations to maintain a grave plot, and temples, especially in urban areas like Kyoto, risk losing revenue if a grave is abandoned. Abandoned graves are easy to spot when walking through a Japanese cemetery. The stones are often crumbling or covered with lichen, and the names etched in their façades have long been worn away, reduced to a mumble of their former bold pronouncement. After some time of neglect has passed, the temple groundskeepers tag the graves with large, brightly colored placards strung around the central pillar (Figure 5). In contrast to its somewhat unceremonious display, the text of these placards is written in the most ceremonious language, asking caretakers to contact the temple concerning the grave, which will otherwise be moved to the common memorial site for muenbotoke following regular temple "maintenance."

The presence of abandoned graves is not ignored by regular visitors. The collective memorial monument for the abandoned spirits is usually located close to the entrance of the temple cemetery. Visitors pass by this memorial and chat as they fill buckets with water from a spigot to clean their family's graves—a kind of

Figure 5. Abandoned graves tagged for removal in Kyoto. Photo by author.

"well-side gossip circle" of the cemetery. One woman I spoke with at a cemetery explained that the reason that so many graves are being abandoned is that couples are having fewer children and the children often move away. "It's so horrible!" she said. "So sad (*kawaisō*) for those who have passed away. These days you have 'memorial parks' (*reien*) where the stones are all neatly lined up for the ancestors, and you don't have abandoned graves."

I myself noticed several billboards for reien "memorial parks" in Kyoto, usually at train and subway stations where they could promote their accessibility and convenience for commuters. During the weeks preceding Obon, when thoughts of the ancestors are close to everyone's mind, I also noticed many more television advertisements for reien, often featuring a healthy-looking couple of middle age (forties or fifties) strolling through the sunny, well-groomed park before stopping at a grave marker and assuming a very traditional Japanese posture of reverence: eyes closed, hands together, and head bowed. One of these television spots I saw ended with the tag line, "Just my memory."

All of the advertisements I saw avoided depictions of both children and the elderly (no three-generation households here), suggesting a changing conception of memorial away from kinship bonds based on generational succession that extend into ancestorhood, and moving toward memorial based on individuation of both the mourner and the deceased. Individuation does not, however, necessarily entail abandonment. As the woman in the cemetery remarked, "you don't have abandoned graves" at the reien. Nor does the aesthetic of the reien necessarily clash with beliefs concerning the intimacy and bonds of care possible with the dead. Kawano (2003), for example, describes a scene in the Japanese film *Ohaka ga nai!* (I don't have a grave!, 1997), where "spreading a plastic picnic sheet and a lunch box, a salesman tells the actress: 'A good thing about a Western-style lawn cemetery is, we can have a picnic with *hotoke-sama* (ancestors)'" (Kawano 2003, 132).[10]

New grave arrangements constitute forms of adaptation, new designs for living and dying that involve the collaboration between mourners and mortuary institutions. Kawano's descriptions of the "Western-style lawn cemetery" are consistent with the images I saw in advertisements, and the revitalization of mortuary practices that recognize both the life of individuals and the personal needs of mourners. In 2005, the first year of my fieldwork in Kyoto, a front-page article in the *Daily Yomiuri* newspaper reported that "western-style gravestones have become more popular than their traditional Japanese equivalents in private cemeteries" in the Tokyo area. Western-style stones are not necessarily associated with Christian burials (many cemeteries in Kyoto had gravestones for Christians, noticeable only by a small carved or bas-relief cross) but may be personalized in a number of ways, including personal inscriptions or inset photographs.

Today there are a multitude of memorial options, including scattering ashes in nature (Kawano 2003; 2010) and, as seen in the case of Kitano-san's mother, "perpetual memorials" (*eitai kuyo*), which promote a new possibilities of post-mortem social bonds among the dead. Perpetual memorial arrangements made with temples ensure the care of an individual's remains regardless of the presence or lack of kin. Several older people I asked about funerary arrangements spoke positively about perpetual memorial as the most practical solution, even when these older adults coresided with and received care from adult children. One woman in her fifties told me that her ideal would be to have her remains placed in a large communal grave managed by the city rather than a temple. She argued not only that this arrangement would prevent the abandonment of the dead, but that the dead themselves would not be "lonely." Her mother's remains, for example, were buried in a grave but without descendants to maintain it, and her father, an ex-sailor, had his ashes scattered at sea.

There are an estimated three thousand perpetual memorial burial monuments in Japan, but many more mausoleums and other varieties of structures for memorialization. The caretakers of some of these arrangements go to great lengths to preserve the deceased individual's memory, provide areas for placing small offerings and observing memorials, and even enshrine memorial tablets for individuals or groups. At one such perpetual memorial site I visited, the tablets for the dead were placed in a large memorial hall alongside the tablets for group commemoration, such as one for the victims of the Great Hanshin Earthquake of 1995.

Mainstream Buddhist institutions are not the only ones adapting to an aging Japan. Many of Japan's various "new religious" groups, such as Risshō Kōseikai, Shinnyō-en, Sukyō-Mahikari, and many others, have strongly emphasized the importance of the spirits of the dead, extending their memorial rites well beyond household ancestors to include all of the dead (Kōmoto 2001; Shimazono 2004; Smith 1999). One member of Shinnyō-en, a group associated with the Shingon sect of Buddhism, told me that he found memorialization so important that he would make a point of remembering the dead and making offerings wherever he traveled, be it those who died at Pearl Harbor when he went to Hawaii or the restless ghosts of American Indian people when visiting the mainland United States. This man was introduced to Shinnyō-en group after his wife had a miscarriage, so that there was continuity between the grief that led to faith and the mourning that sustained it. New religions were also particularly active in efforts to aid and comforting survivors of the March 11 tsunami disaster by conducting memorial rites for the dead (McLaughlin 2013).

Groups like these show how individuation in memorialization seen in perpetual memorials and Western-style graves may also decalibrate identities from the primary institution of the household and open up creative spaces for new kinds of collective commemoration. While I was not surprised that some of my informants told me that they did not wish to have their remains placed in a traditional, household-based grave where the stakes of abandonment might be high, I expected this to come with the worry and disappointment that I saw expressed by Nakamura-san. However, this was usually not the case. Instead those who cited a preference for alternative burial arrangements generally seemed at peace with this decision, sometimes telling me that they believed "real Japanese beliefs" were about the material "return to the earth," and allowing one's energy to cycle through nature in exactly the same manner that participants in Yamada and Kato's research depicted the life cycle. Their narrative could therefore uphold aesthetics of temporality without depending on formal institutions.

While Mori-san, Nakamura-san, and Sato-san all maintained graves for individuals or couples, those graves also marked the potential for reunification with the dead, as a kind of place marker for one's own future hopes. As a form of insurance, they held the risk of abandonment at bay, but did not do away with it completely. Rather, the presence of the grave reiterated the need for continued care. Care of the grave is, for many bereaved, an integral site for cultivating aesthetic discernment to face losses in old age. Whether in the mountains or in the middle of the city, the grave is a site for the affirmation of the past self and the imagination of future possible selves, and each one stands in memory to the those metaphorically abandoned on obasuteyama, and to aging itself as an ethical practice of creating and maintaining social bonds in the midst of loss.

CHAPTER 5

Passing It On

CIRCULATING AGING NARRATIVES

Narratives are continuously shifting toward the aging subject; just as they seem coherent, some ordinary disruption cracks the surface. Psychological anthropologist Byron Good (2012) has argued that investigating subjectivity requires acknowledging the haunting that erupts through these cracks, that reveals in symptoms or other fraught conditions things concealed in the mind. Cultural phenomenologies of spirituality, aesthetics, and mourning are not the only narratives that aging subjects contend with, nor, necessarily, the most prevailing. This chapter examines the ways life course events come to haunt narratives, not literally as spirits and ghosts, but, like obasuteyama, as unsettled stories that repeatedly assert themselves into old age.

"You Can't Take It with You"

When we first met, I was able to look past Mori-san's cluttered machiya home as something merely eccentric and probably temporary, partly because of her chatty charm and generosity—I would rarely leave from her house empty-handed, and I marveled at the variety of small gifts that seemed to appear from everywhere. Even before the move, however, I made some unusual observations. The front room of her machiya would normally be the tidiest and most austere place in the house, containing a decorative alcove for displaying precious objects and works of art, and the butsudan. Mori-san's front room, though slightly more navigable than the others, had not been functional for guests for some time because of the encroachment of objects that had migrated there. As a result, I was usually ushered back to the dining room on occasions when we had interviews, watched television together, or shared a meal.

The dining room had no fewer than six calendars hung around its transoms and walls, some of them outdated by several years but still dutifully displaying their bright photos of cherry blossoms or seated portraits of members of the

Japanese imperial family. A telephone rested on a portable shelf unit overflowing with bills, letters, and other scraps of papers. Whenever Mori-san wanted to illustrate something for me, or clarify a word, she would lean over and ruffle through this shelf, finding a blank scrap to write on, placing it back somewhere in the shelf when she was done. There were at least fifteen umbrellas speared into a bucket by the door, and many more throughout the house. The entryway to the kitchen, long fallen into disuse, was bricked up floor to ceiling by shoe boxes, some containing footwear that never made it to anyone's feet. While some areas appeared to house organized collections, others were more haphazard. Tables and chairs became anonymous surfaces for papers, clothes, and various bags and boxes.

The objects and the spaces they inhabited within and around Mori-san's life seemed to busy the world and blot out the open stillness of ma. They engulfed the house with desires, memories, and affect, overstuffing the story. They were part of Mori-san's process of narrating *ma*, of seeking to fill the experience of loss and abandonment with the material traces of desire. As seen in the examples of the graves, offerings, altars, photographs, and even mountains and rivers, objects and the values they symbolize provide older adults with ways to anchor their process of making meaning out of loss. Interacting with and through these objects circumscribes a locus of agency for older adults, and a chance to order a narrative of the self.

Cheryl Mattingly succinctly writes that the perspective of "narrative phenomenology" aims to understand the ways people "try to make certain stories come true and thwart other possible stories" (2010, 217). Not all narrators are conscious of the narratives they create or thwart, or the aesthetic consequences of their composition. Traditions, values, and hopes compete for attention with the ugly feelings of abandonment, despair, and fear. For older adults, narrating the ma requires the ongoing work of negotiating this aesthetic and affective terrain toward hope and horizons of the possible. Orin's reconfiguration of kinship and of her own body in *The Ballad of Narayama* offers one possible kind of narrative: loss and abandonment in harmony with the beauty of old age and hope for a good death. For many, however, the narrative is incomplete, indeterminate, and dynamic, fraught with obstacles and dead ends produced through trauma, or other narrative disruptions.

Mori-san's obasuteyama narrative seems to begin in medias res, as if she had suddenly found herself at the base of the mountain when she realized the immensity of the task of moving herself and her belongings to her daughter's new house. Abandonment and hope are intermingled here, but in Mori-san's case, past abandonments (mother, husband, father, daughters) seem to have left wounds raw. Over the course of her lifetime, Mori-san developed habits for tending to a self in abandonment that bore the stains of failed relationships, guilt, shame, and grief. As we got to know each other better, I could see these habits in slow-motion collision with the losses of age, as her body weakened, her memory grew more disorderly, and her ability to exercise agency in the family became more attenuated. As with many aging in grief, the line between patho-traumatic symptom and normal aging would become blurred. And then the stuff was piling up.

Returning home from a visit to Mori-san's house on one occasion, I began to think about the ways that I too am sometimes irrationally compelled to keep things that others might not find valuable—sentimental objects, old letters, news clippings, various "files" that I imagined, somewhat defensively, may come into use one day. In gathering information during fieldwork this sort of collection sometimes (okay, often) verges on the compulsive, as every advertisement or architectural detail or chance encounter seems to be loaded with important and ever fleeting cultural meaning that must be documented immediately before the next encounter. I soon had my own stacks of paper everywhere, and little time to organize and tag each one; books, souvenirs, neighborhood bulletins, senior center activity schedules filled the closets. My already cramped room had begun to resemble Mori-san's. Wasn't this because I too was anticipating my own act of abandonment, my departure from the field? Did the papers reassure me that I was present, useful, and even clever? That I wasn't leaving Mori-san and the others behind?

I looked around and immediately started throwing out some of these items. Some, but not all. After all, they might be useful. I might use this clipping in a scrapbook. Maybe this doll would make a nice present. Perhaps I should keep this neighborhood bulletin for the field notes. The rationalizations and excuses for keeping my hoard also stacked up like fortress battlements protecting my cherished belongings from loss.

Psychiatrists have scales and measurements for separating my kind of hoarding from pathology, including the Saving Inventory–Revised, the Hoarding Rating Scale, and the UCLA Hoarding Severity Scale (Mataix-Cols et al. 2010). The fifth edition of the *Diagnostic and Statistical Manual of Mental Disorders*, released in May 2013, classifies hoarding disorder for the first time as distinct from other compulsive disorders, though an estimated 20 percent of patients diagnosed with obsessive-compulsive disorder are also hoarders (Mataix-Cols et al. 2010).[1] Like other hoarders detailed in the psychological case study literature, Mori-san showed a lack of insight about her behavior (only about 15 percent of hoarders have insight about their condition, which they might experience initially as enjoyable and anxiety-reducing). This may have been one reason she was not ashamed to invite me into her home, despite a scene that would make most Japanese people very uncomfortable. But Mori-san's hoarding had, over the course of her life, become maladaptive—even dangerous—especially as she entered old age.

Although it was reasonable that Mori-san would develop emotional attachments to some sentimental objects like her childhood school papers or her parents' old books, it was more difficult to discern at first why she could not bear to part with things like broken umbrellas, old calendars, or scraps of used paper.

Mori-san frequently told me that she did not want to "waste" things, and one friend confided that when Mori-san visited his home she proceeded to ruffle through his trash bin, a behavior that he interpreted as her concern about his consumption of packaged junk foods. If Mori-san disposed of anything, it would be given as a gift. In fact, it was rare that I would leave Mori-san's home without something that she had come across like an old wooden serving platter, some Japanese rice paper screens, or a tiny ceramic jar. There was usually little rhyme or reason to the things she handed off as far as I could tell. She would simply bring something out and ask, "Don't you think you need one of these? Do you think you would use it?"

During the move, I sometimes accompanied Mori-san as she redistributed belongings to friends and neighbors. I carried boxes of assorted clothes to the home of one friend, and an antique dresser and some chocolates to a local noodle shop owner. Again and again I heard the refrain that these things could still be used, or, in the Japanese vernacular, they hadn't completed their life (jumyō). I even helped move the large camillia trees from the front of her house to a tiny patch of dirt in a neighbor's yard. Returning from one of these trips, we sat in the entryway as Mori-san told me in a concerned voice that her daughter Naoko-san had been asking her, "How are you going to use all this?" I waited as she fingered some scraps of paper on the ground, soon answering, "If I think about it, I know that I can come up with a way to use these things in some way. I'm just weak when it comes to useful things."

As if to illustrate, Mori-san leaned over and reached under a nearby pile of books, pulling out a tattered hatbox bursting with scraps of old fabric. She gently removed a few pieces of cream, green, yellow, and light blue fabric and laid them on the tatami floor between us, sighing, "I can't just throw them out." The pieces of fabric were kimono collars that once belonged to her mother. After explaining their age and use to me, Mori-san recalled another argument that she had with her daughter Naoko-san a few days earlier: "That girl [Naoko] says 'what are you going to do with those?' and 'They're stained aren't they?' Well they are a little stained but even so they're very high quality. I can't really say what I might do with them, but I'm sure there are plenty of things that you do with them, it's all written in a book I have. I don't have much choice but to keep them! I just can't throw them out like that. They have memories of my mother." Objects like the old, stained collars seemed to haunt Mori-san's narrative as personal symbols of her unsatisfied desire for dependence. She was haunted by things that existed as potentiality, as memories, as broken ghosts of their former selves. This was not the patina of transient beauty, but the struggle to keep things as they were—to retain. One of Mori-san's common responses to questions about saving was to recall the deprivation during the later stages of World War II, around the time when she recovered from her illness and her mother died. She was also critical of the irresponsibility of younger people's consumption and waste today and resentful of being judged by them. Mori-san's daughters all told me at some point that they came to see their mother's hoarding as a part of her stubborn and oblivious personality. These competing narratives create a seemingly unbreachable divide between mother and daughter, a recapitulation, in a way, of the separation Mori-san experienced from her own mother. Although Naoko-san did not directly place her mother at fault, Mori-san felt constantly on the defensive, and expressed her concern and worry about their fights repeatedly. Understandably, she could not bear the abandonment of losing her narrative, so painstakingly constructed.

Simply putting a diagnostic label such as "hoarding disorder" on Mori-san's symptomatic behavior hardly does justice to her lived experience, nor does it help us to move beyond the particulars of her case to generate broader claims about aging, care, and loss in Japan. Her behaviors tell a story of an entire life course of narrative events that became aesthetically entrenched as she grew older. The idea that hoarding could be one expression of seeking symbolic attachments to guard against the pain of loss, and that the desire to gather objects mediates the ugly feeling of being a burden on others, makes sense if juxtaposed with Japanese narratives of aging and loss such as obasuteyama. If being dependent and burdensome leads to abandonment, then becoming abundantly useful and resourceful is a reasonable response. It also makes sense in the context of the material economy of care of the spirits. The perpetual maintenance and protection of objects like memorial tablets, butsudan, and graves across generations, not to mention the safeguarding of the memories of the deceased, all conform in some sense to a narrative model of retention expressed in Mori-san's hoarding.

Obasuteyama, however, also warns its audience that without yielding, there is no future for aging, no rest in dying, and no hope for liberation. Transience, transformation, and return seem to elude the world Mori-san had built and inhabited, as if thwarted by desires, attachments, repetition that have become a basis for her subjectivity, her way of being in a world of others. Mori-san, unwittingly, has written herself into the tale of obasuteyama, leading her closer to abandonment. From the point of view of cultural aesthetics, the entire scene of the move, from the cluttered rooms to Mori-san's wasting distress, to the fights and estrangement from her daughters, was ugly. And yet, in the objects Mori-san still sought a sense of hope. In some ways, the objects represented a form of waiting, searching, hoping for some tie to the world and to existence that formed part of her subjectivity (see Biehl 2005, 41). Her task, then, was to put her things in order, to reimagine a new relationship between her grief, and her need for kinship and care. She would need to turn her excess of retention into an aesthetic narrative of "protention," or "plans for future actions" (Miyazaki 2004, 19).

Aging does, however, provide other spaces to inscribe a ma, a space that could allow a turning point or "vital conjuncture" (Johnson-Hanks 2002) of life circumstances to emerge in the self-narrative. The disposal of the old graves and erection of new stones (chapter 3) was surprising in its orderliness and sense of organization and forethought. If her narrative phenomenology was fraught, perhaps it was easier to provide the dead with a coherent narrative. Even the dead must have their stories.

Narrative Redemption: The Life-History Project

Narratives are often about correcting inconsistencies or placing uncertainties in an understandable framework that can then be used to do some kind of work in the world, whether that means creating a sense of self, legitimating a claim to authority, healing from an illness, or justifying the terms of an exchange. Dan P. McAdams (1996; 2005) has been one of the leading authorities on using narrative theory in gerontology, observing that well-being in late life is closely related to the ratio of "redemptive" versus "contaminating" sequences that make up important points in their life review (McAdams et al. 2001).[2] McAdams links redemptive sequences to positive adaptation to aging, better health, and greater sense of social well-being. In narratives of grieving and giving, could we also look at sequences of retention and protention to find similar results? What might this tell us about the ways older adults understand their place in the sociocultural world?

The stories about the stories of older people, or the ethnography that I have been presenting in this book, constitute a separate narrative, one with a particular audience and aesthetic storytelling conventions (Jackson 2002). In all of these narratives, however, there is both an effort to "get the story straight," to make it hang together in some temporal sequence that relates to a larger experience of the world. There is also an incompleteness that moves the process forward, calling for an aesthetic approach, a method of abduction, imagination, and creativity, for revision and acceptance (Thomas 2010). After all, if we don't write our own narrative, who will?

But of course others do, and with good reason: we are part of each other's narrative phenomenologies, others' work of filling in the gaps. Agency in old age is not merely an inside job of resolving competing or conflicting self-narratives, but involves "others" who can tell your story back to you (or produce the "virtual self" in Kohutian terms). This is hardly a process that ends in old age or even death, as the memorialization of spirits clearly shows, and it is always embedded in a context of political narratives, ideologies, and cultural scripts that establish how to be in the world with others. These political narratives, however, are also fraught with contingencies, multiple interests, and moments of slippage. I encountered this friction between narratives while participating in a local interview project organized by a youth center in Kyoto. The construction of a kind of "master narrative" of aging here was entangled with other narratives of youth, national history, and cultural identity, and yet, perhaps because the local stakes were relatively low, the execution of the narrative also opened opportunities for older adults to insert another spiritual narrative.

I heard about the local project on conducting life-history interviews with elderly people in Japan about six months into my fieldwork. All of the participants
(except myself) were native Japanese youths between the ages of sixteen and
twenty-nine. The purpose of the workshop was to prepare these younger participants to conduct a series of "life-history" (*denki*) interviews with local elderly
volunteers, eventually compiling, illustrating, and hand binding a short written
biography based on their stories.

My purpose in bringing up the life-history project or *denki-tsukuri* ("biography making") here is to draw connections between the work of the self in old age
as practiced through narrative and life review and broader discourses on aging
and generations in Japan. The municipal youth center's life-history project is
only one example of the various ways local organizations mediate official discourses of aging and the narrative work of the self of individuals, both young
and old. There are literally hundreds of groups in Kyoto alone employed in this
mediating capacity, and while some are direct products of Japan's more recent
insurance and welfare reforms, others, like the ubiquitous *chōnaikai* (block association), have existed in some form for centuries and are at the core of social
organization in places like Kyoto.

The youth center, like the senior community center mentioned in chapter 1,
functions principally to provide a space for leisure activities, but it is also an
important conduit linking different groups under the principle of community
building (*machi-tsukuri*) (cf. Robertson 1994). The life-history project is unique
in these efforts for its recognition and deployment of an intergenerational
model of community building, and was conceived as a volunteer activity that
would harness the youthful spirit of volunteerism and older adults' impulse for
storytelling to provide benefits for all participants.

Though I was initially excited both by the project's goals of intergenerational
communication and life review (not to mention the opportunity to expand my
range of older adult contacts in Kyoto), I began to see additional agendas being
promoted as we drew closer to National Respect for the Aged Day (Keirō no Hi,
September 19), when the young interviewers would finally present the biographies to the interviewees.[3] The project, including the final ceremony, was
covered widely in the Kansai regional media, including television coverage
by the local branch of the Japanese National Broadcasting Agency (NHK).

The workshops and feedback sessions held over the course of the project were
not didactic, but rather encouraged a collaborative construction of aging through
dialogue. For example, the first workshop instructor, Shirakawa-sensei, the director of a day service center in Kyoto,[4] began by asking us from what age one
becomes "old" (using the word *kōrei* rather than *oi*). The first person from the
audience to answer guessed sixty-five, the next person seventy. Another person
answered seventy-five. The numbers, like an auction, only seemed to get higher
with each person called on, but as Shirakawa-sensei continued around the room,
the rest of the participants eventually agreed that the onset of old age is somewhere

between sixty-five and seventy-five. This perception was consistent with national survey data from the Ministry of Health, Labor and Welfare, which reported in 2005 that 46.7 percent of respondents said that old age begins after the age of seventy, while 14.0 percent said after sixty-five, and 19.7 percent after seventy-five.[5] Shirakawa-sensei explained that people seventy-five and older are considered "late old-age" (*goki-kōrei*), and that this is usually when one begins to experience more physical and psychological decline. By "super old age" (*chō-kōrei*), this decline is expected to progress more quickly, and the rates of dementia quickly rise.

He then offered us practical advice on how to conduct the interviews with people in late old age: smile, remember their names, do not avoid eye contact but do not stare, do not try to correct them or point out that they've already told a particular story, "leave a *ma*" instead of jumping in with a new question, and do not joke about fantastic tales that they might tell you. While the idea of the "honorable elders" was not absent in the presentation, it shared space with the idea that the old are also emotionally delicate and even childlike, a tendency that is often seen in the perceptions of the elderly in Japan and elsewhere, especially when they receive care (Hockey and James 1993; Tsuji 1997, 198). The overall message of the presentation was that older adults not only were different from us in many ways, but also will show signs of physical or mental decline, and should be indulged and deferred to.

The narrative of the life-history project also constructed a model of older adults as fragile vessels of an authentic Japanese culture and history to be respected, and archived. While their stories were not ignored, they were crafted in such a way that made them less guides to Japan's future than a preservation of something past its time. This model can also be seen in results of a survey conducted by the Ministry of Health, Labor and Welfare in 2004, published in their annual White Paper on Aging (*kōrei hakushō*). When asked "What is your image of old age?" over 70 percent of total respondents across the age range answered "declining mind and body/great concern with health" (*shinshin ga otoroe, kenkomen de no fuan ga ookii*). Other, far less popular responses were "rich in experience and wisdom" (*keiken ya chie ga yutaka de aru*), "little income, concerned with finances," "not bound to time, can follow anything they want," and "likely to be old-fashioned."[6] Interestingly, the same survey found that older respondents were less likely than younger ones to choose "declining mind and body" (63.3 percent of those over seventy-five, compared with 74.1 percent of those in their twenties), but older respondents were even less likely to choose "rich in experience and wisdom" (28.4 percent of those over seventy-five and 51.9 percent of those in their twenties). Looking at the overall responses, the cultural association of aging with physical decrepitude combined with wisdom of oiru seemed upheld by younger respondents, while older people themselves saw losses across several different categories of life, but have little sense (or do not report) of gains like "wisdom." These results lead to more questions than answers, and demand a different kind of conceptual vocabulary.

At the conclusion of the youth center presentation, we were addressed by the moderator and the director of the project, a stern, bookish-looking woman with bobbed gray hair and black thick-rimmed glasses. She wore a black blouse with white polka dots buttoned all the way to her chin. In her address to the group, she emphasized that the elderly volunteers have had "interesting lives," especially since they lived during the difficult years of World War II and its aftermath, and that we would be doing a wonderful service to them by helping them revisit their old memories. Her address reiterated the Japanese view of older adults as repositories of tradition and history and as embodying a more authentic "Japaneseness" (located in the nostalgic past of the prewar era).

The explicit goals of the interview project were to provide young people with a chance to interact with older adults and also to provide older adults with a social activity and a sense of imparting knowledge to future generations. The rationale was that with fewer coresiding three-generation families, younger people have become uncomfortable interacting with older people and older people did not have anyone young in the household to impart their knowledge to. The project also operated on the assumption that the elderly, while physically frail, were nonetheless socially valuable because they are rich in memories of the pre- and immediate postwar era of Japanese history. It was also assumed that the elderly, who represent the image of memory disintegration in the form of senility, need life review in order to form health and well-being. Thus, the elders were being constructed as cultural curators with fragile bodies and even more fragile memories, while the youth were being socialized to view these memories from a respectful distance, "to leave a ma," the way, we assume, a grandchild would listen to a grandparent.

As a participant in this project, I found the format a little stiff, but instructive: the script was already written, and we simply had to enact it together with our older adult friends. As I consulted with the coordinator, it became increasingly clear that one of the objectives was to develop a particular scripted narrative arc of each person's life, starting from the youthful and happy prewar years, through the difficult (but ultimately character building) war and its aftermath, and eventually to the reestablishment of normalcy, and the current enjoyment of old age. We were learning not only a particular historical narrative, but a prepackaged "redemptive sequence" (McAdams 2005) that we were to then enfold into the personal narrative of the interviewee. I was urged by the coordinator, for example, to ask my interviewee about children's games, school trips, and other leisure activities before the war began. As for the war years, I was told that asking about food rations, mandatory labor, and lost relatives would usually elicit good responses. Then, for old age, I was advised to ask questions about exercise and health regimes, grandchildren, hobbies, and social functions. We were to avoid experiences of loss and thoughts about death. It was unclear whether this scripted subjectivity was meant more for the benefit of the younger people conducting the interviews, the elderly interviewees, or both. Unlike obasuteyama, interviewers and elders were urged to complete the story, enshrining the past in the form of a biography.

On the first meeting with the older life-history participants held at a local social welfare group, I had expected the same values and narratives of the project organizers to be reiterated. I was surprised, however, when the group's president addressed the project participants and other older people gathered there by reading the following passage from *Ikigai no Sozo* (Creating value of life), by popular inspirational writer Iida Fumihiko (1999, 330):

> For us, "death" is surely nothing to be afraid of. It is just that peaceful moment of our homecoming after we've finished our work in this world. The loss of a loved one is certainly not a permanent separation; it is just a brief space of time where we become unable to converse directly before making our joyful reunion [with them] in the other world. Moreover, the souls (*tamashi*) of family and friends that have gone before us are always warmly watching out for us and speaking to those of us who continue to work, as if they are encircling us. Our calls surely reach them as well. Whenever there is no one around but we get the feeling that we are being watched, don't you suddenly remember, for no reason those people who've died? These times in particular are moments when the souls are truly sending us a message. Open your heart (*kokoro*) and please ask "Who is it?" "What are you trying to tell me?" Surely someone's face and words will arise [in your thoughts]. Even if we were to stand by ourselves in the middle of an open field, we are never alone (*kodoku*).

The reading received nods of approval from the older people present, but struck me as out of place since it dealt so directly with matters of spirituality and death in a context that is typically so secular and life-affirming. But with this passage read in the context, I recognized how the significance of memorialization (the idea of "joyful reunion," the listening and watching of the spirits, the visual reminders of connections to the departed) sometimes overflowed individuals and families, entering into other social realms. In the passage, Iida was clearly addressing those grieving in a time of abandonment, calling on them to recognize the ma in times when no one is watching, as if "in the middle of an open field."

The reading at the senior welfare group made me especially self-conscious about my own assumptions about aging and loss in Japan. On the one hand, my emerging thoughts about importance of spirits to older people in the context of national discourses of the aging Japan seemed to be affirmed by the reading. On the other hand, I had to reexamine my assumptions about life course development and face-value acceptance of metaphors of redemption, faith, and wisdom. Given that ancestor memorial has been used to organize and promote the goals of the state and other interests in the past, is it presumptuous to think of my project as fundamentally different? Isn't the redemptive sequence promoted by the youth center in some ways the story of the creativity of loss?

I am not sure if I have found the answers to these questions, though I do recognize my own role in constructing a cultural narrative around aging in Japan here. Ethnography itself is an inherently narrative venture. The older adults I spoke with were also not impervious to cultural scripts when reflecting on their own aging and life-course experiences; like many of us, they too can be sometimes moved to accept a certain version of their life, a subjectivity, for good or for bad. My hope, then, became that after repeated interactions and triangulations, the events of a life course and their narration from the point of view of old age would sometimes interfere with these scripts, including my own, revealing the creative work of the self embedded within them. It was these moments that I try to focus on in this book, moments when the work of the self was engaging with possibilities, fragments, partially articulated discourses like those on death and loss, which seemed to emerge in an uncharacteristic turn of affect, often after a long pause.

Young interviewers in the life-history project communicated their relationship to the narrative by not only producing the text itself, but also carefully constructing its wrapping: printing, illustrating, and hand binding the final copy. This required attention to the older person's aesthetic tastes (since the woman I helped interview mentioned a fondness for a particular kind of hyacinth and often wore the color yellow, we included these elements on the cover of the booklet). Interviewers would then take on the role of substitute grandchildren on Respect for the Aged Day, performing a ritual of filial gratitude. It was an emotional day for all, as the well-dressed older participants accepted their books and the interviewers gave teary-eyed testimonials of their experiences. The life-history project and its mediating scripts formed one narrative of aging and generations in Japan clearly linked to the discourses of the national crisis of a super-aging society, but as enacted through the ritual structure of the project, these discourses became aligned with an experience of emotional catharsis. The books were aesthetic materializations of this narrative catharsis, of a past that, although lost, has the ability to return through the thoughtful reflections of future generations. Like the material exchanges in memorialization of spirits, the books became their own narrative of concern and the creativity of loss.

THE SOULS AND STORIES OF THINGS

As we took a break from packing boxes, Mori-san told me over a cup of tea that she was worried, not about herself or her daughters, but about an acquaintance who was seventy years old and had been complaining of fatigue all autumn. The woman, who had been seemingly healthy, suddenly just stopped eating. Mori-san's eldest daughter Haruka-san overheard the last part of the story as she came in from another the room. "When you get old, it's all sad stories!" she said as she sat down at the table and poured some tea for herself.

Haruka-san's childhood friend, Yuri, was over this morning as well, and soon came over to the table after text messaging a friend outside. Mori-san began to serve her a glass of tea, but the teapot was empty. "Aren't you BOKE (senile)? You forgot the water!" Haruka-san scolded as her mother shuffled in the direction of the kitchen.

Yuri-san seemed unfazed by the scene, quietly commenting, "Obāchan [Grandmother] hasn't changed, has she?" Haruka-san complained that her mother "lives in garbage," but Yuri-san countered that it looked better than before, and has opened up a lot. Indeed it was one of the last days I helped with Mori-san's move, and things were starting to look clearer inside. Mori-san, however, was still trying to cope with her health problems brought on by the stress and strain and winter chill.

One of my last tasks was carrying several dozen potted plants out of Mori-san's garden and lining them up in a neighbor's yard. It was yet another tedious process, and most of the plants seemed shriveled and dead, some with long brittle tendrils winding around still more pots. When I suggested that the job might be easier if we dumped out the old soil and dead plants from some of the pots, Mori-san admonished me that even the pots that seemed to have nothing in them sometimes had seeds or roots buried in them, and just needed some care to be revived. Looking down at the gray dirt filling the pots, I couldn't see anything that resembled life, but I reluctantly complied with her request. Perhaps even these poor neglected plants did not deserve to be abandoned, or perhaps she sympathized with them in some way; they were, like Mori-san herself, not as inert or useless as they appeared.

When I was finished moving all of the plants, I stepped inside and rested at the doorway to take out my notebook and jot down some notes. Mori-san, who had been packing in the house, came into the room and, seeing me there, told me excitedly that she wanted to show me something that she had come across while packing. She led me inside the house and reached up to a shelf next to her butsudan, pulling down a small wooden box stuffed with yellowed cloth. She took out the cloth and slowly unwrapped a short dagger, the handle missing and the blade now rusted. She explained that it belonged to her mother's father's brother, and was a symbol of his high status. Mori-san had never known this man personally, but the stories about his life and his official prominence in her mother's household made her careful about disposing of it. She explained that the dagger held this man's "heart" (kokoro) and "soul" (tamashi) but that it could not be buried with him since it would be too pitiable to be buried with something that cannot be cremated, but will only slowly rust and disintegrate. It was, in a way, representative of something that resisted signs of transience that were necessary for the peaceful transition of the spirit.

Mori-san first tried to give the dagger to one of her other relatives, but none of them knew what to do with it or refused to take care of it. "Besides," Mori-san said with an air of disappointment, "people disappear" (ningen ha kieru mon). She also tried to take it to her parish Shinto shrine, but found that it no longer accepted objects for ritual disposal. Finally, she asked the priest at the Buddhist temple where her graves were located. Those at the temple agreed to take the dagger and conduct a ceremony for its disposal. "Young people don't know how to do these things," she explained. "Old people like me understand; I *listened* and learned."

For Mori-san, turning her collection of old and broken sentimental objects over to shrines and temples was a surprising discovery. Even the very ordering and prioritizing of objects needed to carry out this task was a rare occurrence throughout my observations over months of packing and cleaning. It showed that Mori-san could find relief from her anxiety and hoarding by redistributing the heart (kokoro no kubari). When I looked around at the rest of the room, I wondered how she was going to ever finish the move without throwing away much more. My excitement was immediately tempered by a creeping sense of concern. Should I have more hope?

My experience of helping Mori-san move was a turning point in my thinking about aging, loss, and memorial. Once I was able to look past the symptoms of age, such as her absentmindedness and her hoarding, I came to see other things that shaped her subjectivity and provided her means of expression, agency, and life. I began to look at other older adults differently too, looking not only at what was lost or what people held onto, but how they circulated objects as a means of distributing dependence and infusing meanings of age into the economy of care. A photograph, a festival float, a dagger all worked their way into the experience of aging, the relationships with others, and the ability to discern worlds beyond.

Listening and Watching

Like the life-history project biographies, the gifts circulated in an economy of care transformed into memories and bonds; they were means of expanding or strengthening dependencies and subverting risk. Whenever I had an interview, for example, I would make sure to never arrive empty-handed. Gifts were part of the aesthetic of encounter, performing my concern and opening up a space for other exchanges by putting everyone at ease. The standard gift on these visits was one that could be consumed, and if the interview was held at home, these gifts would be placed in front of the memorial tablets at the butsudan, whether I had brought traditional Japanese sweets or a small box of French cakes. The ancestors, after all, enjoy cake as well, as they share in the general social and material matters of the household from their place on the altar. This circulation of the gift was part of the flow of care, and as with the living, I could understand it as expressing the same desire to give to oneself through giving to others, waiting, in the meantime, with a sense of possibility.[7] Like small payments on the loan of life, they might be a way to buy oneself time to hope. Some people explained that the spirits consumed the scent of the food, the substance of the gift we shared in anticipation.

In contrast to the retention of Mori-san's hoard, the material life of Nakamura-san was much more consistent with the flows of value between living and the dead. And yet like Mori-san, these flows were contingent on a principle of shared aesthetics, on a kind of sensorial empathy that Nakamura-san referred to as "listening and watching," just as Mori-san claimed that aging allows one to "listen and learn." Listening and watching were means of embodying a narrative of loss through rituals of memorialization and aesthetic discernment, which not only constituted aged subjectivity, but extended loss as debt into the next generation.

In Nakamura-san's house, the hotoke and ancestors were not the only ones seized by the economy of spiritual care. Scattered throughout the rooms and courtyard were no fewer than sixteen shrines to different kami, most consisting of little more than a small platform, a container for offerings, and an image representing the kami, such as a small fox statue for the kami Inari. Every morning Nakamura-san went to each shrine and presented the kami with fresh water or tea, putting his hands together and bowing his head in veneration or saying a short prayer. This ritual cycle would take about an hour to complete, and always began with the ancestors on the butsudan, which Nakamura said were the most important of all:

> We make offerings and pray [to the kami]. Something like "May we live in health again this year," right? "May business be good." Well, we pray like that. And then on the twenty-first is the death anniversary so the monk comes to visit us. And we ask "May we live in health, one more year" [laughs loudly]. That's the kind of thing we ask for! [whispered and trailing off] Well, it's like they say: if there weren't any ancestors, then I wouldn't have been born. We have to respect those ancestors, you know? We have to take care of them. That's the feeling they give me. . . . So, in the morning, every morning, I pray (*inoru*) to the hotoke-san. I wake up in the morning, and before eating I wash my face and then I go to the hotoke-san and then to Benten-san [turning and gesturing around the room], and then next the bath kami-san, the toilet kami-san and bow (*ogamu*) to all the rest of the kami-san. It really—it really is hard to take care of all of them!

Certainly there was a sense of duty as the eldest son to perpetuate the traditions of his ancestors, and his "hard work" of upholding this tradition underlines the self-sacrifice embedded in the acts of offering, just as the numerous shrines and altars are embedded in the architecture of his machiya. This hard work was material, but extended the giver beyond the house while remaining contained within it. As a daily practice, it had become so naturalized that Nakamura-san and his wife simply laughed at the thought of ever stopping. However, it is precisely the material nature of the rituals and shrines that make them vulnerable to loss as the Nakamuras age. Objects and actions that require an investment of space and time materialize care (Langford 2009); they are produced and sustained by reiterative symbolic actions (such as kinship rituals that link the shrines in the home to sites of worship "out there").

The rituals at the domestic shrines are situated within the same social and political context as community-based matsuri, initiating the play among intimate objects, narratives, memories, and larger institutional interests. They are also strained by the same context of an aging Japan. In Nakamura-san's case, the materialization of memorial is challenged by the aging body itself, its health and longevity as well as its need for care. If he is not cared for in the home, or if he must give up his home to receive care, the sixteen shrines will also be abandoned. The anticipated demise of the gods and ancestors call out for a cause, invoking the burden of longevity. Although his eldest son may return to care, in some fashion, for the shrines, his absence in the meantime weakens his ability to listen and watch. As a result of a model of longevity that holds up independence as the reward of health and financial stability, Japanese families sometimes stretch the distance and time between generations, allowing successors to abandon not the frail elder, but the healthy one.

The effect of this kind of abandonment is loosening bonds of exchange that incorporate individuals within a system of kinship and enable the flow of generational debt through ancestors, elders, and descendants. As in the case of Nakamura-san's shrines and household graves, these loosening bonds have material-spiritual consequences. Listening and watching means more than imitation; it is an observation that conjures the calming presence of the ancestors. As with the rituals at the family graves, the "hard work" of memorialization in the home also contributes to the uncertainty in old age:

EMIKO: Where the bride is from, it's kami-san. They worship (*matsuru*) kami-san. And we're Buddhist, right? The hotoke-san side. That part is completely different.

NAKAMURA: I think that the things you do are a little different.

DANELY: Yes, but, don't you have quite a lot of *kami-san* here? [all of us laughing]

NAKAMURA: When you say that kami-san and hotoke-san are different, well, but the kami-san and the hotoke-san are exactly the same. [Emiko laughs a little] They're both exactly the same but, the, the kind of way you worship, the holidays—these thing are of course, the things you do seem to be a little different.

DANELY: I see.

NAKAMURA: Yes. So that's the kind of thing that's difficult [for her] to comprehend. So if she were to say I don't really want to be giving water and tea every morning, well then [the tradition] will have remained until then. Even if she says we didn't do that sort of thing at my house so I'm not going to keep [your traditions], well that's just that. [Emiko laughs a little] Right? That's just the end, right?

From Nakamura-san's perspective, "the end" of traditional household ancestor memorial practices (difficult to verbally articulate) and the decline in traditional family-provisioned care are directly related to the loosening bonds between kin and communities in Japanese society. Both trends weaken the conditions for the transmission of family traditions and family history. Just as there is no "insurance" that his children will tend to the family graves, there is also no insurance that Nakamura-san's children will care for him and his wife in their old age.

In chapter 4, Nakamura-san referred to this risk of kinship with the shrug of "the passing of time," a shrug that I interpreted as a kind of gateway to a larger temporal framework that includes multiple generations of the ancestors. Elsewhere I have argued that narratives of aging in Japan reveal a comforting sense of resignation to a greater temporal order, something not directly known, but perpetually hoped for (Danely 2013). But Nakamura-san's shrug was also a gesture of ambivalence; he was not entirely resigned to the "deculturation" of his traditions (Gutmann 1987). After all, it was not merely the performance of the rituals or the bonds of kinship and place symbolized by the house and graves that were at risk of being abandoned. More crucially, what was being abandoned was "listening and watching," the processual guts of the narrative process that engage aesthetically with the material world. The narrative gained through listening and watching is the source of the spirits' agency, or of their ability to bridge the past and the future continuity of the household. To the extent that this agency is entangled in the agency of the Nakamuras, the threat of abandonment strikes deep.

For many older Japanese adults, the multigenerational coresiding household ideal was either unrealistic or undesired. For Nakamura-san and others who have made a lifelong investment in the economy of caring for the spirits, listening and watching are essential for shaping the affects and desires, or "appreciation" for tradition:

NAKAMURA: For generations this is, well, if my son who is the successor doesn't keep [traditional customs] then that's a problem, but. . . . [laughs] Well, you know, we don't live together so he doesn't understand. Two generations, we lived together so that's why I think you have to do this sort of thing. Well, you're *allowed* to do these things.

Now, even my son has left. He's living separately so doing this sort of thing is. . . . [trailing off] Maybe he saw some of that when he was a child, but, since he got married, well, whenever a little break comes, it's not like he's going to come over her. So, well, there's a lot of things to it. He stops in on O-higan and O-bon and such. After all, you have to take care of the hotoke-san. That—well, it's nice if he comes around then but. . . . He's living separately so you just can't pass things on so easily. There's all these things that well, depending on the sect, there are different things to do. Passing those things on just isn't—It's just become difficult in this day and age. More and more.

Well that has to do first of all with coresidence. When you don't coreside, it's a little difficult.

DANELY: Coresidence?

NAKAMURA: Living together. In the same living quarters. It's called two-generation coresidence. It's because it's gotten more difficult to have two-generation coresidence. Young people these days, well, it's like "We want to have a house for ourselves, we want to have our own domain" It's hard because they want to have their own domain or house and so these nuclear families are leaving. It's not an absolutely bad thing but, it's just like that. It isn't that they're doing the wrong thing either. The reason that the ancestors aren't important is really because there isn't a household (*ie*). I think that sort of thing, I guess you could say that lately it's weakening a little. The appreciation (*kanshin*) has, you know?

DANELY: The appreciation has weakened?

NAKAMURA: Well I think, isn't it because the appreciation has weakened? If you place importance on the household—well when you say household it means two generations coresiding or else three generations, you listen to what your parents say, or else while your grandfather and grandmother are still alive. Because they teach you good things. They would absolutely never teach you the wrong thing. Oh, it's the best if you hear these things from when you are little.

More and more older people like the Nakamuras are living in single-generation households, either alone or with a spouse. While 41 percent of older adults lived with children in 2010, only 8.4 percent of households fit the three-generational model, about half the number in 1975 (16.9) (MHLW 2011). In addition, 20 percent of households were composed of at least one older adult in 2009, compared to 10.1 percent in 1994 and only 3.3 percent in 1975 (MHLW 2011). Looking at these statistics in light of Nakamura-san's feelings about coresidence and the value of the old and the ancestors produces questions about the changing ethical boundaries of care, about care's relationship to a sense of indebtedness and to materiality and sacrifice, and about the possibility of intersubjectivity among the young, the old, and the dead. To care and not to abandon is hard work.

The hard work of keeping up with ritual obligations is, in a way, the heart of the hard work of the self in old age, echoing Orin's work to manage her family in anticipation of her departure to Mt. Narayama. But everywhere around me, it seemed, people were hard at work: Mori-san slowly and painfully discarding her hoard, Sato-san and others keeping dependence at bay at the community center, and even Nishida-san with her busy schedule of funerals and memorial services. They were more than just "busybodies" (Katz 2000); the material exchanges, debts compiled, and credits extended in the hard work (and creativity) involved or presumed in these encounters invite listening and watching, if only by the spirits.

SPINNING TIME, WEAVING LIFE

Nishida-san's sense of continuity and integrity in her later years cannot be understood without first understanding her relationship with the past and the future, with both reminiscence and hope. In chapter 2, I described how Nishida-san attributed her health in old age to a life-threatening incident following the birth of her first daughter. During that time, Nishida-san saw a vision of the other world, desiring to stay there, but "listening" to the voices of her family calling her back to life. The daughter then died before she was a year old. When World War II had finally come to an end, Nishida-san's husband, who had always had an interest in English and would read only English-language newspapers, took a job as a translator for the occupying government. The long hours of work and frequent trips to other cities wore him to exhaustion, and in 1951, after only eight years of marriage, Nishida-san's husband died of acute pneumonia. Their sons were five and three years old.

In Nishida-san's account, her devotion to her family did not waver even after the death of her husband. The interdependent sense of self that Nishida-san developed in her childhood continued on after her husband's death. Nishida-san raised her two sons with the help of her mother-in-law in the same house where we sat to conduct our interviews. Still unfamiliar with most of the aspects of running a weaving business, Nishida-san relied on the help people in her community, and learned accounting skills and marketing practices through working with them. Times were difficult, but in the end her strong community ties gave her the ability to sustain her business until today. Her eldest son attended college and soon after returned to run the business for his mother. Although Nishida-san was officially retired, we were interrupted on numerous occasions at her home when longtime customers would call and ask to speak with her. She was still an integral part of the business in many ways. The interdependent structure of the silk-weaving community in the Nishijin district of Kyoto (Hareven 2002) helped Nishda-san to develop her ability to cultivate social networks, her credit and perpetual indebtedness. As a baffled Japanese professor of economics at Kyoto University once told me, in defiance of standard economic theory, "people in Nishijin *try* to remain in debt!"

The scale of Nishida-san's redemptive narrative is incredible, but the more I spoke with her, the more I understood how clearly it followed from the relationships she held with important people in her past as well as the relationships she continued to build with those she hopes to meet in the future beyond death. If there was any overarching theme that emerged from our conversations, it was that she approached her life from a perspective of deep humility and gratitude that generated and sustained interdependent relationships, and although circumstances may have shifted over the course of her life, it was almost as if the space of her grief opened her even more toward others. Over time, what may have begun out of necessity became a lifelong pattern.

Nishida-san was born in central Kyoto in 1923, and as the youngest of seven siblings, she was constantly doted on by her brothers and sisters. This was particularly so because while the other siblings were born only one or two years apart from one another, Nishida-san was born nearly ten years after her closest sibling and nineteen years apart from her eldest sister. As a result, she never thought of her siblings so much as peers, but rather as pseudo-parents.

Nishida-san's parents were somewhat distant after retiring, moving to the outskirts of the city when Nishida-san was still attending a girls preparatory school at the age of nineteen. This was once a typical pattern for older people, removing themselves from the home of the successor and obtaining a "hidden residence" (*inkyo*) on the periphery. Recalling her father's declining health that quickly led to his death, Nishida-san remembered his rebukes when she offered to stay with him at his place of retirement outside of the city. He demanded that she finish her education in Kyoto and live there with her older sister. The death of her father, who refused her care so that she could have an education, drew Nishida-san closer to her siblings as guides and role models, so much so that her eldest brother stood in for her father to broker her marriage and provide the customary dowry of furniture and kimono.

Nishida-san remained close to each of her siblings and their families as they became older. With all of the attention from siblings throughout her childhood, Nishida-san felt a strong sense of care, security, and trust, to which she credits her own capacity for compassion and love today. In one interview, Nishida-san elaborated on her feelings about love, smoothly linking together love and care of children and for the elderly, experienced not only by listening and watching, but also through bodily warmth and embrace:

> NISHIDA: It was my father, mother and then the five siblings, out of whom I
> was the youngest, so I remember being thoroughly loved (*kawaigaru*).[8]
> DANELY: Oh, they didn't leave you alone?
> NISHIDA: They loved me and cared for me, and however old I get, that
> thought stays with me . . . So you see, my love (*aijō*), love, that is, rather,
> something like warmth (*nukumori*) I suppose you could say? I think that
> I've really received *so much* of that. So I want to take care of other people
> (*daiji ni shitai*). . . . I always want people to take care of each other and get
> along. So whenever someone like a relative has a child I'll say hug them
> *tight* and love them! If you care for them like [makes a quick squeezing
> sound], then that child won't become jaded or feel strange don't you think?
>
> You see—my older sister died when she was ninety-two years old. And
> I watched over her until the very end. She was all alone you see, and I just
> can't abandon (*hottorakasu*) someone who is alone. . . . I put her in an old
> folk's home, but I'd go and visit her every week, and then in the end, when
> she really started feeling worse, I went and got her and brought her to the
> hospital. The home sent her off. . . . [trails off]
>
> Love has to come from love, right?

In the middle of Nishida-san's exposition on love, she explained that she "just can't abandon someone who is alone." For Nishida-san, close attachment is a vital part of love, and like Sato-san, abandoning or letting someone go completely is strange and almost incomprehensible to her. As I have hinted at in earlier chapters, dependence, love, and exchange all fit within the domain of ancestor memorial, and each of these transformed and adapted in response to experiences over the life course.

When she was a child, Nishida-san's family had a butsudan, and she remembers being taught to honor the ancestors enshrined there. The importance of reverence and gratitude to the ancestors and hotoke is something that she now passes on to her own grandchildren:

> In my case, since I was little [I was raised to believe] you have to honor the hotoke-san. And then if you get something tasty, if you get something special, first of all is the hotoke-san. Well that's just become natural to me. I don't think twice about it. My—even the granddaughter here, ever since she was little, from the time she was a baby, I'd say, "Okay, go pray" so she'd pray. That's just become natural, so even now when I make some warm rice, [I think] "Grandma liked rice, I ought to give her a bowl," and heap some rice in a bowl and go make an offering. But anyway, we're all allowed to live now because of the grace of the ancestors. Or you could say we have been brought to life, whatever. But you mustn't make light of the ancestors. [You should] do your best not to worry the ancestors. Saying that, even if you have something you're worrying about, [the ancestors] will protect you! [laughs]

Giving to the ancestors and hotoke not only means "honoring" them, but also deferring to them, remembering them, and, most of all, being grateful to them. This gratitude is an acknowledgment of sharing agency with the departed, of the past becoming one's present self, as in the statement "We're all allowed to live now because of the grace of the ancestors." The seeming passivity of her language and the deferral of agency also acknowledge the space, or ma, between the living and the dead that provides the conditions for individuation and respect.

It is also notable that Nishida-san refers to the hotoke as "grandmother" (obōsan), and talks not of her sons or daughter-in-law, but of her own granddaughter. The special tie between grandparent and grandchild can be especially potent in a three-generational household, where the old and young may be able to form a coalition to balance the power of the "sandwich" generation, but it is also important for socialization, as seen in the special relationship Kitano-san had with her grandmother (chapter 4). Nishida-san also had a special affection for her grandmother, and told me that the earliest memory that she had (ever) was pressing her body against her grandmother's back and feeling the warmth (nukumori). This was the same word she used when talking about the feeling of "love" ("love, that is, rather, something like warmth"). The shared sensation of bodily heat and the merging of young and old bodies had another feeling of passivity, but I find it difficult to imagine a better aesthetic anchor for a life narrative of interdependence than the warmth of this image.

Interdependence between generations as well as between members of the community has became a vital part of Nishida-san's life narrative, her adaptation to old age, and her religious outlook. Her community ties were an extension of her experiences growing up, and as she tells it, they gave her the same feelings of humility and support that have helped her to persevere through the years. Nishida-san recalls feeling "small," in comparison to her siblings, and compensates for this by maintaining a different kind of confidence in herself that could not be any more different than Sato-san's hypermasculine John Wayne self-image. Her modesty makes her feel that this confidence amounts to being a selfish or "an irresponsible person" (*iikagen na hito*), someone who doesn't place himself or herself in a position of accountability. Fulfilling her responsibilities to the dead, then, becomes a way that she can reframe herself in terms of other people whom she has depended on:

> I'm thankful to my parents, I'm thankful to my brother, and I go to their graves now. [quiet laugh] [My brother said] "You have the worst of these [motions to face] than any of our five siblings. Have a good heart," he said . . . "because you have the worst face among the five siblings, if you don't have a good heart (kokoro) you'll never make it in the world." [Danely: Is that what your brother said?] Yes, my brother. My eldest brother. He was the most handsome. Out of my five siblings, he was the most handsome. My elder sister was also pretty. She wasn't like me with all these little marks on her face. [laughs] I understood that. My brother was tall, he was built, he had a pointed nose. He was very good-looking. And my sister was beautiful; she had that quintessential Japanese hair—so beautiful. And I was *small*, I was the third [sister] so there was nothing left. I was the worst. . . . [trails off]
>
> But anyway, whenever people said something about me, bullied me, I was, in the end, for myself, my personality was sort of confident. So going straight ahead, on some path, I'd say, "Oh, I'll go along on this path." That was my way. I'd go along—confidently, well, "confidently" sounds a little too presumptuous, but . . . I guess you'd say I'm an irresponsible person. I don't know if it's right, but I just go along with it for the time being, so I just go on some different sidetrack. I'm irresponsible. If you want to put it badly, I'm an irresponsible person. Well, anyways, in the end, for myself, [I don't think about] "Oh I've had this has happened to me, that has happened to me, my husband died, my child died, my relatives have all this problems, fights, divorce, affairs. . . ." This thing and the other thing—what is it all? Well, I've come to my conclusion. I've had some good kids, but well, I've been through some tough times, so I've gotten stronger for it, right?
>
> I don't have a husband here to consult with about things. . . . [trails off and pauses] That's the only thing I can't really help. . . .

PART III

Abandonment and Care

CHAPTER 6

Aesthetics of Failed
Subjectivity

In the last chapter, I began to delve further into what I have called the "economy of care" in order to better situate the ethnographic narratives of aging, loss, and dependence in contemporary Japan introduced in the first half of the book. In this chapter I look at how economies of care can collapse into forms of social, political, and bodily abandonment. My argument here, as throughout this book, is that the sociopolitical and economic conditions of contemporary urban Japan are producing aged subjectivities suspended between abandonment and hope. For some older adults, these subjectivities become meaningful and intimate through aesthetic practices of ritual memorialization. In this way, the political context is not merely in the background of the older adults' spiritual life, but at the heart of it. What I call "the creativity of loss" is the way older adults exercise agency over their narratives of loss, recalibrating and transforming its value, and producing new possible selves and relational worlds and form a sense of well-being.

In examining how something stays together and works, be it an engine, a marriage, or a narrative, it is often instructive to look at how it breaks. By tracking the circulation of discourses of abandonment, we can see how older adults' fears are more than fantasy, but grounded in experiences of neglect and violence that are often rendered invisible through isolation and liberal forms of "Japan-style" welfare. Just as memorialization works to put a life together by incorporating an aesthetics of loss into the personal narrative, abandonment presents a picture of failed subjectivity, where the older person becomes unable to exercise agency. We can blame neither the state nor the families and individuals complicit in the event of abandonment. However, we can learn something from examining the ways abandonment becomes possible for older people. I also show how memorialization seeps into these discourses, how it resists foreclosure, countering abandonment by extending dependencies and providing a source of protection and care.

ABANDON THE OLD IN TOKYO

Zeami's *Obasute* portrays the shame and suffering of maintaining attachments in old age, impressing on its audience the tense *ma* between this world and the next, the suspense between abandonment and hope. The event of abandonment, however, is hidden in this story, recalled only as a rumor; the problem is not how to avoid abandonment, but how to find hope in a state of abandonment. In a similar way, Imamura's *The Ballad of Narayama* seems to distribute the guilt of abandoning Orin by linking old age and death in an economy of care and generational yielding to tradition, to household, and to community. Maintaining social integrity through self-sacrifice is not only meaningful for Orin, but for the social integrity of the generations of her household, living, dead, and yet to be born. It functions, in a way, as part of the social contract and the debt ledger of care, operating in synch with the generational and seasonal cycles. Orin's ability to find hope in her abandonment was hard work, but by ensuring the continuity of her family, she could maintain the hope of a "good death" through reunification and memorialization in death.

Obasuteyama can be instructive in these issues, as its many reiterations over the centuries show a degree of play that follows the partial, indeterminate nature of loss, mourning, and concepts of age. In some versions of obasuteyama, for example, the old woman is not even completely abandoned, and is praised for her wisdom (Cornell 1991; Traphagan 2000, 150; Yamaori 1997b: 35); in others, she is freakishly demented and demon-like (Kurahashi 2003, 27–40; Sorgenfrei 1994). While most of these reiterations like *The Ballad of Narayama* retain the basic template of Zeami's Noh play, situated in the dark and yet quintessentially Japanese folk realm of the remote mountain village, others have explored obasuteyama in modern Japan, taking on the problem of the ethics of care in a time when problems of intergenerational conflict, neglect, and abandonment have created new cultural nightmares of loss in late life.

Nowhere is this cultural nightmare of abandonment in old age more striking than in Tatsumi Yoshihiro's obasuteyama story *Abandon the Old in Tokyo* ([1970] 2006), a graphic novel, or manga, set in a grim, modern-day urban Japan. Tatsumi was born in 1935, and began drawing Japanese serial comic books during the 1950s; Tatsumi became a pioneer of manga art and storytelling through a characteristically gritty, dark, black-and-white style that he dubbed *Gekiga* ("dramatic pictures"), which has earned him a status as a cult figure in the manga world (Garner 2009).

Tatsumi's stories blend the angst and ennui of everyday life in a Japan cast adrift in the postwar era (Tatsumi's autobiography is titled *A Drifting Life*). Using surreal depictions of often bizarre, violent, and disgusting imagery, his stories speak of alienation, anger, and helplessness in the midst of Japanese capitalist ascendancy. There is little heroism in this Japan, and little hope for more than brief, desperate episodes of animal pleasure. Tatsumi's work confronts the

Figure 6. Kenichi contemplating abandoning his mother. From the book *Abandon the Old in Tokyo*. Copyright Yoshihiro Tatsumi. Used with permission by Drawn & Quarterly.

existential anguish of life in the gray zones produced by social alienation, and his antiheroes who work in sewers and other dirty jobs can hardly stake a moral position from which to criticize the emotional numbness of the society around them. It may come as little surprise then that his 1970 story *Abandon the Old in Tokyo* directly incorporated the themes and subjects from obasuteyama, setting it within the historical context of the two generations spanning the war years.

Abandon the Old revolves around a troubled garbage collection worker named Kenichi Nakamura, and his mother, who live together in an old, cramped Tokyo apartment. Kenichi's mother is bedridden, and when the reader first sees her, she is lying on a urine-soaked futon after having just soiled herself. Kenichi, who had just finished cleaning other soiled garments, dutifully attends to the mess while his mother laments on how hard it was to raise him, how lonely she is when he goes off to work, and how miserable it is to be old (Figure 6). Kenichi bears his burden stoically. In fact, throughout the short story, the reader does not see him speak a word to his mother.

At night, unable to sleep due to his mother's loud snoring, Kenichi drifts off into a memory of his childhood, the way he was neglected by his mother, who worked as a bar hostess and would stay out late with male customers. The memory ends with his retribution, locking his mother out of the room as she pounds on the door yelling, "I work so hard for you and you turn me away!" The memory establishes Kenichi as a latchkey child of a single mother in the sex trade, unable to trust the person he loved, or trust her love for him with anything more than guilt and shame. Kenichi's thoughts foreshadow the repetition of abandonment when he takes his mother to obasuteyama.

Still lying in his futon, Kenichi opens up a newspaper and reads one of the headlines: "Old person (*rōjin*) discovered two weeks after death in a downtown apartment." The following frames show Kenichi thinking back to something said by one of his coworkers on the garbage truck earlier: "People get rid of anything old. That's modern life for ya" (Tatsumi [1970] 2006, 54).

For Kenichi, caring for his aging mother in a dingy apartment is anything but "the modern life," or any life at all, really. He thinks of his fiancé, seductively saying, "I can't wait to leave home. I can't wait to live with you" (Tatsumi [1970] 2006, 54). Only the upper half of Kenichi's head can be seen in this frame, panicked and sweating. A cough from his mother lying next to him snaps him out of the fantasy. The word bubble coming from him holds nothing but an ellipse.

Kenichi does not waste time, and soon finds a small, secluded apartment to move his mother into. His mother is heartbroken at the news that Kenichi has decided to move her, crying, "I can't believe how ungrateful you are, after all I've done," echoing his memory of her from his childhood. Kenichi leaves to wander the city alone, passing by an overpass marked with a sign that reads "Please don't throw away your car here."

When the day has come to move his mother, Kenichi must lift her onto his back to climb a long staircase up to the apartment. Though his mother is dressed in a simple kimono, her posture is anything but flattering: her legs straddle him, bare feet sticking out stiffly to the sides; her body hunches over his, draped limply like a flesh cape. Kenichi hears the crows overhead, and when he looks up, a full-page frame shows him suspended in the tableaux of the obasuteyama, the streets and buildings have become the dark silhouette of the mountain forest, and Kenichi sweats and grimaces at the skies (Figure 7). Even in the middle of the city, this moment, or ma, in the narrative transforms the landscape and immediately catches the reader before returning to the everyday urban landscape.

The story could just as well end here, as it more or less does in Zeami's *Obasute* and in Imamura's *The Ballad of Narayama*. The old woman has been abandoned by her son, giving him the chance at re-creating himself with another woman who is young, pretty, and modern. Kenichi knows that what he has done is planned mortal neglect. He has even arranged to go on a vacation with his fiancée far away from the city and the sounds and smells of his mother.

But there is a sense that like some gothic Edgar Allan Poe character, he cannot bear the guilt, and his fiancé's advances make the reality of this abandonment unbearable. Just before the train departs, as his fiancé smothers him with affection, he becomes panicked again. When she tells him slyly "I'm never going to let you go," clutching at him with her words, he finally makes an excuse and leaves the train, agitated and ashamed, but also determined, and runs back to his mother. When he opens the door, he finds her body, rigid, next to an open bottle of sedatives (Figure 8). Kenichi is distraught, but soon manages to put himself together and lift his mother's body onto his back once again. He walks down

Figure 7. As he carries his mother up the stairs to a small room he has rented for her in Tokyo, Kenichi becomes enveloped in the tableaux of obasuteyama. From the book *Abandon the Old in Tokyo.* Copyright Yoshihiro Tatsumi. Used with permission by Drawn & Quarterly.

Figure 8. Kenichi runs back to the place he has abandoned his mother, only to discover that she has died of a sedative overdose. From the book *Abandon the Old in Tokyo*. Copyright Yoshihiro Tatsumi. Used with permission by Drawn & Quarterly.

the stone steps where he paused before, and then out into the streets, where he runs into the middle of a large crowd of people who seem to hardly notice the burden he is carrying. Tatsumi's last punch line comes when a news reporter approaches Kenichi with a microphone on the street asking, "Pedestrians are here today to take back the streets. As a dutiful son, would you care to comment on this?" (Tatsumi [1970] 2006, 67). The frame pans back cinematically, and we see Kenichi and his mother in the classic obasuteyama pose; above his head hangs a banner that reads "Pedestrian Paradise" (*Hokousha Tengoku*).

Abandon the Old in Tokyo presents the dull, drudging work of elder care as hopeless: whether in life or in death, Kenichi's mother will continue to haunt, perpetually unsatisfied and dependent. But not only Kenichi is implicated in her death, nor does his abandonment nullify his care of her. *Abandon the Old* depicts the way the "bare life" (Agamben 1998) of aging seeps in through family and through modernity, in memories of the past and uncertainties of the future. The poor conditions and heavy dread that sets the tone of the manga resemble the Brazilian clinic where Joao Biehl observed the socially abandoned. There, Biehl writes, "in the face of increasing economic and biomedical inequality, and the breakdown of the family, human bodies are routinely separated from their normal political status and abandoned into the most extreme misfortune, death-in-life" (Biehl 2005, 38). Aging, stripped of sentimentality, can become a "death-in-life," and for some in Japan, it is.

Living in Japan, I was surprised to see just how frequently stories of elder homicides made the news, many of them perpetrated by adult sons (usually unemployed and in their fifties) strangling or smothering their mothers (usually with dementia and in their eighties) because of caregiver fatigue. One evening after spending the day at an adult day care facility, I turned the television to NHK to find they were airing a lengthy segment on caregiver stress. I shuddered to imagine any of the men and women I had just seen at the day care facility returning home to a family like those on the program, but such stories were frequently circulated at the day care and other places where older adults socialized (Danely 2011). The segment on the news that evening reported the case of an Osaka man who murdered his seventy-year-old mother by strangling her in 2003, after four years as her sole caregiver. In this case, the son, who had inherited a sizable debt when his father passed away, had to forfeit his own job in order to care for his mother. Eventually, according to the care manager, he had only enough money to buy one small lunch box a day, feeding his mother first and eating the leftovers himself. Unable to afford a residential nursing home, he tried to take her to an adult day care center, but his mother would have wild outbursts and tantrums exacerbated by her dementia. She displayed a similar excited state when attended to by a home helper, forcing the son to give up that service as well. The man confessed to the police a few hours after the crime.

While this filial devotion seems completely contradictory to the gruesome nature of his crime, it begins to make sense when we consider Tatsumi's obasute story. In the son's mind, his mother's attachment to the world, her demanding dependence, the damaged and decrepit body of what once was a source of love and nurturance, produced a painful disconnection in the way things were supposed to be. In the despair, abandonment or homicide, although morally ambiguous, emerged into the possible. Ten years after the incident reported on that evening, a wheel-chair-bound woman, eighty-six-year-old Oishi-san, was doused with fuel and burned to death. The son, an unemployed man fifty-five years old, was badly burned as well, and it is suspected that he was suffering from caregiver exhaustion and was attempting suicide after murdering his mother (*Mainichi Shinbun* 2013).

Modern tales of elder neglect, abuse, and even murder like this are frequently seen in Japanese newspapers. In a 2004 study of elder abuse conducted by Japan's Ministry of Health, Labor and Welfare, half of the respondents between the ages of seventy-five and eighty-five reported incidences of abuse resulting in detrimental mental or health effects (*Asahi Shinbun* 2004). Equally unsettling was that according to the same study, 88 percent of care managers assigned to monitor the health and safety of older adults in the home reported that even though they knew that someone was being abused, they felt they did not have the means to rectify the situation. Despite the 2006 passage of the national elder abuse prevention and caregiver support law, which offers assistance, information, and advice to municipalities for the purpose of abuse detection, the first evaluative studies of the act show persistent problems in effectiveness (Nakanishi, Nakashima, and Honda 2010; Obara 2010).

Reliable measures of elder abuse and neglect are notoriously inaccurate, given the difficulty of detection and the fact that in many cases the perpetrator is a family member or caregiver and the abused elder may be unwilling or unable to report themselves. The Ministry of Health, Labor and Welfare does keep track of reports and confirmed cases of abuse in institutions or in the community. In 2010, there were 25,315 cases of elder abuse reported in the community alone (an 8.2 percent rise from the previous year),[1] with the most common form of abuse being physical. In most of these cases the person making the report was either a care manager or a home helper (43.4 percent). In far fewer cases a report was filed by the family of the abused (12.6 percent), or by self-report (10.7 percent) (MHLW 2011). Again, these statistics can show possible trends, but they also constitute a small number of actual cases, since many go unreported at the local elder abuse consulting window.

The shame of abuse, the lack of education about signs of abuse, the reluctance to report, and the lack of knowledge about support services all delay or deter abuse reporting. In newspaper reports and tabloid accounts, the most frequently cited cause of elder homicide or abuse or neglect resulting in death is "caregiver exhaustion" (kaigo tsukare), a combination of physical, emotional, and financial stress incurred from the devotion to elder care. The most common perpetrators of abuse for this reason are the children of the victims.

News stories like these are not limited to this era. An article in the *Yomiuri Shinbun* newspaper printed in September 1933 bears the headline "Old Woman in an Empty House Present Day Ubasuteyama," and tells the story of "unfilial" brothers who left their mother behind when they moved to a new house. The mother was told to wait behind for the nursing institution staff to pick her up, but she was discovered after three days of abandonment in the empty house. In an accompanying statement, one son claimed that he hadn't planned on the abandonment, and that the old mother's "stubborn" attitude and fights between her and his wife resulted in a general unwillingness to make all the arrangements to bring her along and take care of her—a prototypical obasuteyama scenario. In Japan today, the combination of shrinking households, an aging population, and the endurance of cultural values of perseverance and shame have presented obstacles to insuring community-dwelling older adults adequate care and supervision to avoid such fates.

Leaving an elderly member of the family behind at an institution has also taken on the same connotations of unfilial neglect. It is not surprising then that the word obasuteyama has been associated with placing an aging parent into a nursing home, even though many people I spoke to had a more favorable view of nursing homes today. The ambivalence of the tale is evident here, since this can be seen as a modern way of caring for a parent at the same time it runs counter to the value of selfless filial duty (Bethel 1992; Traphagan 2000, 151). Calling a nursing home obasuteyama shows the plasticity and reproduction of the obasuteyama schema in modern Japan. Sometimes it still seems appropriate. Many institutions continue despite abuses or poor conditions because overburdened family caregivers rarely visit and feel they have few other choices. As late as the 1990s, many institutions still routinely placed problematic residents in restraints at rates far higher than in American or European institutions (Ōguma 1996). However, even in such cases, limiting obasuteyama to modern total institutions decouples it from its centuries of repetition, and therefore misrecognizes its underlying force. Obasuteyama, when presented in a graphic form as in *Abandon the Old in Tokyo*, visualizes what is so hard to detect, the intensely affective, visual, and visceral context of abandonment.

Abandon the Old also has a vacant, echoing silence to it. We imagine empathically, rather than read, the protagonist's thoughts. Other postwar stories of elder care, such as Niwa Fumio's "The Hateful Age" (1962), allow us to hear the tension between cultural ideals of care, the reduction of the aging body to a state of bare life, and the possibility of abandonment (Donow 1990, 487). At one point, the son thinks to himself that his old and senile mother had "become just a body, in which it was impossible to detect the slightest trace of a soul, spirit, conscience, or anything that makes human beings worthy of respect" (Niwa 1962, 340). In contrast to Kenichi in the manga, this caregiver sees his situation as produced by a dangerous ideology of the family system: "People had been complaining for years, but the traditional family system still lingered on, with all its inefficiency, hypocrisy, sentimentality, and injustice. It was high time for something to be done—not by sociologists, but by people all over Japan who were themselves suffering from these anachronistic traditions" (Niwa 1962, 340). By setting his story in postwar Japan, Niwa, like Tatsumi, takes the obasuteyama trope out of the "once-upon-a-time" realm of a mythical premodern Japanese wilderness and situates it directly among the concerns of the modern family. And yet, Minobe's references to his mother as "just a body," and something like a "stone idol," recalls a version of obasuteyama in which the abandoned woman physically transforms into a stone (Inoue 1965, 95; Keene 1970, 122). But to be "just a body" is to lack creative agency and be only subject to others and to the putrefaction of the flesh. Older people become "just a body" in contexts of care and abandonment, a "cost" that must be amortized (Neilson 2012). Shades of this death-in-life do not exist on the margins of Japanese society, but fill up its most intimate interstices of everyday experience. Tales of neglect, abuse, and abandonment circulate among older adults frequently in rumors and gossip, in news tabloids, and in social welfare bulletins. Taking Tatsumi's manga seriously, this chapter looks at how older adults attempt to construct places of agency across old age and death in a context of uncertainty about the family-provisioned care, social welfare, and care institutions.

Keep a Clean Altar

When Nishida-san officially retired from the weaving business at the age of sixty, her son, himself fond of skiing and other outdoor excursions, suggested that she take the large initial pension allowance and go on an overseas vacation. Nishida-san decided instead to purchase a new butsudan. After some consultation about having the old butsudan refurbished (at a cost of 1.2 million yen, or about eleven thousand dollars), they decided that it would be better to purchase an entirely new one, and after she and her son picked one out, they arranged for the performance of the requisite rituals for moving the souls (*kaigen kuyō*), literally an offering to "open the eyes." Not only did the purchase of the new butsudan coincide with Nishida-san's retirement, but it also happened to be close to the fiftieth anniversary of the death of Nishida-san's father-in-law (the deceased head of the household), so his memorial and the rededication ceremony for the butsudan could conveniently be observed at the same time.

Nishida-san's choice of purchasing a new butsudan with her pension allowance symbolically announced the connection between her transition to old age and the assumption of greater responsibility to care for the household spirits. Much like Orin in the *Ballad of Narayama*, Nishida-san's strategy reflects her deference to the care of others while preserving her own sense of identity and taking up a new role (ba) in the household as elder. She has materialized the continuity of the household in the future and the memory of her spirits along with the other ancestors. While many are scaling down their butsudan, either to physically manage its bulk in a cramped apartment or because there are fewer generations of spirits to memorialize, Nishida-san's gesture was a powerful example of her desire to be seen and remembered for a long time after she passes away. In this way, the butsudan not only functions as a site of attachment, care, and hope, but, similar to the grave, confounds spatial-temporal states; memorial repeats the past into Nishida-san's future self, and as an object to be inherited, into the future selves of her children and grandchildren.

Nishida-san told me about her butsudan during a brief visit I made to her home in late December, as she went about the usual business of dusting and cleaning it in preparation for New Year celebrations. The butsudan was located in approximately the same location in the house as Nakamura-san's, four rooms back from the entrance of the long, narrow machiya house, on the ground floor, facing east. It occupied a niche in the wall up from floor to the transom, and the wood was smooth and lacquered, contrasting beautifully against the sparse gold-leafed and filigree decorations inside.

One by one, Nishida-san carefully took each item out of the large open space of the cabinet-like altar, beginning at the lower shelves and moving upward, setting them down carefully on a small table next to the altar: decorative candles, offerings of flowers and tangerines, incense, a cup-shaped bell seated on a squat round brocaded cushion, cups for water and tea, prayer beads, matches, and of course the memorial tablets (ihai). The only item that she did not remove from the butsudan before she began dusting was the statue of Amida Buddha set on the highest shelf in the very back. When she took out the ihai, she explained the significance of each one. The largest ihai was for the collective ancestors of the household, the second largest for the mother and father-in-laws, and the next was for Nishida-san and her husband. On this tablet, Nishida-san's posthumous name was filled in with vermilion, rather than gold, in order to indicate that she was still alive. The smallest ihai was for her daughter who died in infancy (chapter 2), and stood at about half the size of a normal tablet.

Nishida-san continued cleaning her butsudan, wiping the folding doors as I asked about the different objects set on the table. The ihai bearing her own posthumous name was particularly interesting to me, since it was not very common for people living in Kyoto to receive one before death.[2] Nakamura-san, for example, assumed that his wife and sons would outlive him and take care of the posthumous name and memorial tablet at that time (chapter 2). Although he believed that his regular donations to the temple would ensure a long, prestigious name worthy of this lineage, his wife half joked about their children not being able to afford such a name.[3]

Seeing Nishida-san's "other world" name inscribed next to her husband's on the long black lacquered tablet seemed somehow romantic to me, like a promise made to a departed loved one—"I will return to you." She received her Buddhist name after she underwent a layperson's ascetic training exercise (shugyō) that culminated in a nighttime enactment of the soul's journey from this world to the next, guided only by a single small candle and the occasional attendant.[4] A long-standing active member of the temple women's group, Nishida-san decided to undertake this training after her retirement. Again, Nishida-san had materialized not only her age, but her postretirement affiliation with the spirits, making these objects of ritual and reflection for herself and her household. These objects formed part of her narrative, entangling it with the narrative of the deceased of the household through the same practices of offering and care.

As she took out a dusting rag and began to wipe the butsudan, Nishida-san segued into a discussion about people in her neighborhood who died without having properly prepared for their own mortuary rituals. Nishida-san knew of many of these cases, having served for thirty years (from forty-five to seventy-five) as a representative of the community's Civic Association (*minseiiinkai*), a position that her father also held for many years (and which Nishida-san also suspected may have contributed to his death). Despite this, she took the appointment and for most of her service was delegated to the community social welfare position, which involved looking after the elderly members of the community, and particularly those men and women who were living alone and were considered to be most at risk of succumbing to depression, illness, and death.

Throughout her years in this position, Nishida-san came to know most of the people in her neighborhood, and was often the first person that would be contacted in the event of a minor dispute or a major crisis, such as a death. As a result of her community service, Nishida-san became a seasoned professional at postdeath arrangements, often instructing bereaved families on everything from cleaning the body and house, to procuring the death certificate.

NISHIDA: [wiping the butsudan] After an individual dies, we have to clean up. If they live in a rented house.

DANELY: Rented house.

NISHIDA: A rented house. If they die there. When one old man died, that's up to the social workers. Even if it is my area, others will come out to help and we'll have a number of people cleaning. So we take all the unnecessary things, put out all the trash—one old man politely wrote it all out—the Buddhist priest, for example, who should come, and from the chōnai, who should come, he wrote it all out, so we followed as best we could, but, if we didn't have something written out like that, and if it was someone without any money, in the end, we'd go around and ask for money, and everyone would put in a little, and we could dispose of all the garbage. For people who don't have any family. The civic group would have to take care of all of it. We'd have to give a simple funeral for the person too. Well, I feel bad, but when someone in this chōnai, an old man died—do you understand "*otsūya*" (Buddhist vigil)?

DANELY: *Otsūya?*

NISHIDA: When we look after the deceased for one night, right next to the body. It's supposed to be the family that looks after the deceased, but if you're alone, there's no one to do that for you, right? So the civic group said we'll have to do this, but I felt like, I'm scared to do this by myself! [laughs] It's a little creepy! [laughs more and pushes me jokingly] to be with a dead stranger! I can't do it! Then the head of the house next door asked me, "Nishida-san, what will you be doing tonight?" and when I said "I'm doing *otsūya*," he said, well, I'll come and keep you company. So he came with about four people and we stayed up drinking tea and chatting! [laughs].

In another story from her days as a community social welfare volunteer, Nishida-san told me about a funeral with only three people attending:

NISHIDA: One time this old man died and his wife was all running around and not really getting anything done saying over the phone, [strained and mocking voice] "Oh, my husband has gotten sick and died!" So I went right away, and after all the funeral arrangements were made, there came another call—"How much should I pay for this?" she said! At the time it was about a hundred forty thousand yen [about fourteen thousand U.S. dollars], so I negotiated with the funeral director and we were able to agree on a hundred forty thousand yen for everything. In exchange, I had to do hold the *otsūya* and watch over the funeral. That was on December 31.

DANELY: New Year's Eve?

NISHIDA: Right. He died on the thirtieth, and so until he was cremated at four o'clock on the thirty-first, and I was there. They depended on me. That's the first time I'd been to a funeral with only the hotoke-san and two other people! I've had a lot of experiences. . . .

As with the previous story, Nishida-san took on a leadership role in making arrangements for the bereaved, reinforcing her reputation as someone you can depend on. The theme of all of her stories seems to be that if you keep up connections with others, you will not face a shameful death that burdens other people. The same could be said for growing older, since old age for most people brings with it increased dependence and fewer personal resources to manage and cope with problems. As Nishida-san interacts with police officers and social workers she brings a practical knowledge of aging and death into the realm of agency:

NISHIDA: At the end of year, an old lady (*obāchan*) in the neighborhood, solo dwelling senior (*dokkyo rōjin*) old lady, when I was going around near the end of the year, I said to her, "Hey take care grandma, come back for New Year!" Then I asked where had she been and she told me that she'd been to the doctor's.

"Oh, well, take care. Let's meet again when New Year is over!" I said, and we said good-bye.

You see? So then after that, a couple of days after New Year, [someone asked me] isn't that A-san's place? When I looked at the door of the house, several New Year cards were under the door. I thought, oh, well she didn't pick them up. After a while I thought that I'd go check-in on her. . . . I thought it was a little odd, so there's a place that has all the house keys and I went over and got the key. I unlocked the door and called her last name "A-san! A-san!" But nobody came. That's odd, I thought, but it was such a big house. She invited me inside once, but anyway, so I said, "Just wait a moment, I'm coming inside!" I went back to the very end where she slept. When I took a look, nobody was there. Then all of a sudden I saw her lying face down in the hallway! [motions with her hands to show how the body was flat on the ground].

DANELY: In the hallway?

NISHIDA: Yes, in the hallway. I thought she had slipped and fallen, but she didn't have a pulse, I checked. So I looked a little bit more and she had purplish spots all over her skin.

DANELY: Spots?

NISHIDA: [motions to her arm, marking little spots with a finger] It's also called *chanōze* . . . well it's something that you shouldn't have. They were speckled all around. Oh, this isn't good! I thought, so I called the police and the ambulance right away, but in the end . . . [trails off] So I did that, and this was interesting: the policeman didn't understand—you see, I have this long string attached to the light? That's so when I go to sleep I can use it to turn off the light, and I don't have to get up. But the police saw it said [with an alarming voice] "Nishida-san! What is this!" I told him, all old people have back trouble so they tie these strings to their lights! "Oh, well in that case, that's a pretty clever thing, isn't it!" [laughs] But anyway, that's the way it is. [said with a sigh] You have to guide the dead through the wheel of life too! [after a pause] One woman, she had all these savings!

DANELY: Savings?

NISHIDA: Savings. . . . When she died, one of the other social workers called me—"Nishida-san! Come quick!" [when I did they showed me] there was all this [money] under the tatami!

DANELY: Money? There was money hidden? A kind of hidden savings (*hesokuri*)?

NISHIDA: [nodding] Hidden savings. . . . Um, you see, well, when you die just like that you urinate.

DANELY: Oh, yes, I see.

NISHIDA: So we took up the tatami mats. And it was just like, well, the younger social workers can't take this kind of stuff, they don't like it. So they called me up and I said "oh, okay, I'll do it." . . . So [when we found the money] I called up some professionals and said I want them to come.

As she finished this last story, Nishida-san had replaced all of the items in her butsudan, like the furniture in a doll house, then paused, put her hands together and bowed. Now, retired from her civic position, Nishida-san had a large, framed certificate of achievement in her home, humbly tucked next to the television in the living room rather than above the special alcove the way Nakamura-displays his. She is modest about her role in the social welfare association, seeing it less as a position of authority than as an extension of her sense of community, and human connection (en) that extends seamlessly into the other world. Her dependability as a community leader and her creation of the altar space and purchases of her butsudan and ihai were preparations for death and ways of dis-burdening dependency in old age. In this space of loss, Nishida-san found ways to create not only a role for herself, but rituals of comfort and concerns for the bereaved. They were material anchors of her care for others and the self's transition to the next world.

As I watched Nishida-san pray, I noticed a small calendar tacked on the wall next to the butsudan with a calligraphic message for the month reading "Didn't you forget something?" (*Nanka wasurete/imasen ka?*) (Figure 9). No, nothing had been forgotten. No one had been forgotten.

As a guardian of her community, Nishida-san had a wealth of information on how her neighbors grew older and how they died. While there is nothing odd about solo-dwelling elders dying alone, for Japanese people such deaths reveal the inability of families and neighbors to take care of older people. The burden of care, constructed as it is through laws, policies, and the system of services, still rests on older individuals and their family. Solitary deaths like those Nishida-san describes are the unsurprising consequences of an increasingly individuated generation of welfare consumers.

Several other current and past self-governing association members I met saw the problem of abandonment and solitary deaths as a failure of unconnected (muen) communities. However, Nishida-san's stories show how, by rallying neighbors to clean houses, make funeral arrangements, and even hold wakes after such deaths, community is reinforced and enacted. The old person's abandon-ment can be reintegrated through spiritual narratives of connection and care.

In the next section I discuss how the modern Japanese state employs a simi-lar symbolic ideology of care, community, and family in order to marshal cheap affective labor of people like Nishida-san. This has been a strategy since the early twentieth century (some Japanese people I've met argue that it harkens back to the seventeenth century), but the scale of Japan's aging population seems to be creating doubts that a community- and volunteer-based elder care system will be sufficient. A brief history of elder welfare in Japan can help us contextualize the experiences of people like Nishida-san.

WELFARE JAPAN-STYLE

Early in her survey of the social history of modern Japanese generations, Merry Isaacs White writes, "Social programs to support equality at the workplace,

Figure 9. Nishida-san arranges items in the butsudan, some of which rest on a nearby table. The calendar posted on the right side of the butsudan reads, "Didn't you forget something?" Photo by author.

child care, and the care of elderly are in place. However, they are scarcely able to manage the gap between needs and services: a lack of community challenges each family to manage its own needs for space and time and resources. Grandparents needing care must be housed in or near the household and teenagers may want separate spaces of their own. From within the walls of the home, the call for help in fulfilling the functions assigned to families has become clamorous" (White 2002, 62). The situation White describes did not arise suddenly, nor should it be assumed that it constitutes simply a failure of state provisioned welfare on the one hand or the breakdown of community- and family-provisioned care on the other. It would be tempting to explain the current insufficiencies of welfare that White describes by pointing to the spread of neoliberalism and global capitalism, which place care in the realm of self-reliance, self-responsibility, and consumer choice, while at the same time dismantling state resources.

However, this explanation is only part of a much longer history of care in Japan, and cannot fully account for the meanings, values, and aesthetic elaborations on care that have developed over the lifetime of my informants, and to which they have been socialized. Here, I provide a brief overview of this development, concentrating less on specific policies and the full historical picture than on the aesthetic ideologies that continue to influence expectations, political views, and life decisions.[5] These fragments of discourses run through the last century of Japanese history, much of which my informants had experienced firsthand.

The Ie System as a Substitute for State-Provisioned Welfare

Over the course of my older informants' lives, they have been socialized in an environment that emphasized upholding responsibilities as members of households in the corporate family system known as the *ie*. The ie has been defined as a "corporate residential group" that acts as a "frame" for understanding hierarchy and in-group/out-group distinctions (Nakane 1970, 4–5). This system, originating in the medieval period and popularized in the early modern period, organized kinship according to proscribed household roles that formalized structures of patrilineal and primogenitural succession and inheritance, and aligned them with the nationalist ideology of cultural identity and promoted a formal standardized version of ancestor veneration (Traphagan 2000, 57; Smith 1974, 69–70). To the extent that the ie structures bonds of interdependence and obligation within the family, others have found that it also has the potential for structuring the kinds of emotional possibilities within these relationships (Hamabata 1990, 33–51; Kinoshita and Kiefer 1992, 46–52).

When I began my research, I considered the possibility that the generational cohort of older adults I would be conducting research with would observe memorial rituals more frequently and with greater investment than younger cohorts as a result of their socialization in the prewar era ideology of the family as ie with the ancestors at its core. In part, my thoughts were influenced by a curiosity about strong statements regarding the ie, like this one from Yanagita Kunio: "It is not the will of oneself but of the *ie*. The ancestors have willed that the *ie* would prosper, and the descendants try to put the will into practice. . . . If the *ie* system disappears, it might make one become incapable of explaining oneself why one should be Japanese" (quoted in Kawada 1993, 39–40).

Anthropologists too had written extensively on the ways that the ie not only anchors cultural identity, but also structures expectations of care and purpose in old age, as in this passage from anthropologist Takie Sugiyama Lebra:

> The aged person is expected to and does depend up on the younger. In the traditional social structure, dependency of the aged is tied to the institutional requirement to perpetuate the *ie*. The aged retired parents depend up on their son and successor and his family for security, comfort, and emotional support. They are also concerned over who will take care of the funeral, ashes and tablets, the grace, and memorial services for them and their ancestors. Attainment of peace of mind in one's late years and salvation after death is thus closely connected with this sense of dependency upon the succeeding generation. The successor is expected to be dependable, willing to prove his filial piety by gratifying their dependency wish. (Lebra 1976, 65)

While the ie provided a familiar cultural reference point, when I began to construct genealogical trees for informants, I realized that in almost every case, sources of care and support did not follow the neat logic or have the cultural weight that Yanagita or Lebra claim. It was not entirely absent, and still functioned in the sense that informants had a strong sense of obligation toward relatives, but care flowed through many sources (kin and non-kin) that lay outside the ie, reflecting in some sense Robert Smith's (1974) findings that memorial tablets for the departed rarely adhered to an orthodox model of kinship or religious custom, but depended more often on personal affective bonds that extended beyond kin. What did the ie do then?

One thing the ie signified was an effort on the part of the modern Japanese state to standardize and rationalize the family in coordination with its aims. As an extension of the attachment and veneration of the ancestors, the ie system, as codified in the Meiji Period (1868–1912) also became the locus of the "Japanese spirit" of mutual care and responsibility, and this was enshrined in legal codes (Kinoshita and Kiefer 1992, 49). This ideology, in turn, was used as a form of governance in the sense that it created a modern bureaucracy of Japanese "tradition," aimed at producing "loyal subjects and filial children" (Tsuji 2002, 182) who would honor their ancestors as they honored the emperor (Hozumi 1901, 36–39). At the same time, the ie, which became a matter of citizenship and patriotism, also became enfolded into the ideology of minimal social welfare, since, as one Social Bureau director put it in 1929, Japan had "for the most part, the beautiful customs of the family system and neighborly mutual assistance" (Garon 1998, 56). Just as households took care of their ancestors, they were responsible for the care of their elders.

Postwar/Post-ie "Japanese-Style Welfare" Society

The pre–World War II Japanese state not only made use of the ancestors to reign in the labor of its citizens to provide care for the elderly, but also mobilized community volunteer associations and other groups to mediate between the state and the ie. These community groups, much like the self-governing association that Nishida-san volunteered in, were encouraged less as an alternative to the ie, than as a way to support and promote the self-sufficiency of the ie and to offset welfare costs of the state. At the time, most older adults who had living family would have been ineligible for state welfare assistance, and social community volunteers would often provide "care" by locating kin rather than assisting in acquiring state assistance (Garon 1998, 51–58). Even when most of the ie-based rules concerning care of the elderly, succession, and inheritance of property including graves were removed with the New Civil Code of 1948, there was little change in these mediating organizations or in Japanese social welfare ideology.

As the Japanese economy expanded dramatically in what has come to be known as the postwar "Japanese Miracle," and nuclear families began to displace ie-based multigenerational households, the population of elderly rose rapidly. The community- and family-based care system that the government had relied on was nowhere near adequate for addressing the health and care needs of this population, and in 1973 the government took the major step of expanding its national health insurance program to provide free medical care to anyone over sixty. Gradually the implications of this major expansion in spending became evident, and the government began to gradually reduce benefits. By 1979, after reigning in earlier commitments toward government spending on programs for the elderly, the "Japanese-style welfare society" ideal was once again openly pursued, officials again citing the strength of the "Japanese family system" and "traditional communal solidarity" (Garon 1998, 215; Kawanishi 2009, 146–147).

This ideology of Japanese-style welfare echoed the prewar alignment of tradition of family with the aims of the state. This approach was constructed not only from within (as the rhetoric of family values might suggest), but also in response to the perceptions of welfare systems elsewhere, such as Scandinavia, where high-level welfare provisions and access to institutional care were reported in Japan as causing "loneliness and isolation" and "cold-hearted human relationships" (Garon 1998, 223). The fears of adopting a non-Japanese welfare system, of course, echoed the fears of an institutional obasuteyama, losing human connections by turning care over to professionals—a kind of abandonment through care. As detailed in chapter 2, the health and long-term care insurance for older adults in the 1990s and early 2000s continued to follow the sort of expand and contract pattern since the 1970s, gradually placing more of the burden of labor and cost on families and individuals and increasing the precarity of late life (Allison 2013; Neilson 2012, 61; Portacolone 2013).

Welfare rhetoric from the 1980s through the period of my research continued to espouse self-sufficiency of the elderly through work, social participation, preventative care and lifestyle choices, and nurturing bonds with family. The social welfare cooperative for my chōnai, for instance, hosted several educational seminars, bringing in police officers to talk about being careful in traffic, and a doctor to talk about Japanese health care insurance. In both of these cases, the speakers emphasized the importance of individual preventative measures rather than community responsibility or support, and reiterated ideas about healthy, active aging as a national project that would distinguish Japan from other developed countries.

If Scandinavian-style welfare policies are perceived as "abandonment through care," some of the older people I spoke with, such as Hasegawa-san (the author of the haiku in chapter 1), might call Japanese-style welfare "care through abandonment." State policies that provide inadequate institutional care or pensions to afford them are perceived as a form of social abandonment, whereas policy makers might see this as providing incentives for older adults to engage in prevention-based activities and to remain close to family. This care through abandonment, however, is not really care at all, but rather what Neilson (2012) observes is a global trend toward the "amortization of the body" that devolves costs of life onto workers, and presupposes a degree of self-reliance and able-bodiedness that underlies much of the marketing of biotechnological investments in bodily "immortalization" (Neilson 2012, 61–62). Older adults who can no longer rely on family or even community networks for support, and who receive only minimal benefits from the state, have limited resources to care for themselves should they become dependent. While care managers and social workers may suggest greater use of eligible insurance benefits, they cannot force institutionalization unless it is evident that the individual's life is at risk.

The "Home" Care Market

The recent emphasis on in-home care services has blurred the line between family and professional care, deploying the idea of the ie as a means to signal tradition, stability, and social legitimacy. One signboard I found in the window of the Tokyo Japanese Nurses Cooperative, for instance, featured a cartoon of a smiling, gray-haired older woman below the words "Of course 'home' is number one. The power of home help aids to support you." (*Yappari uchi ga ichiban. Anata wo sasaeru hōmonkango no chikara*). In the billboard, the word "home" is represented by the character for *ie* with the term *uchi* written alongside it as an alternate reading.[6] *Uchi* literally means "inside," as in the group to which one belongs, and is considered the locus of identity, trust, and purity (Bachnik 1994). It stands in contrast to the perception of care from "outsiders," while preserving the traditional identity of household. Using this play on words conflated the intimate affective labor of elder care, the traditional relational obligations of the ie, and the supportive (bio)"power" of professional services. In another sense, the poster shows how the lineage-based ie system has become displaced by a more modern notion of the emotionally bound family supported by consumer desires.

The rhetoric of self-sufficiency has shifted somewhat from the corporate family system based on ancestor veneration (ie), to the more ambiguous uchi, an interior space that blurs the line between one's group of intimate fellows, to the very inner spaces of body, memory, and consciousness (Schattschneider 2003, 211). Interiorizing the "home" as a locus of care (a kind of "home is where the heart is" sentiment) effectively individuates the older person and places him or her in a role as a consumer of care. Although these two terms, ie and uchi, occupy overlapping semantic domains, as seen in the Nurses Cooperative billboard, the trend can be characterized as a movement of biopower from the ethical to the aesthetic; the welfare for the old is less a matter of ethical duty than the cultivation of an aesthetic of the self and home.

Social versus Spiritual?

Japan-style welfare policy and the emerging market of aging baby boomers have led to an expansion of private care services, further reinforcing the idea of aging as an individual consumer choice. The disconnect between the twenty-first-century economy of care and older adults' affective bonds with the ancestors manifests as what Inoue Haruyo called "a feud between the social and the spiritual" (2003, 3). New burial and memorial options and new religious groups have been very successful at developing new uchi (socially as well as spiritually) for the exchange of care with the spirits of the dead (Suzuki 2005), often incorporating those aspects of conventional memorialization that Lebra noted were essential for "peace of mind in one's later years." And yet these practices and groups remain socially and politically marginalized, difficult for many to incorporate into a personal narrative of loss.

Several older adults like the Nakamuras, who had over generations built a store of social capital based on the ie model and traditional customs, were not ready to consider new options outside of tradition. These adults were concerned with the uncertainty of kin and community bonds and their implications for the continuity of memorial, even without direct reference to ie. Sometimes the grave and the butsudan were the only symbols of household succession left to anchor the ie, the only "places" left for older adults. Even these, however, are being displaced by new ways of burial and memorial that do not require the continued care of descendants. Disentangling the economies of care of the living and the dead introduces new kinds of uncertainty and new possibilities for the experience of loss and abandonment. Do they also provide spaces of hope?

ABANDONMENT AND THE LONELY DEATH

In July 2010, city officials came knocking on Sogen Kato's door.[7] The officials were visiting Mr. Kato to congratulate the 111-year-old man for being Tokyo's oldest resident. However, as the *New York Times* reported, "[Officials in the Adachi ward of Tokyo] said his daughter gave conflicting excuses, saying at first that he did not want to meet them, and then that he was elsewhere in Japan giving Buddhist sermons. The police moved in after a granddaughter, who also shared the house, admitted that Mr. Kato had not emerged from his bedroom since about 1978" (Fackler 2010). Another article describing the case of Mr. Kato reported that rather than giving Buddhist sermons somewhere in Japan, he had literally become a "living buddha" (*sokushinbutsu*), a label usually applied to ascetic practitioners who enter deep meditative states to the point of eventual starvation and death. Such a description, although poetic, was perhaps closer to Mr. Kato's reality.

As officials and communities scrambled to confirm the whereabouts of their centenarians, more stories began to emerge. Two months after discovering Mr. Kato, the Japanese government estimated that at least 234,354 of Japan's oldest citizens on record were missing (Fukue 2010). In one case, relatives of a man listed as 103 years old had not been seen for thirty-eight years, although his seventy-three-year-old son continued to collect pension allowances "in case he returned one day" (Fackler 2010). In another case, Aiko Watanabe, the fifth daughter of Michi Watanabe, turned herself in to police after skeletal remains of her mother, who had died in 1996, were found in the home. She claimed that she used her mother's pension money to cover living expenses (*Japan Times* 2010b). In another instance it was reported that the bones of one centenarian were being stored in her son's backpack (Craft 2010).

In most of these cases, poor record keeping and inefficient auditing could account for the oversight (in thousands of cases records were open for people that would have been over 150 years old), but as other cases show, there were clearly many instances of pension fraud, deliberate or simply negligent. Some commentators suspected that one reason for this oversight was that in order to delete an entry on the official family registry, someone has to personally present a death certificate to the municipal office. The shame of presenting a death certificate for an older person one was supposed to be caring for was, perhaps, enough to keep many people home. As one report stated, "Silence might be a means to preserve face, just as it is a way to collect benefits from the dead" (*Japan Times* 2010a). Also, municipal governments depend on local volunteers to check up on the status of their older neighbors, and these volunteers lack the government's access to individuals' private information, so it is easier for caregivers to turn them away (*Japan Times* 2010a).

Since there are not enough municipally employed social workers or local volunteers to monitor the growing number of elderly residents in each school district, help is sometimes outsourced to other private services. Many convenience stores in Japan, such as the aptly named Family Mart, which have typically been associated with school-age children and working adults on the go, have now initiated food delivery services for homebound seniors, and while they are eager to tap into the growing market of older adults, the service is framed by the same community ethic of care promoted in other "Japan-style" public welfare campaigns. Family Mart's website recalled the statements made by state officials in the previous section, but with a more global, affective tone, calling for "mutually

helping each other, supporting each other, we want to all be smiling together. . . .
If we can smile, our towns will surely become more lively, brighter and more
wonderful."[8]

In another case, the city of Ashikaga, Tochigi prefecture, asked for help from
"Yakult ladies," who distribute the nutritional drink Yakult to homes, usually by
bicycle (Fukue and Aoki 2010), thus explicitly gendering the role of caregiver:
"It's not just about making sure they're alive. It's also about communicating with
them and keeping them from becoming isolated (from the community)," director Junko Akino of the city's welfare division said. "Keeping an eye on the elderly is important, she said, and the project is funded through this year." As this
statement indicates, moral expectations of family-provisioned care and informal
mutual aid that are in part reinforced by Japanese welfare policy and ideology
not only have proved ineffective, but may have generated the widespread shame
and deception that led to the invisibility and abandonment of the old. Social
policies, demographic change, economics, cultural values, and emotions have
slowly collided to produce this future for Japan's older adults. How could this
happen on such a massive scale throughout Japan?

It is not easy to answer questions like this in the ambiguous zone of obasuteyama. Whether the missing centenarian predicament was precipitated by
intentional death hastening behaviors, widespread selective neglect of the old,
everyday fraud, or bad record keeping, it was the older people, lost, dead, or disappeared, who have been silent as more stories and rumors whirled around the
national and even international media. Japanese commentators, however, leaped
at the chance to characterize this as a symptom of larger social disintegration,
the nuclear family, and weakening of neighborhood ties. "This is a type of abandonment, through disinterest," said Hiroshi Takahashi, a professor at the International University of Health and Welfare in Tokyo. "Now we see the reality of
aging in a more urbanized society where communal bonds are deteriorating"
(Fackler 2010). Katsuya Inoue, emeritus professor of psychology at Tsukuba University, was quoted as saying, "People used to take care of their aging parents. But
with rapid changes in lifestyles, the very idea of taking care of one's parents
seems to be waning" (Talmadge 2010).

Interestingly, the case of these "abandoned" elders, most of whom are
assumed dead, brought new attention to the story of obasuteyama as well.
Ishihara Shintaro, then governor of Tokyo, was reported in the press as saying,
"If we don't know their whereabouts . . . maybe we ought to go looking for them
on *Obasuteyama*! If there are flocks of crows and a bunch of bones, it would be
a modern-day ghost story!" (*Nikkan Sports* 2010). This statement's use of the
imagery of obasuteyama followed the exact picture from Tatsumi's manga. It
was shocking, even for Ishihara-san, who is well known for making provocative
comments. But the tale of the missing centenarians is not only a modern-day
ghost story, but a story of modernity's ghosts—the lingering abandoned elders
who did not merely "fall through the cracks" of a modern bureaucratic system,

but were excluded through decisions made at multiple levels of Japanese society, from the family to the state. The abandoned elderly of Japan's obasuteyama are constituted by modernity itself.

Abandonment and aging both seem to imply a state of liminality (the abandoned are neither living nor dead, elders are neither wholly in the world nor separate from it), and yet liminality, that period of transformation between two socially recognized statuses, also implies that there is an overarching structure in which the abandonment makes sense either by the inversion of normative values or the repetition of them (Turner 1967). The loss or leveling of self-identity experienced in the liminal phase is meaningful precisely because it is understood to be a precursor to a particular kind of transformation and reintegration. Traditional Buddhist mortuary rites taken in the first forty-nine days following death and subsequent periodic memorials, for example, attend to the specific liminal state of the spirit (and of the family) and the need to ritually transform and elevate it to the status of hotoke and eventually ancestorhood.

In contrast, the stories of Mr. Kato as "giving Buddhist sermons" or becoming a "living buddha," while depicting the act of abandonment and mortal neglect in terms of positive cultural tropes, do little to change his status or lead him toward a process of reintegration into the larger social context. He has reached his last stop. There is simply no "there" there that can constitute an end to the ambiguity of the abandonment. While I have tried to understand this in terms of psychic and cultural ambivalence brought about by the confrontation with aging, as portrayed in obasuteyama, the case of the missing centenarians also compels us to examine the political dimensions of the work of self that compose the "mountain" of aging today.

The case of the missing centenarians happened because of the paradox of care and abandonment in Japan today: modern systems of care that individuate and problematize the old body not only make it easier to imagine its abandonment, but provide an ethical and economic logic to the abandonment. Pension schemes, care managers, records offices, and other institutions depend on a kind of innate cultural goodness or "Japanese spirit" of mutuality located in informal mediating entities like families and neighborhood organizations to monitor care provisioning. But when dependent older adults are located within discourses of national burden and bodily frailty, and when family caregivers face their own life uncertainties, the exhaustion of self-sufficiency creates the affective stage for the logic of abandonment. Even the discourses implicit in the "oldest citizen" award and institutions like senior community centers occlude the very real problems of dependence and care behind a fog of "successful aging." The only way to recognize the unrecognizable (the abandoned) in this fog is to render them invisible, or from the perspective of the state, as a kind of bureaucratic duplicate haunting the system through continued acceptance of financial assistance.

As a manga, *Abandon the Old in Tokyo* can expose this paradox of care not only through the ma of omitted text, but also through images that evoke a somatic and affective dread. Kenichi's blank expression, frequently interrupted with moments of sweat drenched, mute panic, conveys the unspeakable nature of contending with the paradox of care in modern Japan. In one conversation I had with a few older women at a day-service center, the solitude of family-provisioned care was judged as a far worse fate than living alone. As the women gossiped, one of them brought up the case of a friend who lived with her son and his family but who was otherwise socially excluded from most family affairs like eating meals together. "They even go on vacations without telling her!" she told the others, reacting with knowing nods. "And once," the speaker continued, "when they went on a vacation to Okinawa, she died." As chilling as the story was, it needed to repeated several times in a loud voice for the more forgetful listeners at the table—"She was left alone, and she died!"

As pointed out in Nishida-san's anecdotes, dying alone (kodokushi) has been an increasingly visible phenomenon in Japan, representing a final consequence of the fundamental paradox of care that places old bodies behind closed doors of self-sufficient or family-provisioned care (Kotsuji and Kobayashi 2011). It is estimated that thirty-two thousand people die alone in Japan each year, most of them older adults (Hoffman 2010). While older people and families are encouraged to take care of themselves, public accounts and discussion of kodokushi also warn against the danger of solitude. Older adults in Japan have fewer cultural resources to imagine a resilient self in this state of solitude, and perhaps less motivation than younger men and women to see demise as objectionable. In this way, kodokushi, like suicide, occupies an ambiguous state between care and abandonment even before death (Traphagan 2010). When the dead person is discovered, this ambiguity floods into the space of unanswered questions, and it is often left to volunteers and community members, many of them other older people, to clean the stains and remake the body by arranging for its ritual disposal.

Cleaning up the material traces of the abandoned, the way Kenichi cleans up after his mother in *Abandon the Old* or how Nishida-san cleaned up after her dead neighbors, has the dignified humility of an ethical act that restores the hope of a "good" or "beautiful" death. If the materiality of care is a component of offerings and memorials, then the horror of kodokushi might be found not only in social abandonment, but the material mess left by these lonely deaths. Kodokushi leaves not only dead, decomposing remains, but cluttered houses, unpaid bills, broken promises, regrets, grudges. As one Japanese professional house cleaner put it, "The majority of lonely deaths are people who are kind of messy. . . . It's the person who, when they take something out, they don't put it back; when something breaks, they don't fix it; when a relationship falls apart, they don't repair it" (Nobel 2010). Cleaning up the shameful mess of an ugly solitary death is evident not only in the practices around the everyday yet sensationalized accounts of mortal neglect and kodokushi, but also in the purifying discourses of the medicalized death.

About 80 percent of Japanese deaths occur in hospitals, with a slightly higher rate for older adult and those who die from cancer or suffer chronic debilitating conditions. Hope for a "good death," then, rests on the possibilities available within these settings as they are created and constrained by the cultural scripts enacted by families, patients, and staff. In Japan, the ideal narrative of the "good death" as opposed to a "shameful death" (Kellehear 2007, 213–233) includes several ideals of community and intimacy, or being close to others in one's final moments, and of dying in one's own home "on the tatami" (Becker 1993; Hattori, McCubbin, and Ishida 2006; Kondo 2012; Long 2005; Traphagan 2013). What interests me most about these studies is the way hospital settings, and the medicalization of death in general, catch families in an ethical bind between technologies of an ambiguous and undesirable life extension and the acceptance of death as a part of life (cf. Kaufman 2005). Multiple factors might play a role in these kinds of end-of-life decision making, and the fact that terminal diagnosis is often hidden from the patients themselves puts an additional burden of silence on family members. Each end-of-life choice, whether in the home or hospital, with family or alone, seems to present another path up obasuteyama, but the road is obscured, and hopes must be revised or lost.

When viewed from the perspective of obasuteyama, the difference between such hospital deaths and the abandonment of kodokushi is not entirely black and white. Perhaps the biggest difference is in the material remains, and the possibility of mourning. Nishida-san's stories emphasize the importance of making postdeath arrangements (purchasing a new butsudan, giving a kaimyō, planning funeral arrangements), and the important roles of community members for those who do not. In either case, material remains produce work, but the transition from the work of life (settling debts, cleaning the oozing and putrefying body) to that of death and memorial (the vigil, funeral, etc.) is more easily managed by those who have put things in order, and "kept a clean altar." If the material work of life demands attention, the work of death and forgetting allows one to be memorialized.

PART IV

Hope

CHAPTER 7

Care and Recognition

ENCOUNTERING THE OTHER WORLD

In the last chapter, I referred to "Japanese-style welfare" as an ideology of "care through abandonment," in which obligations and resources of care are distributed among state, community, family, and the older persons themselves, creating both an array of possible dependencies as well as ways to fall through the cracks and become forgotten or discarded on your own. Because this ideology relies on a paradoxical set of ethical demands for both self-reliance and self-sacrificing mutuality, I argued that it produces aged subjectivities unable to uphold human connections, recognition, and care without producing shame, isolation, and estrangement. Abandonment, produced by the indeterminacy of waiting, echoes through both the political and psychological spaces of narrative, bearing aesthetic traces of obasuteyama.

In this chapter, I return to the framework of economies of care, and to an examination of how care and abandonment are reimagined and reconstituted in aesthetic encounters with "the other world," not only in the everyday rituals of memorials, but also in dreams, visions, and consultations with oracles. These events form communicative flows that depend on an openness to care and an sense of intimacy with the felt presence of the departed. The phenomenology of care expressed within and through these encounters resists easy categorization or articulation. Like the moon half hidden behind clouds, care is exposed in the aesthetic of haunting traces, semiobscured metaphors of hopeful reunion, and reflecting surfaces of uncanny presences. They produce a sense of comfort and relief in dependency and loss, anchored by meaningful encounters with the spiritual.

One thing that became particularly pronounced as I listened to the care described in the life course narratives of older Japanese adults was the ways care itself was gendered (closely identified with the mother) as well as how gendered subjectivity over the life course influenced outcomes in older adulthood. The obasuteyama stories, such as *Abandon the Old in Tokyo*, are particularly heartbreaking because they portray deep feelings of ambivalence of the son toward his mother. In fact mothers frequently appeared in the narratives and life histories as pivotal figures that remain most closely associated with the spirits. It is not surprising then that women, many of whom invested strongly in child care and sometimes elder care over the course of their lives (usually as daughters-in-law caring for their husbands' aging parents), typically develop a different orientation toward giving and receiving care than do men, and that this orientation is reflected in a phenomenology of spirit encounters and practices of mourning.

Communication with the "other world," mediated by rituals and other interpretive frames, facilitates the circulation of care in ways that reflect back on and shape aged subjectivity. This care is formed through different modes and moments of recognition, which not only produce a shared narrative, but also hold the potential for social and political agency. This circulation of care and recognition, like the annual cycle of seasons or the generational life cycle, enfolds givers and receivers in an interdependent rhythm of loss and renewal, actively participating in the care of others, while yielding to a greater spiritual sense of one's place in the world.

New Year and the Economy of Care

New Year is typically a time for settling accounts, thanking friends, colleagues, and clients for their good relations in the last year, and committing to a continued relationship in the next year. The year's end is filled with symbols of closure and renewal, as numerous *bōnenkai* (literally "parties to forget the previous year," many of which do result in a good deal of merriment induced amnesia) are followed by meticulously penned New Year greeting cards that ensure the spirit of exchange follows one into the new season. Special visits to household graves, beginning around the time of the winter solstice and continuing to New Year, signal this same renewal of bonds of care and remembrance.

Kinship is at the heart of these materializations of care, bringing together old age and the ancestors by reiterating two essential (though paradoxical) themes: the celebration of a long life (*chōju*) and passing (*yuzuri*) of the older generations to make way for younger ones. The wish for a long life is symbolized, for example, by eating long buckwheat noodles (*toshikoshi soba*) and glutinous lumps of pounded rice (*mochi*), which are (among other things) symbolic of the moon, an offering made to the kami (*kagami mochi*, literally "mirror mochi"). The referent of this "long life" is open, and may be an individual, the generations of the household, or human relationships in general, all of which are conceived of as interdependent on one another and together they constitute origin of personhood.

On the other hand, traditions such as creating a temporary New Year shrine, and giving New Year pocket money (*otoshidama*) emphasize the passing of generations. In Kyoto, New Year shrines are decorated with a *shimenawa* (a woven rope representing the kami), embellished with various elements symbolizing the "fortunes" (*sachi*) of the mountains (persimmons) and seas (dried squid) as well as long life (paper cranes, evergreens) and generations (*daidai*, bitter oranges). Another common feature of these small temporary shrines is a leafy plant called *yuzuriha* (*Daphniphyllum macropodum*), the distinguishing feature of which is that as the young leaves grow, the older ones make way for them (yuzuru), falling off of the branch. As one of my informants explained, "The yuzuriha means that the generations of this household are going to be linked together: from predecessor to the next child, from the next child to the grandchild. And so they'll be linked. So that's why we say it brings good fortune (*engi wo katsuide*). . . . [after thinking for a moment] Good fortune? Well, it's more like *linking*. The previous generation who looked after the household, and then when the next generation comes, they look after it; all the way from parent to child, to grandchild to great-grandchild—continuing all the way. That's what those leaves mean."

Just as the leaves of the yuzuriha tree make way for the new generation, adults are expected to give pocket money (otoshidama) to children and grandchildren.[1] Murayama explains that the tradition of otoshidama comes from the expression of passing on the "soul" (*tama*) from the senior members to junior members of the household (*tama*, meaning jewel or treasure, is a homonym for "soul") (Murayama 2001, 136).[2] The association of the old man giving treasures to children at the New Year represents the continuity in the life cycle that follows the rebirth and renewal for the coming year. Older adults of the household therefore play a special role as a link between its past and future, death and rebirth.

To celebrate the New Year, the Nakamuras invited me to participate in a small neighborhood *mochi-tsukuri* (rice-cake-making) festival. The festival was being held on the grounds of a vacated elementary school that like many schools in central Kyoto, had been closed due to lack of students, and was now used for various community events. When I arrived in the early morning, benches had been set up outside on the school grounds and older women were busy making soups and sauces at tables covered by the civic association portable shelters. Nakamura-san was busy happily chatting with his neighbors, sleeves pushed up and trousers stuffed into a pair of black rubber boots, along with other men gathered on a blue tarp next to the shelter. Everyone there had just participated in a "disaster prevention" drill, held across the city on the last Sunday of the month since the Great Hanshin Earthquake in 1995. The school grounds, though unoccupied by students, were also a safe rallying point in cases of emergency.

Nakamura-san called the event a *fureai matsuri* (literally touching together festival), a term often used for local community gatherings to evoke the special bonds felt through close physical, face-to-face, empathic contact. The main event of the festival was the cooperative effort of making New Year mochi, which involved several older community leaders and members of the local Little League team, easily identified in their white and navy uniforms. Team members took turns stepping up to a large stone pestle set on the blue tarp, to pound the wet, warm rice with an enormous wooden mallet while onlookers talked and cheered them on. Nakamura-san, wearing a bright blue windbreaker and a baseball cap turned around backward, bent over the pestle, reaching in his hand between hits in order to turn the glutinous mass. The ritual, enacted at many other gatherings I attended that month, required a surprising amount of skill and timing, lest the mallet come down too quickly on a slow hand, or too slowly, pulling up the rice up into the air or onto the ground. Eventually, an attentive rhythm of "listening and watching" between the person pounding (often a younger person) and the one turning (almost always an experienced senior member) would produce the desired spectacle of aesthetic harmony between senior and junior, recalling idealized values of past community life and producing an embodied bond between young and old. Once the team had all taken a turn, some of the older men eager to show their strength and skill stepped up to the pestle, earning more cheers and encouragement from the crowd of onlookers. Even small children, barely reaching the height of the pestle, were walked up, their fathers helping them to hold the mallet and bring it down once in a symbolic gesture of participation. The mochi that was produced was then taken by the women, who divided and distributed it among participants like a symbolic body of this intergenerational effort of community spirit.

Mochi-tsukuri and its contemporary counterpart machi-tsukuri (community making) consolidate values in an economy of care by drawing on the symbols that must be interpreted within the aesthetic context of New Year: the celebration of long life and interpersonal bonds, as well as the division of labor between generations and genders that performs an agency of yielding. The mochi (as both an offering made for the continued benevolence of the kami and a wish for continuity shared by the community) was created through the intergenerational effort of the men, while their product was prepared and distributed through the care of the women and consumed by all.

As the men turning the rice in the pestle get old, Nakamura-san explained, they would "step aside" and let the other adult men do it, but since there were so few adult men with children in the neighborhood, it was hard to find people who wanted to continue with events like this. Still, he held onto hope, and as we ate our mochi, he called over a tall, middle-age man who had recently moved back to Kyoto with his family from the suburbs of Tokyo after twelve years. The man smiled and introduced himself as Okamoto. He told me that his family has been in Kyoto for three generations, then pointed to himself and then to his nine-year-old son, adding "fourth, fifth." Okamoto-san had no intention of taking over his family trade (textile dying), but worked as a product manager for a large company specializing in creating biodegradable materials from wood. As we spoke, the man talked about not only wanting to be closer to his parents who lived in the city, but also wanting to raise his children with a sense of community, tradition, and care. "You just can't find this kind of tradition going on in a city anymore," said Okamoto-san, adding that many other people are attracted to the "Kyoto brand" that includes things like the festival. Nakamura-san beamed nearby, finally interjecting, "Okamoto-san is going to be the leader of this festival!"

BURYING THE DAGGER

The festival cheer and sunny glow of the day brightened my spirits as I said goodbye to Okamura-san and the Nakamuras. Anxious that I might be late, I took a taxicab across town to the temple where I had arranged to meet Mori-san for the ceremony to dispose of the dagger she found in her home while moving (chapter 5). When I arrived, Mori-san was not there yet, and I took a moment to sit in the sunny temple courtyard and write some notes on mochi-tsukuri, inter-generational transfer, and the ways rituals open up ways to enact caring. I started to think that the cultural creativity of the event might be similar to the ceremony for the dagger, since both involved renewing bonds and family continuity, at the same time that they seemed to turn things over. In Mori-san's case, yielding meant giving up not only a piece of family history, but part of the hoard that strained the transition to her new home. What the ceremony would consist of and how it would change things, I could not tell for sure, but neither could Mori-san, who was significantly more invested in a favorable outcome.

Mori-san soon met me at the temple along with another woman of similar age, whom she introduced as a younger cousin. The cousin, dressed in a long black wool coat with black fur trim, had come from several hours away by train to visit Mori-san and attend the ceremony, and seemed just as excited as Mori-san. The two women stood at about the same height, but the resemblance ended there. Mori-san's slightly hunched posture made her seem smaller, more frail and anxious, while her cousin appeared both elegant and vibrant. Both took on a polite, deferential tone toward the woman from the temple's staff who came to greet us. Mori-san reached into her bag and produced the dagger, still wrapped in its white cloth, the way corpses are dressed at a wake. After she handed the dagger to the staff, we removed our shoes and stepped up into the quiet temple. We chatted in anxious, hushed voices as we quickly put on slippers from a nearby rack.

The woman on the temple staff who took the dagger soon reappeared and signaled that the ceremony was ready to begin. She led the three of us, shuffling in our slippers on the smooth wooden floor, to the temple's main sanctuary, a large open room surrounded by sliding wooden doors. The abbot of the temple sat in the ceremonial space between the altar and the three folding chairs set up for us at the back of the hall. He was a thin man with a smooth bald head and wispy white eyebrows; his thin white socks peeked from beneath the folds of an ample ochre robe. The abbot did not greet us as we entered the room, but sat meditatively on a red cushioned chair next to a wooden stand for his ritual text and a variety of bells and drums.

A large statue of the bodhisattva Kannon several meters tall, loomed over us alongside statues of other comparatively diminutive Buddhas and bodhisattvas. She stood at the back of a raised platform, her head near dim, shadowy rafters. Multicolored flags and flashing brass filigreed ornaments draped down beside a large central altar of lacquered wood, on which offerings, flowers, candles, and ancient looking memorial tablets were placed on various levels. The central statue was hidden even further by this altar, but this was a common aesthetic arrangement, echoed in the placement of objects in the butsudan, that suggested the hidden presence of the sacred, and the interstitial place of hotoke, ancestors, and places of offering.

The Bodhisattva Kannon, also called the Bodhisattva of Mercy or Compassion, is one of the most revered figures of the Buddhist pantheon in Japan, and certainly vies with Jizō as the most widely represented in Japanese art and statuary (Kalland 1991; Young and Ikeuchi 1997, 243–245).[3] Unlike most other bodhisattvas, Kannon is instantly recognizable as feminine, sometimes represented alongside children, or holding a child or fetus, as in one statue in the cemetery of the Shingon temple complex on Mt. Koya. Sometimes compared to the Virgin Mary in Christianity,[4] Kannon is also seen as a Buddhist version of earlier Japanese mother deities associated more blatantly with fertility and sexuality (Buruma 1984, 8).

Interestingly, Mori-san had a small wooden statue of Kannon, about three inches tall, in her butsudan with a single memorial tablet for her mother. When I asked about the statue, Mori-san laughed and told me that it was given to her mother by a wood-carver friend. She picked up the statue and held it in front of me. "You see the arm is broken here?" She began to giggle. "When I was a little girl, I was playing with it and I accidentally broke it off!" I asked if she was scolded for this, but she didn't remember that, only feeling "ashamed." She placed it back on the shelf.

As we made our way into the ceremonial hall, Mori-san shuffled to abbot's seat, bowing and whispering a few words I could not make out before returning to the back of the room where I sat with her cousin on folding chairs. Mori-san began the ceremony by stepping forward to a small table in front of us where the incense was already smoldering in a censer. In the identical gesture performed at funerals and memorial ceremonies, Mori-san kneeled at the table and took a pinch of incense from a pot, raising her fingers to the middle of her forehead and sprinkling it in the middle of the censer. Still kneeling, she bowed deeply with her palms pressed together and walked back to where we sat. Mori-san's cousin followed this same procedure, and finally she motioned for me to go forward and do the same.

I offered my incense, I took my seat alongside Mori-san, and after a moment the priest began reciting verses, continuing without pause for the next twenty minutes. Although it was difficult to clearly hear or decipher the meaning of the chanting, there did not seem to be any specific reference to the dagger or to the ancestor to whom it once belonged. To my surprise, the ceremony for the dagger was largely indistinguishable from the memorial rituals that might be conducted for a deceased person, and the dagger itself resembled a body, dressed in the white clothes worn by a corpse. The sutras functioned to pacify the spirits of the dead that might still have attachments to this world and to the knife itself. This format stands in contrast to other ceremonies held to dispose of inanimate objects in Japan, such as dolls, which are usually collected over the course of a year and burned together in a giant pyre (Kamiya 2006).

The clanging of bells and gongs that accompanied the priest's monotonous chanting was jarring at times, and I was relieved when it ended and the priest swiveled around to face us. His eyes were relaxed, but his chin jutted out dramatically. "Shaka-sama [Shakyamuni Buddha] even gave sermons on his deathbed, so I think it is important that I give one to you today," the priest's voice rose and warbled enthusiastically. The priest's "sermon" (sekkyō) had less to do with the dagger itself or memorials for objects more generally, than it did with encounters with the other world (reikan): "So I can do a little divination, see? These days people go all over to receive divination, but do they come to the temple? They waste their time going elsewhere and all sorts of problems occur!" He continued telling us about his experiences seeing demons (oni) and ghosts around the temple and performing ceremonies to comfort or extinguish them:

> It was even on television, in a show about what happens after a person dies. You know, people say that they don't need funerals, they don't need monks. Why is that? Monks these days, don't have real belief! They don't even acknowledge the world of the vengeful ghosts (shiryō no sekai)! Among all of the Buddhists priests eighty percent don't acknowledge it! This is not only my sect, but all of Japan. That's why people can't believe in the monks. But I have seen it! And I always tell people who come to see me about the world of the souls (reikon). Why would people do these memorials if they didn't believe in the souls?

Mori-san and her cousin seemed to hang on the priest's every word as he continued his talk, growing more excited as he described the pitch black world of demons and vengeful spirits and the importance of memorials (literally "work" otsutome) for reassuring the spirit in the other world (meifuku). Again, no particular mention of the dagger was made, but Mori-san, inspired perhaps by the sermon, approached the priest briefly as we were leaving the hall, assuring him that the dagger was not used for ritual suicide, but that the spirit must have experienced some restlessness because the knife had not been cared for properly. She apologized for the burden (meiwaku) caused to the temple for bringing up such an embarrassing thing. The priest furrowed his brow in concentration, such that the wiry strands of his eyebrows twitched like antenna, then he nodded and assured her that all would be put right now.

With this, we excused ourselves and were led back to a reception room. Mori-san and her cousin immediately turned to each other saying how "relieved" (anshin) they felt, and how they can now "relax" (ochitsukemasu). Mori-san, began giggling and turned to me saying, "It's a mysterious thing, isn't it? It's just not a good thing to keep leftover things in your heart (kokoro). It's different than when you're young! Life gets shorter." The cousin nodded in agreement and added, "when you get old, you don't know how much longer you'll be here, so you want to resolve these kinds of things quickly." The two laughed some more, and Mori-san turned again to me saying, "This is how you feel when you get old!" (*Sore ha toshiyori no kokoro!*).

Their use of the word *anshin* (relief or peace) stood out to me, since it was the same word that Mori-san and others had used to describe the feelings after visiting a grave. Anshin literally means "peaceful heart," but can also indicate a sense of security or protection. Mori-san's comment, "It's just not a good thing to keep leftover things in your heart," showed the beginnings of a realization that attachments can change, or objects can be abandoned, without posing a threat to the self. The dedication ceremony relieved Mori-san of the burden of the physical symbol of her attachments to a past she felt responsible for, a memory she never had. While the meanings Mori-san attached to the objects in her hoard were lost on others, the dagger could consolidate these meanings in a way that linked their disposal to the memorialization of the restless spirits of her past, and to the ethical practice of offering sacrifice. The abbot's ability to see beyond this world and evoke images of the torment of restless ghosts lent an additional layer of symbolic meaning and value to ceremony. His sermon even went so far as to make this belief in spirits a kind of statement about the secularization of Japanese society and the commodification of divination (*uranai*).

The religiously framed disposal of the dagger was not merely another way of gifting or recycling precious objects, the way she would give me small items when I would visit. The ritual seemed to generate a different sense of consciousness about the meaning of the things that Mori-san saved. This was a crafted disappearance not only of the object, but of its excess, its inconsolable loss, its abandonment. Mori-san had taken on this excess and transferred it to the spirits of the dead, relieving herself of the burden of caring for it and at the same time ritualizing it to provide care for the spirits of the dead. The meaning of things for Mori-san was linked to memory—an almost obsessive, repetitive remembering that each object contained, and that she used to guard herself against the pain of feeling shameful, useless, disposable. Once Mori-san could configure her belongings in terms of ancestral significance, and dedicate the most precious of them to shrines or temples, she seemed much more at ease about discarding other items. It was as if things had become ordered in relation to a different set of possibilities, a different economy of care, and as a result, some internal barrier had been broken down that allowed loss, and an alternate view of the self to flow in.

UNCANNY VISITATIONS

An extensive literature demonstrates that dreams and visions of deceased loved ones are not uncommon in Japan or in non-Japanese cultures, among older and bereaved adults (Casto, Krippner, and Tartz 1999; Erikson, Erikson, and Kivnick 1986, 123–125; Hallam, Hockey, and Howarth 1999, 142–152; Lohmann 2003; Mageo 2003; Mittermaier 2010), and these dreams are especially meaningful in societies with beliefs in the continued influence of the ancestors or spirits after death. Psychological anthropologists have found that dreams and visions can provide symbolically rich gateways to the unconscious of individuals, and to the invisible and concealed forces that animate a person's behaviors. They also function in various social venues as ways of circulating knowledge, revelation, prophecy, and other signs of sacred power, overlapping with the roles of oracles, shamans, sorcerers, and other figures that help us to see differently into "critical spaces and possibilities" of the imaginary (Mittermaier 2010).

In Japan, these spaces are shaped by long-standing beliefs in the nearby presence of the spirits, their tendency to become unexpectedly revealed, their ability to appear strongly to those with a paranormal sense (reikan), such as older people, and other discourses on seeing the dead. Not everyone claimed to have seen the dead in visions (*maboroshi*) or dreams (*yume*), but for those who did, these experiences seemed to solidify a sense of intimacy and ease with the spirits.

Although several people I spoke with mentioned having visions (*maboroshi wo utsusu*, literally "projecting a vision") that included deceased family members, Nishida-san's were perhaps the most varied, vivid, and richly detailed. Some of these made us laugh, but others made us shiver.[5] Nishida-san's sometimes felt or saw more frightening apparitions during her waking moments (when watching a television show about paranormal activities, for example), but most occurred in the moments just before going to bed, or just after waking up.[6] These visions were the most integrated into her self-narrative, and all involved recently deceased relatives and a pattern of interdependence and exchange that linked them together. Her visions also shared a sense of indeterminacy, blurring the lines between day and night, sleep and wakefulness, the visible and invisible, the living and the dead; they did not give answers, but opened spaces for imagination and creativity.

Nishida-san eagerly responded to my questions about dreams and visions of the other world:

> NISHIDA: Dreams? Oh I have them all the time. Well, but for me, I have dreams when I'm sound asleep, then when I open my eyes they disappear just like that [laughs] . . . but that aside, um, how should I put this? Well I don't know if you're going to believe Jason-kun, but [it happened] when I was sleeping here [points to the room behind her where the butsudan is]. Since grandma died it hadn't been forty-nine days and all, so it wasn't the time for her to have become a *hotoke*.
>
> DANELY: Become a *hotoke*?
>
> NISHIDA: Right. See you can't become a *hotoke* until after forty-nine days. After forty-nine days you do the *kimei* ceremony and then the person who

died becomes a *hotoke*. So it was before then, and, well, always—See the matriarch of this place, my husband's mother, and I, we lived together. So when she died, I didn't have any way of depending on her. Until now I was always saying, "grandma this, grandma that," [and] depending on her. . . .

Well then I had to wake up early in the morning and leave for some business. So before I went to bed I said to the *hotoke*-san "grandma, I'm sorry, but tomorrow early in the morning, I have to wake up by five. I'm a late sleeper, so if I oversleep please wake me up!" Then I slept. Then, well, I would have turned on the alarm clock. But [this time] I forgot to put on the alarm clock, so it wasn't going to ring. I just prayed to the *hotoke*-san and slept.

Well however early [I go to bed], I can't wake up before six. Not until six. Then I heard a voice say to me [gently, in a slightly hushed, voice] "Wake up! Kaori-chan, wake up! . . . I opened my eyes, and I heard the voice over here, so I opened [the door] and there was grandma, right there! So I said "Oh grandma, thank you!" (*ookini*) "Thank you for waking me up!" Things like this are real!

Nishida-san showed no sense of fear or apprehension at seeing her deceased mother-in-law, expressing only a desire to continue everyday bonds of intimacy and interdependence with her. Nishida-san felt dependent upon her mother-in-law while she was still alive, and the same expectation of dependence was carried on after her death, even though the spirit of a recently deceased person is still dependent on the actions of living. The fact that Nishida-san had spent several years caring for her aging mother-in-law is not noted in this narrative, but the reversal of dependency is an important function of ancestor memorial (Fortes 1976, 14; Ooms 1977). In her vision, the relationship of caregiving returned to a prior state where Nishida-san could feel legitimately dependent on her mother-in-law.

The spirits in her visions did not always appear in response to requests for care, but sometimes had requested care for themselves. In a second vision experience, Nishida-san described a visit from the ghost of one of her sisters, whom Nishida-san also looked after in late life. Like her mother-in-law, the sister is identified as an "old woman" (obāchan), rather than by a specific name, suggesting that she is closely identified with Nishida-san herself, or at least with the general category of "old woman":

One time—my sister lives in the town A___. My sister who always looked after me died in A___ . . . um . . . she was properly interred in the grave of another one of my elder brothers. So I hadn't been able to go [to do a memorial for her] for a while. Then, um, at the time too, it was in the morning before I had [fully] awoken. The dreams I have when I am fast asleep at night disappear just like that, but maybe it was when I couldn't tell if I was dreaming or having a vision, and that sister came over here.

"The flowers at my grave are withered," [she said] and I was totally shocked! "Oh dear old woman (*obāchan*)!" I thought— [perhaps seeing some confusion on my face] Oh, well she's my sister but ever since I was a child, I'd call everyone "obāchan, obāchan."

It's my obāchan here! [motions to the other room], but when I suddenly opened up [the screen door of the room], there wasn't a trace of her.

Anyway, I thought that it was strange that the flowers at the grave would be withered, since the wife of my brother [whose husband] is buried in that grave, is just not the type who would let the flowers wither. She goes out of her way to care for the ancestors, so I was concerned about it and I called over there. I even called over to the house, but I couldn't get an answer. So I called some other places and couldn't get though there either. And so it was getting to be the afternoon, and I'll never forget it, it was November third in the late morning on a holiday, so I was just relaxing, doing as I pleased and taking it easy. And then after noon I thought that I'd try calling over to her niece's place.

So I called her niece and when she answered I said "Is this Hana-chan? Hana-chan, has anything happened?"

"Goodness, grandma how did you know?" she said. "How did you know?" she said to me. "Is there something wrong?" I said, and then she told me "Grandma Yoshi-san had to have heart surgery and was taken to the hospital!" That's why they weren't able to go to the grave.

The water—that's why I had a vision of my sister coming to me saying that the flowers on her grave were withering. So I was surprised, and it was November third and even though it was a holiday I asked my son to take me right away, and so I went to pay her a get well visit." Oh, Kaori-chan, how did you know?" she said to me. So I told her, "Well, this morning obāchan came up to my pillow and told me that the flowers on her grave were withering." And when I said this, she was surprised, saying, "Really?!" [laughs] Nobody had gone to the grave. The flowers were withered and bone dry. I went to A___ and then I went to the grave and changed the flowers.

It is reasonable to interpret the vision of her deceased sister as an indication of Nishida-san's guilt and shame for abandoning the grave. Rather than asking Nishida-san directly to visit the grave, the ghost says that "the flowers at my grave are withered," as if she too were dying along with them. Skord points out that the symbol of "withered blossoms" has long indicated the stubborn clinging to the world and the distaste for the ugliness of old age (1989, 132). Here, however, Nishida-san is able to see what others look away from in fright or disgust, and to restore the flowers to a vital and beautiful state.

John W. Traphagan, who noticed a similar pattern of ancestral visions among the older women he interviewed in rural Akita Japan, interpreted spirits' requests as older women's strategy for maintaining the caregiver role by acting as a messenger on behalf of the ancestors (2003, 135–137). Traphagan's findings that these visions (he uses the word "dream") are gendered and occur mostly among the old is consistent with normative cultural assumptions about visions as well as my own findings. The rest of Nishida-san's story appears to support Traphagan's conclusions, since upon inquiring about her deceased sister's dilemma, Nishida-san ended up caring not only for the grave, but also for the other relatives who were responsible for the grave. Visions created opportunities to contribute to the economy of care by making up for what had been lost.

If, as I suggested earlier, Nishida-san also identifies with her sister, then her visit to the grave may be seen as a way to symbolically manage her own desire to be cared for as well. The uncanny visions of the spirits are instances of mutual recognition; caring for the deceased is also caring for the aging self. The self that Nishida-san is able to imagine is not that of the reluctant prophet of calamity, but a self that calmly and affectionately honors her bonds. In a third vision, Nishida-san describes an experience of seeing the ghost of her sister-in-law. Although the ghost's appearance was disturbing, Nishida-san did not seem frightened by it at all:

> NISHIDA: Just the other day, In Y, I was told to come for the forty-ninth day [ceremonies] but I couldn't go. So she said we'll wait until sister [Nishida-san] comes before interring the remains. She waited until the hundredth day for me. She was also ninety-four years old. [Nishida-san's sister had also passed away at this age.]
>
> DANELY: Ninety-four too? That's chilling.
>
> NISHIDA: Yes but she was vigorous, up until the last evening she was vigorous. I went for the funeral, but for the forty-ninth day, the timing was bad, I couldn't go because I so many things to do piled up, so I said I'd come on the hundredth day. I promised. Then, the day before [the hundredth day memorial service], in the evening, I went to the store, and I thought, I have to go tomorrow, I'd better tidy things up. So in the evening I finished everything up. I went over there and shut out the light, and I was going to the kitchen when I looked back for a moment and my sister that I was going to visit the next day was standing there, dressed as she always was, stooping over and shuddering. I looked over quickly and she was holding something like a rope. I looked up and I said, "Oh, it's Kiku-san!" That's her name. "Kiku-san, you've come to get me? I'll be there tomorrow without a doubt." When I did this there was nothing there. No shadow or form. When I told my daughter-in-law that when I went to the shop, Kiku-san came to get me for tomorrow she was so scared she wouldn't come to the store! [laughs] "Grandma, it's so scary!" [she said] "There's nothing to be afraid of. She only came to say come tomorrow" I said. She had come to tell me I absolutely had to come.

Like the previous dream, this vision is a condensation of the desire to care and be cared for. The spirit *comes* to Nishida-san to ensure that Nishida-san goes to the memorial service. This coming and going, departing and returning, is central to the practice of *omairi*, which not only indicates the ritual observance itself, but literally means "a coming." The spirits in Nishida-san's visions require reassurance that they are not abandoned, just as Nishida-san herself gains assurance in the existence of the other world, and hope for her own future memorial.

When Nishida-san described asking the spirit "You've come to get me?" I felt a shiver run up my back, since at the time it seemed that Nishida-san was referring to the ghost coming to take her away to the "other world." Such fears are not uncommon in Japan, especially when discussing the spirit of a newly deceased person, and can be seen in the avoidance of conducting funerals on days marked as "tomobiki" or "friend pulling," since it is considered easier to be taken on these days.[7] I was relieved when Nishida-san explained that the spirit came only to confirm that she would be at the memorial service. In other words, the spirit was a visual projection of a reminder to memorialize—to remember to remember. In this sense, Nishida-san was not only looking back on the memory of the deceased, but looking forward, or anticipating her own future. The request to be woken up in the morning in the first vision and the somewhat prophetic message of the withered blossoms in the second echo this future-oriented nature of visions of the dead, and underline their role as opening possibilities and securing the sense of hope in things unseen.

For Nishida-san, visions bring the departed to the foreground of everyday decisions, and thus toward future actions that ground the experience of the self. These visions give her hope that she too will be cared for after she dies, and that her spirit will not only reunite with lost loved ones, but also be able to return to see and communicate with the living. Her early experiences of grief and the weight of her daughter's death, which left her feeling a sense of helplessness, contrasted with the lightness and hope of these later visions, which provided opportunities to express the anxieties about aging and abandonment and to provide care and acceptance for the spirits.

Love and the Labor of the Unseen

For some, like Nishida-san, the creativity of loss in old age had narrative precursors in prior experiences of grief and mourning. These early experiences may have helped her to cultivate a sense of aesthetic discernment and not only to refigure the narrative of her daughter's and husband's deaths, but also to carry on this labor of care through memorialization over the life course. Her labor of love was evident not only in her care for their spirits, but also in the ways she accepted the support and care of others and the ways she extended that care through her volunteer community work. This lifelong orientation toward cultivating mutuality and her devotion to spiritual practices has even produced a visual and auditory awareness of things that for most people are unseen and unheard, but which for Nishida-san constituted an undeniable sign of the ongoing work of care between the living and the departed.

For others, and more often for men like Sato-san, uncomfortable feelings of dependence and shame brought about by losses earlier in life were countered by projecting an image of autonomy and independence (associated with other forms of occupational labor), which presented additional obstacles to mourning as they grew older. Older men, on the whole, struggled with yielding in old age, partly because their meaningful ties were bound up in relationships outside of the family. Older men who have devoted much of their lives to work and who do not have hobbies or interest often feel a loss of meaning in postretirement years, becoming a burden on spouses who are often eager to enjoy their later years free of responsibility of child care. The divorce rate for men and women over fifty has increased in recent years even as overall rates have declined, and the image of older retired men as "large trash" or "wet leaves" indicates something undesirable that is nonetheless hard to get rid of.

The kinds of work that men and women engage in over their life courses, including the work of care for children, elders, and spirits, will influence the meaningfulness of rituals for the departed as a means of adjusting to old age. Not only is mourning a lifetime's work, but the aesthetic organization of one's life course trajectory, the opportunities and disruptions that arise within it, and the resources to adjust and creatively reconstitute subjectivity are shaped by cultural norms and institutions. For Sato-san, earnest efforts at self-improvement, participation in activities at the senior center, and his focus on independence and self-reliance throughout his life appeared to be ways of coping with feelings of grief, survivor guilt, and impotence, past and present, but these strategies were also predicated on and vulnerable to the anticipation of a future of dependence and loss.

Since Sato-san's grief, and indeed his most secure sense of self and aged subjectivity seemed to be found in the enduring love and mourning for his wife, I asked about how he felt he had changed after her death:

DANELY: How is the Sato-san before your wife died and the Sato-san afterward different?
SATO: My personality was bad.
DANELY: Bad?
SATO: It became worse!
DANELY: Became worse?
SATO: Looking at myself, how can I say it? This is also a little difficult . . . *before, I was BIG. I got smaller. People became smaller* . . . [he appears excited or angry]
DANELY: Did you feel anger at the time?
SATO: More than anger, more than anger, I'd say [in English] depression. [in Japanese] The feeling of depression was stronger. . . . [in English] WHY? WHY? WHY MY WIFE? [in Japanese] That feeling . . . I didn't do anything wrong, right?!

At the time, I was not entirely sure of what to make of this exchange, but Sato-san's description of himself as becoming smaller did strike me as peculiar.

On reviewing this exchange in light of our other encounters, however, this statement became the key to understanding Sato-san's association among grief, shame, and abandonment. It would also help me to see the significance of the obasuteyama tale and its relationship to the experiences of many of the other older adults I spoke with as well. Both Sato-san's statements and the obasuteyama tale address feelings of loss—of a self that was once "big" becoming "small," or the visible becoming concealed. This sense of loss was tied not only to Sato-san's grief over his wife's death, but also to his adjustment to growing older and more dependent.

Just as grief has a weight (see chapter 2), it also has size. Loss of control over his sense of size recalls Sato-san's comments and concerns about height (his wife's reservations about him being short and his admiration for John Wayne's impressive stature) as well as feelings of shame associated with obasuteyama narratives. Feelings of "smallness" (both physical and psychic) or the sense of frustration and helplessness in relationship to a larger, powerful figure (such as a parent) can have profound effects on the ability to maintain a stable sense of self and the ability to transform this self in mourning (Kilborne 2002, 21). If this is the case, how did the smallness of grief haunt Sato-san as he transitioned to an identity as an older adult?

Sato-san's desire for autonomy and individuation, which he depended on to achieve a sense of fulfillment in old age, meant that he remained in some ways haunted by the shame and grief of being abandoned. Japanese cultural sensitivity to exposure and "loss of face" has been observed by several anthropologists (Benedict [1946] 1974; Creighton 1990) and remains fundamental for understanding the kinds of frustrations that arise in the construction of the self (Kitayama 2007; Kawanishi 2009, xvii). This sensitivity has been convincingly traced back to Japanese socialization patterns and the symbol of the mother in Japanese culture (Allison 1996; Caudill and Weinstein 1969; Ozawa de-Silva 2007). Psychologists Miyake and Yamazaki noted that Japanese mothers "try to make the children aware and conscious of the 'eyes' of other people—other children, friends, and teachers" (1995, 493). In contrast to earlier experiences of indulgence and attachment, children between the ages of three and five begin to be treated as separate beings who must align their desires with those of others. While living in Japan, I noticed several instances where mothers would turn or walk away from misbehaving children rather than scold them, sometimes leaving the sulking child alone outside or crossing a busy street without looking back. These kinds of socialization experiences may seem neglectful or even dangerous to those unfamiliar with Japanese culture, but are considered necessary for the maturation of the child and a sense of individuation and interdependence (Hendry 1986; Peak 1991; Tobin 1994). The painful sense of inadequacy in the child's self-image, accompanied by a fear of disconnection, separation, and abandonment, is utilized to form a sense of self consistent with a cultural environment that demands constant attention to the needs of others (Creighton 1990, 285). When seen in light of obasuteyama narratives and the recurring themes of separation from the mother, these observations become useful for understanding the psychodynamic processes at work for older adults, such as Sato-san, and for understanding the relief found in the practice of memorialization.

Sato-san's sensitivity to shame (of feeling "small") was not unusual in the context of Japanese culture, but it also made it difficult for him, and other men in general, to construct a healthy sense of dependence in the postretirement years. His life history, in contrast to that of someone like Nishida-san, lacked evidence of early models of dependable adults. This became evident in his omissions and gaps in his narrative. Although we talked together on numerous occasions, including a dozen interview sessions lasting at least two hours each, Sato-san rarely spoke of his early childhood, his siblings (both living), or his parents. Sato-san described his father as being "absent" from the home, saying, "My father was not there at all. Some of my friends had [curfews] in their house, but my father didn't do anything like that with me. Not even [telling me to] study. I just [had to] take care of the house." Before I could ask more, he quickly followed his comments with others on the importance of "independence" from parents, citing the example of his own sons who he says still "mooch off of him" (*oya no sune kajiri*, literally "gnawing at one's parents' shins"), and his refusal to put himself in debt to another person, declaring dramatically "I'd rather die!" Such virulent refusal to become indebted, while based in a kind of adaptive strategy for adult life, stood in sharp contrast to the views of others such as Nishida-san, for whom debt opened up flows of exchange and care, and Nakamura-san, for whom debt to his ancestors secured his sense of obligation to the household traditions.

As for his mother, Sato-san did not speak about her directly, but he did often compare her to his late wife, who also "did not wear makeup" (chapter 3). In another interview, Sato-san compared his wife with his own mother in appearance and temperament:

SATO: Boys need their mother.... They need discipline. I was too soft on them. But, really, it would have been better if I died than my wife, really. I've always thought that.

DANELY: You really think that?

SATO: I really think that. For male children it really is more about the mother than the father.... I don't know why. For me, in my case, in my situation, my parents lived till they were in their eighties or seventies, and when your parents die in their eighties, well that's another thing, but, I've always thought that way ... that is if one were to die, it should be the father.

Sato-san's own mother was present and the disciplinarian of the home (unlike his father), and this role was repeated by his wife in his own family. The script was, however, disrupted; his wife died young and his parents grew old. On the other hand, his wife could remain constantly held in time as in the photograph (chapter 3), or kept "unforgotten" and "unchanged in [his] heart." The gradual internalization of the image of his wife was mirrored by his treatment of her funeral portrait, which he describes in terms of a process of aligning his personal feelings with his practices.

> SATO: I have that hotok—hotoke—that butsudan in my home, right? For these things—in other words, what day should I take the remains to the grave or whatever—there are a lot of opinions. But for this kind of stuff, I—I make the decisions. I do. You or other people can't decide for me.
>
> DANELY: It is based on how you feel?
>
> SATO: Right. If you're by yourself, the picture—like my wife's picture, right? You hang it above the place with the buddha [motions up by the ceiling], and if it's just by itself—well there are places where people line up [the memorial photographs] grandpa, grandma, and so on, right? Well that's fine for them. I don't think there's anything wrong with it. I am always, to some extent ok with that. [very quietly] But I took hers down. I just did it based on how I felt. That's part of being modest (*kenkyo*). [suddenly much louder] It's not at all like my feelings toward her are going away because she died so early! That's totally wrong! I will have feelings for her until I die. I will be thinking of her every day up until the day I die. I don't go and offer incense every day or anything, but on my wife's birthday, and the end of the year, and then, as you remember this Jason, do you remember? Ohigan, and the "dead spirits come back to my house" everyone in Japan believes that, right? So we [motions as if muttering a prayer] Well, if I get the chance, I'll stop by and bring some flowers or something. I'm satisfied with that.

As with the visits to her grave, changing his practices at the butsudan also allowed Sato-san to embed the memory of his wife in his own narrative identity. His insistence that memorialization should be up to the individual and emerge from his or her own feelings and circumstances reveals the importance of creativity, flexibility, and agency in spiritual practices.

As his frequent confessions of affection for his wife indicated, memorialization allowed Sato-san to regain a sense of loving mutuality with the unseen, and to imagine, if only temporarily or partially, a more integrated sense of self by reuniting with her in death. As he grew older and the avenues of autonomy became attenuated and the desires for the glory days of past selves became less comforting, Sato-san's love for his late wife offered a means for enacting a new relationship with the maternal, caring, comforting part of his self. This recovery of a sense of maternal care offered an alternative to feelings of abandonment and shame that follow loss, and a comforting sense of humility, dependence, and care (*amae*), which many have argued stands at the core of the Japanese psyche (Doi 1973; Johnson 1993; Kim et al. 2006; Niiya, Ellsworth, and Yamaguchi 2006; Tomita 1994). Sato-san's case shows that recovering a sense of the amae may be different for men and women in adulthood. One Buddhist priest explained to me that "strength" is easier for women to achieve since they give birth, but for men it required rigorous religious practices on the mountains (*shūgyō*), which, as pointed out earlier (chapter 3), is the superior feminine symbol of the womb (and tomb). In the mountains, he explained, "men can cry 'mommy!'"[8]

Memorialization has a highly gendered psychodynamic quality that links cultural symbols to psychological dispositions based on family relationships and images of mothers. Tatsumi's graphic reiteration of obasuteyama points this out most explicitly by including a back story of the protagonist's traumatic feelings of abandonment as a child, which led eventually to his effort to abandon his mother in her old age. Unlike some children's versions of the story, where the son reconsiders his actions and saves his mother, Tatsumi's story ends with the tragedy of the mother's death and the unresolved desire for care. In order to adapt to old age and to loss, to form a future self capable of receiving care, Sato-san, like Mori-san, was peeling through the accumulated layers of past selves, memories, and identities and, as he labored in the work of self, creating the open aesthetic of ma.

While it was obvious among some informants that memorialization brought ease to this process, I wondered how Sato-san, a self-confessed "unreligious" person, felt. One morning, as we looked in the window of a shop selling Buddhist prayer beads, I asked Sato-san if he thought that people need religion. Again, his reply was based on his own experiences with his wife:

> It's not that you don't need [religion]. [You] can't be like [you] don't need it at all. Of course, ordinarily . . . in ordinary, normal, everyday life you don't need it at all. However, my wife, when my wife died . . . I didn't have any belief in kami or hotoke. . . . That was my frame of mind, you know? What's a buddha? What's a kami? *Why did my wife have to die?* That's all that I would think about, you know? For years. . . .
>
> Now my thinking has changed a little. It changed. . . . How did it change? Well, basically, until now that feeling [of faith] has been there a little but, of course, [the fact that] my wife is dead, and I am still alive is—of course . . . there must be some sort of *power* (*chikara*) in me that I can't rationally understand, you know? I go on. . . . [trails off]

For Sato-san, the endurance of the self ("I go on") is processual, contingent upon his own capacity for aging and changing. Aging and grief call into question not only the existence and agency of buddhas and kami, but the very meaning of the aging self. In this way, rituals for the dead opened up possibilities for the unexplainable loss, a "power" for conjuring hopeful returns to bridge the visible and invisible worlds and cultivate a mature sense of shame, humility, and dependence through the labor of care.

DIVINING CARE

The ritual disposal of Mori-san's dagger was interesting to me not only because it revealed Mori-san's beliefs concerning the spirits, but also because it provided her an occasion to consult with the Buddhist priest and to visit the family grave.

The juxtaposition of these practices with the ceremony for the dagger produced a link between different contexts of recognizing the unseen or unknowable future foreshadowed by the experience of old age, loss, abandonment, and shame. Divination, as a "way of knowing" that sees the unseen, is a narrative technology that provides what Barbara Tedlock called a "superabundance of understanding" (Tedlock 2001, 192), which diviner and client collaboratively work through to develop transformations in subjectivity.

For Mori-san, whose hoard composes its own superabundant narrative, the trust in a supernatural world held a hope of finding a way to a clear, unburdened heart, that could open up the ma. Mori-san often spoke of the meanings of horoscopes, palmistry, and other divination techniques and believed the priest who conducted the ceremony for the dagger to be unique for his sense of the paranormal (reikan), as evidenced in stories like those he told following the ceremony we attended. In an earlier interview, Mori-san had told me about this same priest, repeating many of the words we heard in the ceremony for the dagger:

> People these days, even the Buddhist priests say "There's no such thing as the other world!" Even priests, you see? Those priests say there's no other world, no paradise. The only reality is living here and now. That's life. That's what priests today say.
>
> Even so, in one of those temples is a head priest who goes out of his way to say that there are MANY mysterious things and MANY experiences you can have . . . in other words, what you might call a paranormal sense? When we say someone has a paranormal sense (reikan) for example, on higan we had a ceremony right? Well, a person who has a clear heart (kokoro), a pure person, a person whose thinking is deliberate, surprisingly [that person] will understand.
>
> Of course, if you think something really seriously, that sort of thing happens, right? You might be right. I think this is true; it's even in Christianity, right? Prophecy (yogen). Of course, it's as if, people have things that they know and things they don't know, but there are people who get it.

Mori-san clearly believes in the power of the unseen supernatural world, accessible to those with a "clear heart." This echoed the statements she and her cousin made after the dagger ceremony about the "heart of and old person" who has learned to let go of things. Mori-san still had concerns, however, for what would transpire once the move was finally finished. At the time of the dagger ceremony, she was already two months behind schedule and the house was still a mess. Just as Sato-san sought a connection to a greater "power" to make sense of his abandonment, Mori-san was hoping that the abbot would be able to find answers using his skill for divination. Their consultation, however, provided much more that this, giving Mori-san a chance to express and symbolize her feelings about growing older and being emotionally or possibly physically abandoned by her daughter.

After the dagger ceremony, Mori-san, her cousin, and I waited in a small reception room where we were soon joined by the priest, who had removed his ceremonial garb and was dressed in a simple grey kimono and a loose black vest. After standing and thanking him again, we were seated and the priest cordially asked after Mori-san's family. Mori-san seemed nervous and excited and began giggling when the priest recalled the personal details of her life, her daughters, and so forth. After a few minutes Mori-san mentioned the move and the toll it was starting to take on her health. She mentioned the help that everyone had been giving her, turning to me and recalling the familiar Japanese saying, "Better to have strangers nearby than relatives far away!"

She then told the priest about her daughter's marriage adding that the son-in-law was born into a temple family, and educated at a Buddhist university, but did not become successor at his father's temple. The priest listened carefully, lips slightly parted with a gentle, if flat expression as he held his hands loosely in his lap.

After several more minutes, Mori-san's cousin finally mentioned that they wanted to ask a favor of the priest. Mori-san continued at her cousin's prompting, saying that what she is worried about most these days is what will happen when she moves to the new house.

MORI: I'm going to be taken care of by my daughter. . . .

PRIEST: She's married, and you're going with her, right? She's going to live with you, right?

MORI: Yes, but. . . .

COUSIN: They're going to be living together. . . .

PRIEST: So will things go well there or not . . . . [is that what you are asking]?

MORI: No, no, I'm an old lady, so that's not an issue! [laughs]

COUSIN: [laughing] Oh! You shouldn't call yourself that!

PRIEST: Oh, you're not an old lady. . . . [laughs]

MORI: Oh, but I don't want to live a long life and be a upsetting everyone! [laughs] If I live too long!

COUSIN: [to priest, bowing] Really, if you could help. . . .

The exchange was filled with nervous laughter, and all three frequently spoke over each other, heading off sentences before ideas were fully elaborated. The majority of the laughter concerned jokes about old age and dependence, topics that might be considered shameful and unpleasant, especially when voiced in public settings.

After the discussion, the priest left the room, returning with his divining tools: a black stone tortoise with a holder on its back from which several long, thin wooden sticks protruded and a wooden box holding six black wooden blocks with notches carved in the middle of each one.[9]

He took out the blocks and lined them up to his left. These would keep track of the hexagram formed by successive readings of the stalks. He then asked Mori-san once more about her family situation and other aspects of the move. When he realized that Mori-san was moving in with her daughter, and that the son-in-law's parents lived separately, he reassured her again that there shouldn't be a problem, as if he felt like there was little need to conduct the divination ceremony. Mori-san, however, persisted, telling him that there are "other matters," and that "young people have different ways of thinking these days," the phrases I had come to recognize from our talks when rebuffing her daughters' comments about hoarding.

The priest resumed, taking up the long sticks in his hands, mixing and shuffling them around, then holding them still while he closed his eyes in concentration. His jaws visibly clenched and then relaxed as he drew out a few sticks and moved each of the blocks slightly left or right. The three of us waited silently entranced in nervous expectation while he repeated this procedure until the reading was completed.

After about five minutes, the priest turned to us with a pensive voice, saying, "Well, I can't say that there won't be any problems, but . . . anyway, you can't acquiesce to everything that your daughter tells you. If you don't voice your own opinions there may be problems." He studied the results again and added, "How is the father [of the son-in-law]?" Mori-san replied quickly, stumbling and stuttering her words as she told him that the father was eighty-three, but was not well and has been undergoing dialysis for nearly thirty-one years. The son-in-law, she added once more, is the third son, and that is why he did not take over his family's temple, but since the other sons are employed elsewhere, the temple may have to close.

The priest took in this information with a furrowed brow and resumed the divination procedure, shuffling the sticks once again, closing his eyes. When he completed this next round of divination, he frowned at the blocks on the table saying, "Oh this doesn't look good . . ." But before he could continue, Mori-san suddenly interjected saying, "If I live too long—if I live too long I feel I'll be trouble for the family [my daughter married into]! Next year I'll be 80, so maybe after six or seven years is fine for me! Living too long is difficult!"

The priest did his best to console Mori-san, who seemed to have been pondering the situation to herself in those long tense minutes of the divination. Although it was left unclear what the priest was indicating with his foreboding remark, I had been under the impression that he was referring to the son-in-law's ailing father. Indeed, most of what was said during the divination was difficult to follow, partial, and unsettled.

Mori-san expressed concerns about growing older and depending on care from her son-in-law, whom she perceived as abandoning his own ailing father. Were she to become more dependent in old age as well, what would happen to her? Her identification with the son-in-law's father helped to explain the final outburst about living too long and the uncertainty she sought to ease through the divination. While the result of the reading seemed far from conclusive or comforting to me, to Mori-san it opened a space to imagine alternative possibilities, at the very least reaffirming the legitimacy of Mori-san's concerns and acting to reflect them back to her, creating a sense of agency. The priest indicated that he had done all he could, and we thanked him for his help and Mori-san told him that she did much feel better.

We left the room and headed toward the rear of the temple to the graves. Mori-san had forgotten to bring flowers, and purchased a few branches of evergreens (*shikibi*) and some incense sticks from a table just inside the temple's entrance. As we entered the cemetery, I offered to fetch her bucket at the gate of the cemetery, and filled it up at the spigot next to the gravestones of the connectionless spirits.

At the grave, Mori-san and her cousin washed each stone by gently pouring water over the top with a plastic ladle and then proceeding down to the lower surfaces. The wet polished surfaces of each of the new stones cut clean lines through the crisp winter air. The deeply inscribed names on the newly purchased stones did not reveal the ages of the remains nor traces of wear. The sun would be setting soon and was already casting long shadows over the stones. We didn't speak, and the slow, gentle dribbling of water was almost meditative after the tension of the divination ceremony. However uncertain the outcome of the divination, the peace of the graves seemed to give a sense of closure. The last stone washed belonged to Mori-san's mother. Mori-san's cousin helped place the evergreens into the carved vessels on either side of each stone. Finally, Mori-san lit some incense with a match and knelt before her mother's grave whispering gently.

REFLECTING SURFACES

When I first arrived in Kyoto, I stayed at a temple inn, figuring that it would not only provide a quiet respite from my excursions around the city, but also give me the opportunity to begin observing some of the everyday life of a working Buddhist temple. Setting down my bags, I breathed in the comforting grassy smells of tatami and incense, and when I drew open the curtains and looked out my window, I saw row after row of neatly arranged gravestones, some dressed with fresh bouquets of flowers.

The temple inn was run by a sweet white-haired woman with a sturdy posture and round face named Fujii-san, who radiated grandmotherly warmth. I continued to meet and chat with Fujii-san during my stay, and when I had finally found permanent lodging, her husband generously offered to drive me and my luggage there. I returned to the inn several times during fieldwork to visit with Fujii-san, who, at seventy years old, was beginning to feel that she could no longer keep up with the busy schedule of responsibilities around the temple.

"Getting old is tough! You get so worn out, so very tired!" she sighed as she took a break from her work to talk with me. Though she sometimes joked about her age in passing, when I asked her about it in our interview she told me, "I look at my own hand, and think 'Oh, that's the hand of an old lady. Oh! It's just like my mother's hand! They've become the same, haven't they?' I look in the mirror and think 'I have an old woman's face!' but then I think, 'Oh, my mother had this same kind of face, didn't she?' There are a lot of things that make me remember my parents. Of course, I am here today because of the ancestors from all the way back have continued until now, right?" Fujii-san took some comfort in the fact that although growing older meant that she was unable to do everything that she had grown accustomed to, she was realizing a newfound sense of intimacy with her mother and with the "ancestors from all the way back" as she put it. Her perception of the world has begun to shift as she sees herself in the mirror of her ancestors, in the mirror of memory.

Barbara Myerhoff wrote that for the older adults she studied, and perhaps all of us, "knowledge of self is requisite to complete consciousness; consciousness requires reflecting surfaces. Cultures provide these opportunities to know ourselves, to be ourselves, by seeing ourselves" (1978, 148). While aging is often marked by its social concealment, or efforts to delay and mask it, culture also provides these "reflective surfaces" to visualize aging. Like dreams and divination, the mirror illuminates new understandings of the self and its image. For Fujii-san, the wrinkled skin of her face in the mirror, that "old woman's face," led her to identify with her mother, and thus to see in herself something of her own spirit. This facial communication with her mother (what Schattschneider 2004, after Wittgenstein, terms "family resemblance") has long been a traditional form of contact with the invisible world of the spirits, buddhas, and kami, a materialization, perhaps of the visions and dreams. Nishida-san's visions, for example, gave glimpses into her identification with the departed, and in doing so became a vehicle to exercise agency and extend the aging self past death.

The idea of reflecting surfaces also recalls the psychoanalytic concept of the uncanny and its ties to old age (DeFalco 2010; Ivy 1995; Schattschneider 2004, 144; Woodward 1991, 63–68; 1999). As the object of the gaze reflected in the uncanny double, Kathleen Woodward (1999), expanding on Lacan, notes that old age presents itself as an opportunity for a second "mirror stage" and, as such, is a time to differentiate the self symbolically from the past through the reflections of oneself in others. Woodward and others who take mostly Western literature and cinema as their subjects reiterate the psychoanalytic interpretation of the mirror as producing despair turned back to the self in dangerous, aggressive, and psychotic reactions (DeFalco 2010, 99; Woodward 1991, 67). Woodward, for example, writes that "the mirror stage of old age may precipitate the loss of the imaginary, with the result that identification becomes a real and perhaps impossible problem that can only be 'solved' . . . by repression" (1999, 109–110).

Examples of this kind of reflective despair abound in Western literature (see Kundera 1991, 33–34; Stabile 2004). In Japan, however, the reflecting surfaces that one must come to depend upon include the spirits of the dead. Just as Schattschneider observed in Japanese bride-doll ceremonies, aesthetic rituals of memorialization create a doubled image; metonyms of the spirit (such as ihai memorial tablets or funerary portraits) both represent the deceased person and are the spirit itself (Gerhart 2009). Although these spirits are not exempt from dangerous associations, given the intimate and loving nature of spirits commonly expressed among the old, it would seem that their cultural value is strong enough to suppress such dangerous associations, or at least provide a more hopeful alternative.[10]

Only a few months prior to this talk with Fujii-san, I had had a similar conversation with a woman attending the neighborhood social welfare association meeting for my school district. These meetings, called the *Sukoyaka Gakkyū* (Scholarly Well-Being), were held in an unused room of an old local elementary school. After lunch, I strolled the halls with the other attendees. An older woman approached me and we chatted before she paused, wistfully gazing over the peeling paint of the stairwell, before turning to me again saying,

> After we graduate, we don't come back to the elementary school building, but really after junior high school, we cut off our ties with our school. Then we get to be over seventy, and we are given this opportunity to come back here. Then I think, "I myself was once young!" and we remember all those old things. There's no way of avoiding getting old [pointing to her cane] getting old is harsh! But there is the other world! Every day you look in the mirror and your appearance changes little by little, and you think about going to the next world. You don't think about it when you're young, but as you get older, you start thinking about it.

She flashed me a huge, bright-red, lipsticked smile, and I felt slightly stunned by this stranger's sudden concise summary of aging, reflections, memory, and the other world. I smiled back. As was the case with Fujii-san, the mirror for this woman was a disconcerting reflection of old age, one that challenged the viewer to reconcile feelings and memories of youth with the undesirable image in the reflection. But inseparable from this alienation was the entry into the imaginary, the "other world" that offered solace and a sense of order to old age suspended between past and future selves.

The mirror of age allows the other world to become embodied as an image of possibility. Like the moon, itself a mirror to the sun, or the sacred mirrors enshrined in Shinto places of worship, the desire to see oneself reflected in others can become a source of hope in old age. The mirror of the ancestors defies the shame of decrepitude, by bringing another form of recognition into being.

CHAPTER 8

The Heart of Aging

AN AFTERWORD

About two weeks before I was to return to the United States after a second field-work stay in Kyoto, I went to visit Fujii-san, the woman who managed the temple inn that served as my first lodging in Kyoto. As I walked to the door of the inn, a small present of Japanese cakes in hand, the overcast sky spread a muted light on the cobblestone entrance to the temple, and a light breeze swayed the deep red lace of maple leaves in the courtyard.

I had been unable to contact Fujii-san directly to arrange a meeting by telephone, so I decided to come by unannounced and drop off my gift if she was not there. When I arrived at the door of the inn, however, a staff woman whom I recognized from my previous stay greeted me with a strange expression of concern and told me that Fujii-san had stepped out for a doctor's appointment, but that I could wait for a few more minutes in case she returned soon. I took a seat on the wooden steps, their surface polished smooth with the patina of age. As the minutes passed, I grew more impatient and anxious, but I was interested in finding out just what the staff person could have been so concerned about. I waited a bit longer.

Just as I was about to leave, I saw Fujii-san entering the temple gates, clutching her cane and slowly making her way up the cobblestone path toward me. Relieved, I got up to greet her, and as she saw me coming, she stopped in mid-stride, breathing heavily. She stood straight and looked up at me for a moment, before slumping down again, looking tired. "I've become an old lady!" she said, as if relaying a doctor's diagnosis. I noticed that she has lost some weight, no longer able to cast the figure of the plump matron of the house. She moved more slowly and carefully; her body was much weaker than just one year earlier. She took a seat beside me on the steps, politely thanking me and putting the bag of cakes I had brought to her side without opening them, while the other staff

woman brought in two cups of warm tea. Fujii-san took a sip and turned to me
again, saying,

> Fujii: I've grown old (*oitte kita*). When I think of this in a Buddhist way,
> every living thing grows old and dies. I want to think like that too but. . . .
>
> Danely: Yes, in Buddhism they teach that every living thing grows old. . . .
>
> Fujii: [after a pause] I think I might have what they call *depression* (*utsu-
> ubyō*). That's what's become of me.
>
> Danely: Is that so?
>
> Fujii: All of a sudden.
>
> Danely: So have you experienced things like not wanting to do anything or
> not feeling motivated?
>
> Fujii: Right. One day, all of a sudden. Just now I went to the doctor and got
> some medicine. Depression is pretty common, especially among older
> people. I can't do my job or work like I used to. . . . Getting old is sad. But
> if I talk for a while with someone, little by little I start to remember.

Though Fujii-san had memories, her feeling of hope was fleeting. I had difficulty
understanding how this woman, who had for decades cared not only for the
temple and priests but also for visitors like me from all over the world, could
"forget" how to be with others. So overwhelming, so excessive are the losses of
age; so fragile was the economy of care.

"Old age (*oiru*) is sad," she repeated, her shoulders heavy with fatigue. She
avoided looking me in the eyes, perhaps having lost some of her own eyesight, perhaps too embarrassed to bear her face. I offered to return later with my wife, but she
told me that this was not necessary, and that she does not want to have many visitors these days. I thanked her for all she had done, and she struggled out a smile.

A few days later I boarded an airplane bound for the United States, wondering when or if I would see Fujii-san and the others who had been so vital to this
research. Was I now abandoning them too? This thought haunted me as I wrote
New Year cards each year, as well as birth announcements, moving notices, and
other occasional letters. Sometimes there would be prompt replies and reassurance, but at other times nothing.

In 2013, when I returned to Kyoto, I set out to follow up with as many people
as I could still find. Hasegawa-san and his wife still lived separately from their
children, and chronic health problems had meant fewer days at the community
center and more time at home caring for each other. Hasegawa-san still rails
against the government in haiku, and occasionally makes it out to public
demonstrations. Sato-san still lives with his son's family, and spends most of his
days in care-prevention activities like ground golf and social dance. He still eats
at the reasonably priced lunch buffet of a hotel near his house nearly every day,
alone. He asked if I remembered visiting the grave with him, and then told me,
somewhat embarrassed, that he had begun going to temples more often lately,
even participating in services and chanting.

Nakamura-san had not decided when to consolidate his family graves, though he did sound more confident that this would happen at some point. He continued to work and had no immediate plans for retirement, though he was already in his mid-seventies. He also continued to participate in neighborhood events and festivals and for the first time was selected from his block association to wear the medieval regalia of a court noble in Kyoto's Festival of the Ages (Jidai Matsuri) parade. This alone might have been considered a top honor for Nakamura-san, who often spoke about the "passing of the times," but even more significant was the fact that participants had to represent several generations. Beaming at the memory, he explained, "You don't have to live together in one house, but you must have a parent, child and grandchild, all in good health. Three generations!"[1]

Nishida-san greeted me at her door, announcing, "I haven't gone to the other world yet!" She reached out her hands and squeezed my arms, smiling with satisfaction. At ninety years old, she was much as I had remembered her, still enjoying her social outings with old friends, her weekly massages (twice a week), and her regular exercise for the mouth. Her memory was not as sharp as it used to be, but she enjoyed the fact that it kept her in the moment (*ima no toki*), remarking,

> I go to these presentations for senior learning, and they put chairs right in the front for people like me! I am just so grateful, and it I just listen and learn new things. Afterwards my son will ask me what it was about and I can't really recall. Was it about water? Maybe giraffes? [laughing] Well I just remember being there and feeling that I was learning something. I was happy that they would do this sort of thing for us. And they were so nice to put chairs out, right in the front!

Nishida-san and I talked for hours, but even though we sometimes looped back and repeated some details, we also seemed to cover most of the topics we had discussed years before, sometimes down the exact words. It was as if the narrative had become even more succinct than before. Once again she told me how she had saved her pension money to purchase a new butsudan, then saved up once again to receive a kaimyō on the memorial tablet. She ran her fingers over the tablet, inscribed with her late husband's name as well, before placing it back in the butsudan. She rarely made it all the way to the graves, but she kept her butsudan clean. The losses that accompanied advanced old age seemed to distill the narrative, purifying and concentrating it at the core of her sense of self.

Finally, I met Mori-san, whom I had last seen about two years after she had moved into her new home. In the years since the move, I learned through letters with her and her daughter that things had become even more difficult than before. In the winter, the snow in the mountains was impossible for Mori-san to clear, and the cold gave her more problems than it had in the past, from aching knees to difficulty breathing. She complained about swelling in her face and fading eyesight. "The cold is scary," she said, adding that so many old people die in the winter that sometimes people have to wait a week or more before they can cremate the body.

On New Year 2011, I received the usual celebratory postcard from Naoko-san, and was surprised to read that Mori-san had moved out of the house, not to an institution, but to an apartment in a town nearby. Naoko-san did not give any indication of fights or other conflicts that may have precipitated this major decision, but mentioned only that it was situated at the bottom of the mountain, closer to the train station, a more convenient location for making the regular trips to the graves and to her doctor in Kyoto. The next year, Naoko-san's surname had changed back to her maiden name, and there was a new address on the New Year card. Earlier in the year she obtained a divorce from her husband and was once again living with her mother, hoping for a "new start" and proclaiming that she had "turned over a new leaf." Not only that, but they were joined by Naoko-san's younger sister and her two-year-old daughter as well. "Mother and Hina-chan [the grandchild] eat so much food and are incredibly healthy!" the postcard announced.

When we met again, Naoko-san confided that Mori-san had indeed been showing some unnerving signs of dementia before she moved out. The forgetfulness and fights were becoming more common, and she seemed to complain more aggressively. On one occasion, Naoko-san discovered the bathroom smeared with feces. After Naoko-san's younger sister and niece moved in, these symptoms seemed to evaporate. Naoko-san could hardly believe seeing her mother take the hand of her three-year-old granddaughter and announce that they were going shopping, as if everything was back to normal. As I walked with Mori-san, she talked about how nice it was to live with her granddaughter, and how much she enjoyed tending to her small garden. "Do you remember that move?" she asked me. "I had to get rid of everything, even the trees!" She stopped in front of a flower shop, something catching her eyes again. "I know I shouldn't really be getting anything more, but these are just so nice," she said as she picked out a couple small potted mums and handed them to the vendor. "Now we just live in a very small house, but I am eighty-seven. I don't need as much," she added as she counted out her change.

In each of these cases, and several others, what struck me most was the ways in which episodes from both the recent and distant past were repeated and restoried, sometimes on occasions years apart, yet still recollected and reiterated anew. These stories were hopeful, not in the sense of being free of loss, fear, or worry, but in the sense that they reshaped losses by punctuating them with points of creativity and moments of connection. These may not be stories of an "aging society crisis," but they are stories of the aging self; they reflect what Mori-san called "the heart of aging" (toshiyori no kokoro), of giving, lightening, and healing. In the last sections I consider the ways this heart of aging allows us to rethink the ways mourning and loss might allow the self to extend beyond the individual, into matters of political subjectivity.

THE AGING SELF

The idea that the aim of a self-narrative or life review in old age is to establish the sense of continuity and self-sameness, to find a constant, steady, and reliable "me" that perdures in spite of changes and losses, is based on a culturally constructed notion of the self that most Japanese people would find difficult to accept. Nonetheless, it has become a popular and persuasive model for many, as evidenced by Sharon Kaufman's (1986) fieldwork on the West Coast of the United States. This "ageless self," as she termed it, was one way in which older people organized and integrated their life choices into a sense of self that often departed from the roles, expectations, and bodily experiences of being "old" (Kaufman 1986, 26–27). Kaufman's work, which introduced empirically grounded critiques of gerontological assumptions of old-age-related changes, spurred the conversation on age away from narratives of decline. It showed that although people may look old from the outside, based on cultural expectations, their selves, and what really mattered, could be experienced as ageless.

Lawrence Cohen (1994), in a larger critical evaluation of the anthropology of aging as a whole, expressed reservations that "The Ageless Self" (and similar work during that time) may not have fully addressed problems of "political and psychodynamic questions of denial and resistance," as well as the cultural and class contexts of the subjects' experiences of aging bodies and selves. Including these facets would require situating subjectivity more fully in the context of power (both the hegemonic power of culture as well as the power of psychological and somatic life), exposing, as Cohen himself did in his ethnography of aging and loss in India, ways that aging "engages in larger debates" of political economy and public culture (1998, xvii). Cohen's critique is also a call for growth in the ethnographic study of aging, one that critically examines culturally and historically situated subjectivities of old age.

The notion of an "ageless self" that could somehow persist independently from the aging body and mind, has little resonance with either everyday social customs or Japanese aesthetic idioms of feeling and experience, which overlap body, mind, and spirit (Lock 1986; 1993; Ozawa de-Silva 2005; 2007). If anything, the Japanese are more predisposed to generate "aging selves," that might exist in temporal simultaneity with other selves. Japanese narrative styles do not assume a singular self that defines the person's identity or a linear emplotment of events (Kabir 2011; Kitayama 1998; Kondo 1990; Rosenberger 1994). Rather, selves are located within human relationships (*ningen kankei*) and bonds (en) of interrelatedness that are upheld through performances and rituals that may require a degree of dissemblance, discipline, formality. An ageless self is a detriment rather than a benefit in this cultural context. These performances extend the self through bonds, enveloping actors in the space of ma in ways that make social identification and action possible. Ma and en are critical for understanding Japanese selves as they emerge through collective engagement and personal connections. It is helpful to think of en through its alternate reading, *fuchi*, which refers to an "edge," a "verge" or "hem"—the place where two things are stitched together at the very limit of their self-sustainability. From the metaphor of stitching together edges, en has come to represent other forms of connectedness that arise through karma, fate, or destiny; it is referred to passively, as something that happens to people, rather than something that is sought or acquired (Rowe 2011).[2]

Longevity allows, among other things, the time for possible selves imagined through relatedness to develop and find harmony with each other (Markus and Herzog 1991; Markus and Nurius 1986). The creative process of mourning and memorial sets the stage for the feelings and experiences of the heart of aging. Over and over, older informants related their desire for memorial with a change of feeling and perceiving the world. As they entered their eighties and nineties, this world became more dependent on the sense of connection with those who had passed, and with acts of passing on. Aging often meant a literal and metaphoric yielding and purging (danshari), actively performing loss. In cases such as that of Nishida-san, a safe, stable sense of interdependence and connection to the hitherto and hereafter of her life narrative eased the process of yielding in old age. For Mori-san, yielding was complicated by a turbulent past, haunting grief, and a complicated memorial system for family. In both cases, cultural images and discourse like obasuteyama and the aging society crisis come to bear at each turning point in the story.

Understanding the ways aging selves maintained these seemingly contradictory orientations of connection and yielding required an examination of aesthetic practices. It is not an exaggeration to say that in Japanese culture, the aesthetic pervades every aspect of being and every human interaction, from speech to dress, from religion to family life, from relationships with the natural world to those with technology (Saito 2007). Aesthetic details, like the weathered masks of a Noh play, reveal the potentiality of the world, stories of human agency and ethical values; or as I was often told, they have a "soul" (*tamashi ga haitte iru*). Aesthetic activities, sensibilities, objects, and landscapes tell a story of the past repeated into the future, placing transience and loss together with a sense of potential, liberating subjectivity. Memorialization at temples and graves, festivals, and butsudan provide ways for older adults to recognize loss and uncertainty in their own lives and to transform this experience of loss into the basis for building a secure connection to the other world, a sense of hope. Hope and comfort in old age come with seeing the faces of the departed, feeling their presence, opening oneself up to their power and care.

Obasuteyama stories present another cultural narrative of old age, one that, like memorialization, hinges on the aesthetic suspense between abandonment and hope. Taken as individual stories, it might be tempting to try to draw didactic lessons or morals from these stories, either on filial piety and respect for the old, or Buddhist views of impermanence, suffering, and detachment. Rather than attempt to circumscribe them in this way, however, I have tried to present them here as a constantly changing loosely bound genre of aesthetic modalities and possibilities that come together and condense into narratives at certain moments of interpretation. Like obasuteyama, the precariousness of living a long life in an aging society emerges in the stories of the abandoned, the burdensome, the isolated, and, like Fujii-san, the disconnected, lonely, and depressed. These stories, I suggest, are not failures of autonomous individuals, nor are they merely the failures of the state, but rather, they are failures on the level of subjectivity, of the ability to mourn in a time of excessive loss.

AGING PERSONHOOD, POLITICS, AND POSSIBILITIES

For older adults, navigating these ambivalent structures and stories of aging and "living out one's natural life" means having the agency, the creativity, and the resources to endure loss and maintain positive bonds to others. Aesthetic practices of aging also open possibilities to challenge political marginalization and encourage a diversity of aging trajectories. In describing the individual lived experiences of older adults in this book, I have tried to show that mourning and memorialization are not merely inner processes, but constitute and are constituted through relationships with others. They are what Amira Mittermaier calls "interlocutory events" (2010, 171) that produce ethical actions and effects. Through memorialization, older adults engage in an economy of care that links them to the dynamics of the family, the community, and the state by engaging models of care, dependence, and place/role of old age in contemporary Japanese society. They represent ways of letting in and keeping out narratives of aging and loss that circulate through these institutions and relationships by cultivating an aesthetic discernment that creates meanings of personal significance in place of symptoms and struggle.

The past decade has seen both a growth in and a heightened backlash against research on "successful aging" (Rowe and Kahn 1987). Although a review of the literature regarding this concept shows diversity in its definition, application, and precise measurement (Depp and Jeste 2006), it is nonetheless a concept that has gained traction in research on aging and well-being (including spirituality) worldwide (Baltes and Smith 2003; Davey and Glasgow 2006). The concept is "seductive," admitted Molly Andrews, but is unfortunately "devoid of social structural critique" (1999, 315). Anthropologist Sarah Lamb has similarly argued that rather than suggesting age-related decline and transience are "failures," gerontology should examine the ways they hold meanings and hint at alternative ways of aging. Lamb's notion of "meaningful decline" (2014, 48), which arose out of research conducted in India and the United States, resonates strongly with the Japanese aesthetics of loss and mourning I have described throughout this book. While I hope that this research initiates a fuller discussion of concepts like successful aging, I do not pretend to have done so with this book. Memorializing the

deceased is not a universal prescription for individual success in aging or anything else. It was what some older Japanese adults told me was important to
them and was behind their fears, concerns, hopes, and moments of comfort in
old age.

I do hope, however, that in recognition of this work, the conversation on
aging develops in such a way that it can provide space for experiences of loss,
mourning, and abandonment as realities of individuals' lives. The changed social
landscape of aging in Japan has produced the necessity to imagine alternative
forms of care and recognition, or as Han puts it, to "draw on a wider network of
dependencies" (2011, 9). This has resulted in changes in caregiver roles, living
arrangements (Long 2009), and communication strategies (Nussbaum and
Fisher 2011) as well as innovations in institutional forms of care such as intergenerational day centers (Thang 2001) and co-housing communities (Godzik
2009). These modifications mirror adaptations in memorialization, expanding
not only the range of ritual forms and monumentation, but also the kinds of
relationships that are potentially drawn into practices, from community and
religious groups to ecological and spiritual relationships (Fujiwara 2012; Inoue
2003; Kawano 2010; Rowe 2011; Suzuki 2000).

While it is easy to focus on the ways that care is rendered inaccessible to older
adults, the proliferation of creative forms of care tells a story of possibility for
new subjectivities. The narratives of older adults in this book show that the cultivation of aesthetic discernment, of a mature sense of transience, interdependence, and openness in everyday life, can ground these subjectivities within a
meaningful sense of being in the world. They also show that this requires not
only the hard work of mourning, but also connections with others that extend
the self into a secure economy of care. A society that cares for the old must also
find ways to care for caregivers, for families, and for communities that link them
to larger systems of connectedness and value.

I end this book on a note of hopeful suspense. The last New Year postcard I
received was from Fujii-san, the woman in the anecdote that began this chapter.
She illustrated her message with a simple hand-drawn self-portrait of herself
smiling sweetly beneath the words "I am 78 years old but my life [is] happy."
At the end of her message Fujii-san wrote,

> These days I am able to live together with my daughter, so I am happy. There
> are a lot of isolated old people (*kodoku rōjin*) in Japan these days, and it's really
> become a problem. I would like to see you if you have the chance to visit Kyoto
> again. Although, I don't think I'll be able to make it to 100. I pray for your
> happiness.

Notes

INTRODUCTION

1. This was also the burial posture of Japanese corpses before the practice of body burial was considered unsanitary and cremation became the only acceptable mortuary procedure (Bernstein 2006).

2. The character for en contains the character for "thread" (ito), as in a thread that ties things together.

3. Source: Bloomberg (2012).

4. The phrase "cultural nightmare" is taken from David Plath (1982, 109), who writes, "By cultural nightmare I mean a condition that we make extraordinary efforts to avoid or deny, for it places a fearsome strain upon our heritage of ideas that bind together human effort and reward. . . . Our secular era, having defined death as a transition to no-where, an alchemy that turns something into nothing, a no-fault accident on life's limited access highway, is left to symbolize old age with metaphors of disaster and terminal disease."

CHAPTER 1 — LOSS, ABANDONMENT, AND AESTHETICS

1. Although the title suggests that the old woman is "aunt" (*oba*), in most versions she is the mother or woman who has acted as a mother to the head of the household (see Yamaori 1997b).

2. This approach to narrative and subjectivity draws on Cheryl Mattingly's (2010) formulation of "narrative phenomenology," Michael Jackson's (2002) "narrative imperative," Markus and Herzog's (1991) "self-concept," and Somers's (1994) concept of "narrative identity." In each of these works, narratives are both personal and shared, imaginative and constrained, embedded in a context of tellers, listeners, and readers, all of whom engage in the "opportunity for a fragmented self-understanding" (Ochs and Capps 1996, 21–22). This narrative process over time produces the intersubjective aging self (Cristofovici 2009, 5–6). "Narrative medicine" (Charon 2009), "illness narratives" (Kleinman 1988), and various works in the field of "narrative gerontology" (Birren and Hedlund 1987; Cohler 1982; Kenyon, Clark, and De Vries 2001) build on the indissolubility of narrative and the embodied self in applied settings. Narrative processes are therefore both fundamental and contingent. They are shored up by cultural institutions, aesthetic tastes,

habits, and norms, and constitute a form of adaptation to uncertainly in social encounters. That said, life disruptions (Becker 1999) and an erosion of support can lead to "narrative foreclosure" (Bohlmeijer et al. 2011). Although there may be normative models of
life's stages, age grades, or "timing," this research is interested in the ways individuals'
experiences converge in what Jennifer Johnson-Hanks called "vital conjunctions" in the
life course (2002).

3. Haiku is a popular form of Japanese poetry that follows a five-seven-five syllable
structure difficult to compose in English. It is meant to capture the essence of the
moment in the fewest words possible, and in this way is not unlike micro-blogging.

4. *Oi hitori / yakusho no oni ga / shine to iu.* Poem reprinted with permission of the poet.

5. This sense of "emptiness" is not to be confused with the Buddhist concept of *ku*,
which refers to a particular ontological philosophy of "emptiness," and "no-self."

6. There are a large number of studies that have examined the relationship among
various aspects of religion, spirituality, aging, well-being, and health in anthropology and
social gerontology. Some of the more recent include Atchley (2009), Bouwer (2010),
Eisenhandler and Thomas (1999), George et al. (2013), Kimble and McFadden (2003),
Krause et al. (2002), Krause et al. (2010), Manning (2012), and Moberg (2001).

7. For more on the history and anthropology of Japanese funerals and mortuary
rituals, see Ambros (2012), Becker (1993; 1999), Bernstein (2006), Inoue (2000; 2003),
Kawano (2005; 2010), Kenny and Gilday (2000), Rowe (2000; 2003; 2011), Sasaki (2002),
Smith (1974), Stone and Walter (2008), Suzuki (2000; 2005; 2013), Takahashi (2004),
Traphagan (2004), Tsu (1984), Tsuji (2006), Van Bremen (1998).

8. *Ekō* is sometimes translated by Buddhist scholars as "transfer of merit" to the souls
of the dead or as "prayers" for the dead. Nakamura-san and his wife obviously have a very
different idea of what this term means, and I have chosen the English word "requiem,"
which still contains the notion of ritual done for the rest of the soul.

CHAPTER 2 — THE WEIGHT OF LOSS

1. Machiya, a traditional Japanese townhouse design common in Kyoto, are sometimes
described as "eel beds" because of their narrow street front façade and long interior.
Junichirō Tanizaki (1977) rhapsodizes about this architectural design and the way it mutes
the indoor lighting, creating aesthetically pleasing effects when combined with
traditional building materials.

2. In Japanese, *Bushi ha onore shijin no tame ni shinu.*

3. The style of the platforms, vases, incense burners, and other paraphernalia decorating the *butsudan* can vary widely according to personal taste, but in more traditional
households, like Nakamura-san's, they are often modeled on the head temple of the
owner's sect affiliation—Zen sect butsudan tend to be simple and sparse, while the True
Pure Land sect butsudan are opulent and glittering.

4. Dead bodies were typically taken out the rear door of the hospital, and Nishida-san
implied that this was a shameful experience. The infant mortality rate in Japan for 1940 was
90 per 1,000 live births. In contrast, the infant mortality rate in 2004 was 2.8 (MHLW 2005).

5. When Nishida-san describes the feeling of taking her child home, the word that she
uses for "heavy" (*omoi*) is actually a homonym of the word "thought" or "consideration"
(*omoi*), as in the words for "empathy" (*omoiyari*) and "remembrance" (*omoide*).

6. Ellen Schattschneider (2003, 21) also notes how a Japanese spirit medium's "heavy
body becomes 'light,'" as she communicates to her ill companion the words of the pos-
sessing divinity." Being possessed, in this case, might be thought of as similar to giving
(up) of oneself to the divinity.

CHAPTER 3 — LANDSCAPES OF MOURNING

1. The closeness to nature depicted resembles Durkheim's ([1912] 1996, 49) argument concerning the emergence of animism from the cult of the dead, in which the spirits of nature become mechanisms to exert agency over the spirits of the dead.

2. I take this term from a personal communication with gerontology and humanities scholar Anne Basting (June 1, 2010), describing her work on creativity and aging titled the Penelope Project, a yearlong collaborative dramatic project with staff, administrators, and clients/residents of an institution for older adults in Wisconsin. The theme of the project was "waiting" and "hope," as symbolized by Penelope's waiting for her husband Odysseus to return from the Trojan War, and her endless project of fending off unwanted suitors by weaving all day and secretly unraveling the work at night. This hidden undoing, I would argue, allowed Penelope to stay in waiting, suspending herself between abandonment and hope—an apt metaphor for the work of memorialization. It also might be compared to the Japanese folktale of the Crane Wife and the "Prohibition of Don't Look" (Kitayama 2007) in Japanese psychotherapy. In this story too the hope is maintained through dissemblance associated with self-sacrifice weaving behind closed doors.

3. While Jizō has principally been studied in relation to mourning rituals for deceased children or aborted fetuses (Hardacre 1997; LaFleur 1992), he also takes a much broader role in the care of all spirits of the dead and is frequently found in cemeteries across Japan. For more on the role of Jizō in Japanese beliefs of the afterlife, see also Bays (2002), Danely (2012a), Glassman (2012).

4. *Namu Amida Butsu* is said in praise of Amida Buddha, or the Buddha of infinite light, who is thought to have made a vow to save all beings who recite the chant.

5. Most supermarkets and even convenience stores carry near the cash registers a rack of inexpensive flower arrangements that are specifically made for graves. They are typically small, hearty arrangements that will keep for a long time (such as carnations or chrysanthemums). Flowers that wither and die quickly (such as roses) or whose blooms drop off the stem all at once (camellias) are generally avoided.

6. Prince Shōtoku (574–622 CE), whom the priest identifies as the founder of Buddhism in Japan, was also regarded as a principal figure in consolidating the power of the fledgling Japanese state (Matsunaga and Matsunaga 1974, 12–17). As symbolic ancestral founders often are, Prince Shōtoku was as much the transmitter of a tradition (Buddhism) as the product of tradition (through the subsequent mythologization of his biography). Interestingly, Nakamura-san himself had a picture of Prince Shōtoku on an heirloom scroll in the special alcove next to the butsudan, and when I inquired about it, he told me that it represented the "founding ancestor" of his "lineage," who did not have a portrait.

7. Yanagita's "unconscious tradition" (*muishikidenshō*) was influenced by European folklore scholars, such as E. B. Tylor, A. Lang, and G. L. Gomme, as well as the work of the Grimm brothers (Itō 2006, 135–139). Yanagita believed that the essences of "Japaneseness" (*nihonjinrashisa*) could be found in the "unconscious" or hidden subtext of songs, stories, and customs that continued throughout Japan.

8. *Kimo ni meizuru* is translated literally here, but some translate it by replacing "liver" with "heart," "mind," or even "memory," in the way that you might say that some experience gets "engraved in your memory" or "taken to heart."

9. In Lacanian terms, we might suggest something similar: that the absence of the "mirroring" mother produced a disavowal, or a failure to accept the lack that perpetuates her desire, resulting in part, in yielding.

10. Of the thirty older adults whom I interviewed, only five married their spouse without an *omiai*. While omiai is often interpreted as "arranged marriage," it is mostly

characterized as a matchmaking chance, with no explicit obligation for marriage, and either party may decline the arrangement (De Vos 1973, 13–19).

CHAPTER 4 —— TEMPORALITIES OF LOSS

1. The National Institute on Aging supports several longitudinal studies of global aging in places like India and Korea (see http://www.nia.nih.gov/research/dbsr/initiative-global-aging). There are many other U.S.-based longitudinal studies, such as the Wisconsin Longitudinal Study, which has been running since 1957, and studies run by the Centers for Disease Control and Prevention (see http://www.cdc.gov/nchs/lsoa.htm).

2. I do not mean to suggest that Japanese culture is singularly unique in their understanding of temporal duality. Stasch (2009), for instance, notes that temporal heterogeneity underlies the expressions of "otherness as relation" that he found among the Korowai of West Papua. Stasch notes that among the Korowai, loss, separation, and abandonment (and their constant obsessive threat) characterized the processes, motions, and dynamics of social relation making: "People's lives are a whirl of the making, measuring and loss of attachment" (2009, 272). The cycle of gift giving cultures noted by Mauss (1990), Munn (1986), and others seems to predispose itself to adopting multiple coexisting temporal orientations as well as selves that can inhabit these worlds without conflict.

3. *Itsu no ma ni ka* is a common expression often translated as "Before I knew it," but more literally it means something like "In what space of time, I couldn't say."

4. Many Shinto shrine festivals typically have a taboo against female participation, especially in regard to contaminating contact with the *mikoshi*, or portable shrines. Although the Gion Matsuri floats are not mikoshi and may have female musicians or other participants on them during the parade, no women are allowed to pull the floats. Shinto has often been described to me as a masculine religion, and care of the household kamidana shrine is more commonly done by the male head of household, while women care for the butsudan (enshrining the household dead). Some Shinto festivals, like the one in my neighborhood, developed smaller mikoshi for women to carry, but this is not common. Often the brawn of matsuri is even outsourced to organized crime groups (*yakuza*), who tend to support a conservative, nationalist Shinto traditionalism, and who are sometimes thought of as supporters of the working-class community (Lebra 1976, 169–189).

5. See Ivy's (1995) description of the role of older people in the revival of a local festival, and Traphagan's (2004) description of male power and authority in a festival in rural Akita.

6. Although the staff with leadership positions are often called on to resolve local disputes or give advice concerning minor neighborhood matters, the major activities of the *chōnai* association are things such as park maintenance, litter removal, and organizing holiday events and local festivals. Neighborhoods are more or less defined as school districts (*gakku*), and each school district is composed of a number of block units (*chō*), then units (*kumi*) each with its own type of self-governing association (see also Akiyama 1975; Nakagawa 1980).

7. See Hashimoto (1996, 13–17) on the "social contract" in caregiving relationships built on reciprocal gifts economies.

8. Hirokazu Miyazaki (2004) finds religious models mediate this exchange, holding agency in abeyance through deferral to superhuman agents. We might say that ancestor memorial in Japan serves a similar function, but this might be jumping ahead.

9. In this last case, the great-aunt was Nakamura-san's father's father's younger sister. Her husband was an apprentice carpenter under the tutelage of Nakamura-san's

paternal grandfather and not only adopted the household name, but also married into the family.

10. While *Ohaka ga Nai!* is a bit of a light-hearted comedy on the problems of finding a suitable final resting place, the salesman's remark is not meant to be out of the ordinary. Rather, it is humorous because it exposes the assumptions that Japanese people already have about the closeness of the spirits, including sharing in food and drinks like beer or sake that might be left at the grave for offerings. Death and the rituals that surround it seem to be rich sources of comedy in Japan, as seen in popular movies like *Osōshiki* (The Funeral, 1990) and *Nezu no Ban* (A Longest Night, 2001), about the vigil. Films about memorialization, in my experience, tend toward drama rather than comedy: for example, *Mogari no Mori* (The Mourning Forest, 2007), *Aruitemo, Aruitemo* (Still Walking, 2008), *Okuribito* (Departures, 2008).

CHAPTER 5 — PASSING IT ON

1. PET scans suggests the possibility that hoarders may possess a different pathophysiology than other OCD patients (Saxena et al. 2004; Saxena and Maidment 2007). Other studies have found that there is a high degree of hoarding in family history (84 percent among first-degree relatives in one study; Zhang et al. 2002). Diagnosis for compulsive hoarding has been verified for Japan by Matsunaga et al. (2008).

2. See Randall and Kenyon (2004) for an extensive review of narrative and time in gerontology.

3. Celebrated on September 19 every year, Respect for the Aged Day was originally celebrated only in Hyogo prefecture on September 15 and was called Older Person's Day. This became nationally celebrated from 1938 as Day of the Aged. In 1966 it became a national civic holiday and was renamed once again Respect for the Aged Day (Kawabata et al. 2001, 12). Half a year prior to the establishment of Respect for the Aged Day, the suicide of an elderly person living alone sparked discussion in the Japanese cabinet, prompting then Prime Minister Sato to call for an increase in retirement homes and other elder care facilities.

4. "Day service" provides inexpensive morning to afternoon services (baths, activities, meals, and occasional field trips) to eligible older adults who lack the capacity to participate in the more active and independence-oriented senior welfare centers, but who do not require full-time nursing care or hospitalization.

5. "Kōreisha tte Nan Sai Kara?" ("At what age does 'old age' begin?") (*Asahi Shinbun,* 2005). A survey in 2005 by the Ministry of Labor found that more than 40 percent of respondents in all age ranges considered old age to start around or after seventy-five. Those in the sixty-five to seventy-four category were the most likely to respond seventy, and those older than seventy-five were the most likely to respond seventy-five or older, indicating a self-identification beginning at about seventy with old age. All survey respondents noted, besides chronological age, "loosing physical ability" as the chief marker of having reached old age. The age at which most people think old age begins has increased since the last survey was taken, in 1999.

6. 2004 White Paper pt. II, p. 309, table 2-(2)-9. Respondents could answer up to three categories. Full results at http://www.mhlw.go.jp/wp/hakusyo/roudou/05/dl/04-03.pdf.

7. See Marcel Mauss, who writes in *The Gift* (1990) that "by giving one is giving *oneself*— one's person and one's goods to others" (1990, 46) and, elsewhere, that "the producer who carries on exchange feels once more—he has always felt it, but this time he does so acutely— that he is exchanging more than a product of hours of working time, but that he is giving something of himself—his time, his life" (77). Both of these are telling passages and can be

linked to Nancy Munn's (1986) observations on value transformation and exchange, especially in regard to the way it shapes experienced temporalities and subjectivities.

8. *Kawaigaru* is difficult to translate but refers to the feeling of care and love that one might give to something or someone small and helpless. *Aijō* is a more general term for love, literally meaning "the emotion of love." Nishida-san also uses the term *daiji ni suru,* which, when referring to persons, means to acknowledge and appreciate, and is less emotionally inflected as the prior two terms.

CHAPTER 6 — AESTHETICS OF FAILED SUBJECTIVITY

1. Because of the poor conditions in Iwate and Miyazaki prefectures after the earthquake and tsunami of March 2011, these prefectures were excluded.

2. This practice may be associated with geographic region or sectarian affiliation. When I visited an island off the coast of the Ise Peninsula (Mie prefecture) I noticed that a number of gravestones were engraved with the name of both spouses (the living spouse having the letters filled in with vermilion). Although I visited several cemeteries in Kyoto, it was extremely rare that I would see even one gravestone like this. Many members of the Jōdo Shinshu sect often receive the equivalent of a posthumous name (*hōmyo* rather than *kaimyo*) before they die, but perhaps because of the emphasis on laity, I have never seen the names of the living engraved on the stones or memorial tablets of any Shinshu followers.

3. In 1999 it was estimated that the average price for receiving a Buddhist posthumous name in the Kinki region (Kyoto and Osaka) was about 400,000 yen, slightly lower than the 498,000 yen average for Japan, according to a survey by the National Funeral Association of Japan (Zensōren).

4. *Shugyō* is closely associated with the notion of selfless discipline (Schattschneider 2003; Kondo 1990) and, while rooted in Buddhist ascetic training rituals, is also used for nonreligious forms of intense training where one is forced to put aside one's own emotions for the sake of a larger goal. One priest I met said that all women who give birth have undergone shugyō. Shugyō is also the term used to describe the soul's journey into the afterlife.

5. Specific policy matters related to aging in Japan in recent decades have been extensively reviewed by others, including Campbell (2000), Coulmas (2007), Knight and Traphagan (2003), Long (2000; 2009), Maeda (2000), Matsutani (2006), and Tamiya et al. (2011).

6. Japanese characters often have multiple phonetic readings that can be discerned only through context or the use of *furigana,* transcribed syllables written alongside the character. The character for *ie* has many phonetic possibilities, but *uchi* is not among them. Rather, *uchi* and *ie* bear similar meanings only for "home," with no other linguistic connection. The poster uses a common linguistic tool to make a link between the words based on a new semantic construction.

7. The Kokinshu, a tenth-century imperial poetry anthology, lists the following appropriate poem: "If only, when one heard that old age was coming One could bolt the door Answer 'not at home' And refuse to meet him!"

8. As advertised on their website, the Smile campaign also recalls similar suggestions to improve social relationships and intergenerational communication, such as practicing "greetings" (*aisatsu*). Some convenience stores have made additional efforts to draw in older adults by employing older workers, providing "generational" foods more suitable to the tastes of older people, and providing larger areas for sitting and socializing within the store.

CHAPTER 7 — CARE AND RECOGNITION

1. *Otoshidama* is also a way for extended families to share wealth by giving and receiving gifts among branch families. Interestingly, otoshidama used to be mochi rather than money.

2. Murayama's interpretation of the otoshidama is even stronger in light of Yanagita Kunio's assertion that the identity of the New Year's *kami* (*toshikami*) must be a kami of good fortune, and therefore "there may not be *Kami* other than ancestral spirits who can be relied upon to protect and support each [family]" (Yanagita [1946] 1970, 57). Furthermore, Yanagita, having made the association between the New Year's kami and the ancestral spirits notes that in some parts of Japan, the "New Year's deity [was] the old man of good fortune" (Yanagita [1946] 1970, 58). Elsewhere New Year's is celebrated with Grandfather New Year, whom Yanagita compares to Santa Claus—a gift-giving and life-giving old man (Yanagita [1946] 1970, 58, see also Yamaori 1990, 72 for comparison of Japanese deities to Santa Claus).

3. A bodhisattva is an enlightened being who remains in this world in order to aid all beings toward the path of enlightenment. Like saints, they might act as intermediating figures in a time of the degradation of the dharma, when enlightenment for ordinary people is considered too difficult. They are also petitioned for this-worldly benefits, such as safety from calamity and disease or the prosperity of the household and ancestors.

4. Indeed the "hidden Christians" of southern Japan kept statues of Mary disguised as Kannon (Mullins 1998, 241n31), often represented holding a child.

5. In contrast to other "ghost stories" I had heard from other informants in Japan, these visions were all isolated incidences; they were not repeated unwelcome visits by unconnected spirits, and they did not indicate threat or the need for an exorcism. Such stories did circulate among the young and the old alike, but I believe they have different functions that require other approaches. See Iwasaka and Toelken (1994).

6. See Mittermaier's (2010, 147–148) analysis of this type of dream typified in Freud's interpretation of the boy on fire.

7. A woman working in a modern funeral home confirmed that this belief is still quite strong, and funerals are rarely scheduled on these days. One man told me that should someone have his or her funeral on "tomobiki," a doll or effigy will be placed in the casket as a substitute to satisfy the spirit. See also Kalland (1991).

8. While there is bound to be individual variation, I found it striking in the cases of the men and women I spoke with that hotoke and buddhas were frequently associated with mother figures, which in the case of Sato-san and Mori-san at least were symbols of dependence and legitimate care (*amae*). Grossberg (1999) argued that in the case of at least one Buddhist woman's spiritual beliefs, the Buddha (Amida) served as a substitute for working through mourning related to the father. While this interpretation seems consistent with some interpretations of Japanese ancestor veneration beliefs (cf. Spiro 1994), I do not think such an interpretation is apt in these cases, perhaps because of the nature of the memorialized persons themselves or other life course circumstances.

9. This kit of divination tools is a version of the Chinese Yijing oracle, referred to as the "yarrow stalk method" (*I Ching* [1950] 1967, 721–724).

10. Hozumi (1901), for instance, writes that in Japanese theater "when a ghost appears to the parent, sons, daughters, friends or lovers, those who meet it never show signs of dread, but those of joy for the meeting, mingled perhaps with sorrow and sympathy" (quoted in Plath 1964, 310). Elsewhere Hozumi connects this sentiment to Japanese ancestor memorial: "The theory of the 'dread of ghosts' and 'ghost-propitiation' seems unnatural so far as the worship of ancestors is concerned; and however strange the expression

may sound to Western ears, I deem it nearer the truth to say that it was the 'Love of Ghosts' which gave rise to the custom of ancestor worship" (1901, 54).

CHAPTER 8 — THE HEART OF AGING

1. The procession of the Jidai Matsuri departs from the grounds of the old Imperial Palace and ends at Heian Shrine. Like the Aoi Matsuri (chapter 1), which also begins at the palace, the departure of the procession can be seen as a birthing, since the emperor is thought to be the mythic divine origin of all Japanese people, and remains a motherly figure even today (Bellah 2003, 176). Heian Shrine (est. 1895) is unique among most shrines in that it is considered a city-wide rather than a strictly local shrine. The deities enshrined there are two former emperors (Kanmu 737–806, and Kōmei 1831–1867), making it, in a way, a mausoleum—a proper ending to the procession of the ages from birth to death (and rebirth), but importantly, one accomplished only as a three-generational family.

2. On the other hand, "cutting ties" is something that requires human agency, often in ritual forms, such as the case of divorce or exorcism.

Bibliography

Agamben, Giorgio. 1998. *Homo Sacer: Sovereign Power and Bare Life*. Stanford, CA: Stanford University Press.

Akiyama Kunizō. 1975. *Kyoto "chō" no Kenkyū* [Research on Kyoto's "chō"]. Tokyo: Hosei University Press.

Allison, Anne. 1996. *Permitted and Prohibited Desires*. Boulder, CO: Westview.

————. 2006. *Millennial Monsters: Japanese Toys and the Global Imagination*. Berkeley: University of California Press.

————. 2012. "Ordinary Refugees: Social Precarity and Soul in 21st Century Japan." *Anthropological Quarterly* 85 (2): 345–370.

————. 2013. *Precarious Japan*. Durham, NC: Duke University Press.

Ambros, Barbara. 2012. *Bones of Contention: Animals and Religion in Modern Japan*. Honolulu: University of Hawaii Press.

Andrews, Molly. 1999. "The Seductiveness of Agelessness." *Ageing and Society* 19: 301–318.

Aoki, Mizuho. 2012. "36 Foreign Caregivers Pass Qualification Exam." *Japan Times*, March 29.

Ariyoshi Sawako. 1972. *The Twilight Years*. M. Tahara, trans. New York: Kodansha International.

Asahi Shinbun. 2004. "Kōreisha gyakutai no 'kagai sha,' 3 wari ga musuko kōrōshō chōsa" ["Perpetrators" of elder abuse, 30 percent are sons, Ministry of Labor study]. April 19.

————. 2005. "Kōreisha tte Nan Sai kara? '70 sai' Hansu '75 sai' ni wari" [When does senior citizen begin? Half say "70" twenty percent "75."]. July 26.

————. 2013. "Yoshien Sabisu Ikan Shukusho" [Support Benefits Services to transfer authority, restrict]. November 13, 1.

Ashkenazi, Michael. 1993. *Matsuri: Festivals of Japanese Town*. Honolulu: University of Hawaii Press.

Associated Press. 2013. "Aso Says Elderly Should Be Allowed to 'Hurry Up and Die.'" *Japan Today*, January 22. http://www.japantoday.com/category/politics/view/aso-says-elderly-should-be-allowed-to-hurry-up-and-die, accessed September 3, 2013.

Atchley, Robert C. 2009. *Spirituality and Aging*. Baltimore: Johns Hopkins University Press.

Bachnik, Jane M. 1994. "Indexing Self and Society in Japanese Family Organization." In *Situating Meaning: Inside and Outside in Japanese Self, Society, and Language*,

Jane M. Bachnik and Charles J. Quinn, Jr., eds. Pp. 143–167. Princeton, NJ: Princeton University Press.

Baek, Jin. 2006. "Mujō, or Ephemerality: The Discourse of the Ruins in Post-war Japanese Architecture." *Architectural Theory Review* 11 (2): 66–76.

Baltes, Paul B., and Jacqui Smith. 2003. "New Frontiers in the Future of Aging: From Successful Aging of the Young Old to the Dilemmas of the Fourth Age." *Gerontology* 49 (2) (March): 123–135.

Barthes, Roland. 1982. *Empire of Signs.* Richard Howard, trans. New York: Hill and Wang.

Battaglia, Debbora. 1990. *On the Bones of the Serpent: Person, Memory, and Mortality in Sabarl Island Society.* Chicago: University of Chicago Press.

Bays, Jan Chozen. 2002. *Jizō Bodhisattva: A Modern Healing and Traditional Buddhist Practice.* Boston: Tuttle.

Becker, Carl B. 1993. *Breaking the Circle: Death and the Afterlife in Buddhism.* Carbondale: Southern Illinois University Press.

———. 1999. "Aging, Dying, and Bereavement in Contemporary Japan." *International Journal of Group Tensions* 28 (1/2): 59–83.

Becker, Gaylene. 1997. *Disrupted Lives: How People Create Meaning in a Chaotic World.* Berkeley: University of California Press.

Befu, Harumi. 1991. *Hegemony of Homogeneity: An Anthropological Analysis of "Nihonjinron."* Portland, OR: Trans Pacific Press.

Bellah, Robert. 2003. *Imagining Japan: The Japanese Tradition and Its Modern Interpretation.* Berkeley: University of California Press.

Benedict, Ruth. [1946] 1974. *The Chrysanthemum and the Sword: Patterns of Japanese Culture.* New York: New American Library.

Bernstein, Andrew. 2006. *Modern Passings: Death Rites, Politics, and Social Change in Imperial Japan.* Honolulu: University of Hawaii Press.

Bethel, Diana Lynn. 1992. "Life in Obasuteyama." In *Japanese Social Organization,* Takie Sugiyama Lebra, ed. Pp. 109–134. Honolulu: University of Hawaii Press.

Biehl, João. 2005. *Vita: A Life in Social Abandonment.* Berkeley: University of California Press.

Biehl, João Guilherme, Byron Good, and Arthur Kleinman. 2007. *Subjectivity: Ethnographic Investigations.* Berkeley: University of California Press.

Biggs, Simon, Ariella Lowenstein, and Jon Hendricks, eds. 2003. *The Need for Theory: Critical Approaches to Social Gerontology.* Amityville, NY: Baywood.

Birren, James E., and Bonnie Hedlund. 1987. "Contribution of Autobiography to Developmental Psychology." In *Contemporary Topics in Developmental Psychology,* Nancy Eisenberg, ed. Pp. 394–415. New York: John Wiley.

Bloomberg. 2012. "Bloomberg's List of Rapidly Aging Countries 2012." http://www.bloomberg.com/visual-data/best-and-worst/most-rapidly-aging-countries, accessed November 17, 2013.

Bohlmeijer, E. T., G. J. Westerhof, W. Randall, T. Tromp, and G. Kenyon. 2011. "Narrative Foreclosure in Later Life: Preliminary Considerations for a New Sensitizing Concept." *Journal of Aging Studies* 25 (4) (December): 364–370.

Bokhoven, J. 2005. *Sōgi to Butsudan: Senzo Saishi no Minzokugakuteki Kenkyū* [Funerals and butsudan: Ancestor veneration and folklore studies research]. Tokyo: Iwata Shoin.

Bouwer, Johan, ed. 2010. *Successful Ageing, Spirituality and Meaning: Multidisciplinary Perspectives.* Walpole, MA: Peeters.

Brown, Naomi. 2003. "Under One Roof: The Evolving Story of Three Generation Housing in Japan." In *Demographic Change and the Family in Japan's Aging Society,*

John W. Traphagan and John C. Knight, eds. Pp. 53–71. Albany: State University of New York Press.

Brumann, Christoph. 2013. *Tradition, Democracy, and the Townscape of Kyoto: Claiming a Right to the Past* (Japan Anthropology Workshop). New York: Routledge.

Buruma, Ian. 1984. *Behind the Mask: On Sexual Demons, Sacred Mothers, Transvestites, Gangsters and Other Japanese Cultural Heroes.* New York: Pantheon Books.

Butler, Robert N. 2002. *Why Survive? Being Old in America.* Baltimore: Johns Hopkins University Press.

Campbell, John Creighton. 2000. "Changing Meanings of Frail Old People and the Japanese Welfare State." In *Caring for the Elderly in Japan and United States: Practices and Policies,* Susan O. Long, ed. Pp. 82–97. London: Routledge.

———. 2008. "The Health of Japan's Medical Care System: 'Patients Adrift?'" *Japan Focus,* April 26. http://japanfocus.org/-John_Creighton-Campbell/2730, accessed April 24, 2009.

Casto, K. L., S. Krippner, and R. Tartz. 1999. "The Identification of Spiritual Content in Dream Reports." *Anthropology of Consciousness* 10 (1): 43–51.

Caudill, William, and Helen Weinstein. 1969. "Maternal Care and Infant Behavior in Japan and America." *Psychiatry* 32: 12–43.

CDI. 1973. *Kyoto Shomin Seikatsushi* [History of the lifestyle of common people of Kyoto]. Kyoto: Kyoto Shinyō Kinko.

Charon, Rita. 2009. "Narrative Medicine as Witness for the Self-Telling Body." *Journal of Applied Communication Research* 37 (2) (May): 118–131.

CIA. 2013. *World Factbook.* https://www.cia.gov/library/publications/the-world-factbook/rankorder/2102rank.html?countryname=Japan&countrycode=ja&regionCode=eas&rank=3#ja, accessed November 30, 2013.

City Planning for Kyoto City. 2005. *City Planning Section, City Planning Bureau, Kyoto City.* Kyoto, Japan.

Cohen, Lawrence. 1994. "Old Age: Cultural and Critical Perspectives." *Annual Review of Anthropology* 23: 153–178.

———. 1998. *No Aging in India: Alzheimer's, the Bad Family and Other Modern Things.* Berkeley: University of California Press.

Cohler, Bertram. 1982. "Personal Narrative and the Life Course." In *Life Span Development and Behavior,* Paul B. Baltes and Orville G. Brim, eds. Vol. 4, pp. 205–241. New York: Academic Press.

Cole, Jennifer, and Deborah Durham, eds. 2007. *Generations and Globalization: Youth, Age, and Family in the New World Economy.* Bloomington: University of Indiana Press.

Cole, Thomas R. 1992. *The Journey of Life: A Cultural History of Aging in America.* New York: Cambridge University Press.

Conklin, Beth. 2001. *Consuming Grief: Compassionate Cannibalism in an Amazonian Society.* Austin: University of Texas Press.

Cornell, Laurell L. 1991. "The Deaths of Old Women: Folklore and Differential Mortality in Nineteenth-Century Japan." In *Recreating Japanese Women, 1600–1945,* Gail L. Bernstein, ed. Pp. 71–87. Berkeley: University of California Press.

Coulmas, Florian. 2007. *Population Decline and Ageing in Japan—The Social Consequences.* New York: Routledge.

Craft, Lucy. 2010. "Tracking Down Japan's Missing Centenarians." National Public Radio, September 20. http://www.npr.org/templates/story/story.php?storyId=129992827, accessed July 10, 2012.

Crapanzano, Vincent. 2004. *Imaginative Horizons: An Essay in Literary-Philosophical Anthropology.* Chicago: University of Chicago Press.

Creighton, Millie R. 1990. "Revisiting Shame and Guilt Cultures: A Forty-Year Pilgrimage." *Ethos* 18 (3): 279–307.

Cristofovici, Anca. 2009. *Touching Surfaces: Photographic Aesthetics, Temporality, Aging.* Kenilworth: Rodopi.

Cruikshank, Margaret. 2009. *Learning to Be Old: Gender, Culture, and Aging.* Lanham, MD: Rowman and Littlefield.

Csordas, Thomas. 1994. *The Sacred Self: A Cultural Phenomenology of Healing.* Berkeley: University of California Press.

Curtis, Bruce. 2002. "Foucault on Governmentality and Population: The Impossible Discovery." *Canadian Journal of Sociology* 27 (4): 505–533.

Daily Yomiuri. 2005. "Western Gravestones Gaining in Popularity." September 10, A1.

Dalby, Liza C. 1983. *Geisha.* Berkeley: University of California Press.

Danely, Jason. 2011. "Art, Aging, and Abandonment." *Journal of Aging, Humanities, and the Arts* 4 (1): 4–17.

———. 2012a. "Encounters with Jizō-san in an Aging Japan." In *Studying Buddhism in Practice* (Studying Religions in Practice Series), John Harding, ed. Pp. 118–129. New York: Routledge.

———. 2012b. "Repetition and the Symbolic in Contemporary Japanese Ancestor Memorial Ritual." *Journal of Ritual Studies* 26 (1): 19–32.

———. 2013. "Temporality, Spirituality, and the Life Course in an Aging Japan." In *Transitions and Transformations: Cultural Perspectives on Aging and the Life Course,* Caitrin Lynch and Jason Danely, eds. Pp. 107–119. New York: Berghahn Books.

Dannefer, Dale. 2003. "Cumulative Advantage/Disadvantage and the Life Course: Cross-Fertilizing Age and Social Science Theory." *Journal of Gerontology* 58B (6): S327–S337.

Davey, Judith, and Kathy Glasgow. 2006. "Positive Ageing—A Critical Analysis." *Policy Quarterly* 2 (4): 21–27.

Deal, William, and Peter J. Whitehouse. 2000. "Concepts of Person in Alzheimer's Disease: Considering Japanese Notions of a Relational Self." In *Caring for the Elderly in Japan and United States: Practices and Policies,* Susan O. Long, ed. Pp. 318–333. London: Routledge.

de Certeau, Michel. 1984. *The Practice of Everyday Life.* Steven Rendall, trans. Berkeley: University of California Press.

DeFalco, Amelia. 2010. *Uncanny Subjects: Aging in Contemporary Narrative.* Columbus: Ohio State University Press.

Depp, C. A., and Dilip V. Jeste. 2006. "Definitions and Predictors of Successful Aging: A Comprehensive Review of Larger Quantitative Studies." *American Journal of Geriatric Psychiatry* 14 (1): 6–20.

De Vos, George A. 1973. *Socialization for Achievement.* Berkeley: University of California Press.

Doi, Takeo. 1973. *The Anatomy of Dependence.* John Bester, trans. Tokyo: Kodansha.

Donow, H. S. 1990. "Two Approaches to the Care of an Elder Parent: A Study of Robert Anderson's *I Never Sang for My Father* and Sawako Ariyoshi's *Kokotsu No Hito* [The Twilight Years]." Gerontologist 30 (4): 486–90.

Dore, Ronald P. 1958. *City Life in Japan: A Study of a Tokyo Ward.* Berkeley: University of California Press.

Dougill, John. 2006. *Kyoto: A Cultural History.* Oxford: Oxford University Press.

Drusini, Andrea G. 2006. "The Hiding-Places of Health: The Elderly in the Age of Technique." *Studies in Historical Anthropology* 4 (2004): 17–24.

Durkheim, Éemile. 1996. *The Elementary Forms of the Religious Life*. Karen E. Fields, trans. New York: Free Press.

Eisenhandler, Susan A., and L. Eugene Thomas. 1999. "Introduction: Research on Religion and Aging—Mapping an Uncharted Territory." In *Religion, Belief, and Spirituality in Late Life*, L. E. Thomas and S. A. Eisenhandler, eds. Pp. i–xvii. New York: Springer.

Erikson, Erik H., Jane M. Erikson, and Helen Q. Kivnick. 1986. *Vital Involvement in Old Age: The Experience of Old Age in Our Time*. New York: Norton.

Fackler, Martin. 2010. "Japan, Checking on Its Oldest, Finds Many Gone." *New York Times*, August 15.

Fitzpatrick, Michael. 2011. "No, Robot: Japan's Elderly Frail to Welcome Their Robot Overlords." *BBC News Tokyo*, February 3, 2011. http://www.bbc.co.uk/news/business-12347219, accessed August 17, 2013.

Fortes, Meyer. 1967. *African Political Systems*. London: International African Institute, Oxford University Press.

———. 1976. "An Introductory Commentary." In *Ancestors*, William H. Newell, ed. Pp. 1–16. The Hague: Mouton.

Francis, Doris, Leonie Kellaher, and Georgina Neophytou. 2005. *The Secret Cemetery*. New York: Berg.

Fridell, Wilbur M. 1973. *Japanese Shrine Mergers 1906–12*. Tokyo: Sophia University Press.

Fujiwara, Kuniko. 2012. "Rethinking Successful Aging from the Perspective of Jizō with Replaceable Heads." *Anthropology and Aging Quarterly* 33 (3): 104–111.

———. 2013. "Coping with Anxiety in a Long-Living Society: Elderly Japanese Pilgrims and Their Life Design for 'Living Happily Ever After.'" In *Anthropology of Aging and Well-Being: Search for the Space and Time to Cultivate Life Together* (Senri Ethnological Studies 80), Nanami Suzuki, ed. Pp. 109–122. Osaka: National Museum of Ethnology.

Fukawa, Tetsuo, and Itaru Sato. 2009. "Projection of Pension, Health, and Long-Term Care Expenditures in Japan through Macro Simulation." *Japanese Journal of Social Security Policy* 8 (1) (August): 33–42.

Fukue, Natsuko. 2010. "234,000 Centenarians in Registries Are Missing, Lack of Periodic Followup and Slack Record-Keeping Blamed." *Japan Times*, September 10.

Fukue, Natsuko, and Mizuho Aoki. 2010. "Cities Scrambling to Find Centenarians." *Japan Times*, August 6.

Fukuzawa Shichihiro. [1956] 1981. *Narayama Bushikō; Fuefukigawa* [The ballad of Narayama]. Tokyo: Shinchosha.

Garner, Dwight. 2009. "Books of the Times—Manifesto of a Comic Book Rebel—Yoshiro Tatsumi." *New York Times*, April 14.

Garon, Sheldon M. 1998. *Molding Japanese Minds: The State in Everyday Life*. Princeton, NJ: Princeton University Press.

George, Linda K., Warren A. Kinghorn, Harold G. Koenig, Patricia Gammon, and Dan G. Blazer. 2013. "Why Gerontologists Should Care about Empirical Research on Religion and Health: Transdisciplinary Perspectives." *Gerontologist* 53 (6) (February 26): 898–906.

Gerhart, Karen M. 2009. *The Material Culture of Death in Medieval Japan*. Honolulu: University of Hawaii Press.

Glascock, Anthony P., and Susan Feinman. 1981. "Social Asset or Social Burden: An Analysis of the Treatment for the Aged in Non-industrial Societies." In *Dimensions: Aging, Culture, and Health*, Christine L. Fry, ed. Pp. 13–21. New York: Praeger.

Glassman, Hank. 2012. *The Face of Jizo: Image and Cult in Medieval Japanese Buddhism*. Honolulu: University of Hawaii Press.

Godzik, M. 2009. "Choosing New Places to Live: Alternative Housing Solutions for the Elderly in Japan." Paper presented at the Fourth Australasian Housing Researchers Conference, Sydney, August 5–7, 2009.

Goldman, Marlene. 2012. "Aging, Old Age, Memory, Aesthetics: Introduction to Special Issue." *Occasion: Interdisciplinary Studies in the Humanities* 4 (May): 1–6.

Good, Byron. 2012. "Phenomenology, Psychoanalysis, and Subjectivity in Java." *Ethos* 40 (1): 24–36.

Good, Mary-Jo DelVecchio, Sandra Theresa Hyde, Sarah Pinto, and Byron Good. 2008. *Postcolonial Disorders*. Berkeley: University of California Press.

Graham, Janice E., and Peter H. Stephenson, eds. 2010. *Contesting Aging and Loss*. Toronto: University of Toronto Press.

Grossberg, John Barth. 1999. "Formulating Attitudes toward death: A Case Study of a Japanese Jōdō Shin Buddhist Woman." In *Lives in Motion: Composing Circles of Self and Community in Japan*, Susan O. Long, ed. Pp. 207–242. Ithaca, NY: Cornell University East Asia Program.

Gullette, Margaret Morganroth. 2004. *Aged by Culture*. Chicago: University of Chicago Press.

Gutmann, David. 1987. *Reclaimed Powers: Toward a New Psychology of Men and Women in Later Life*. New York: Basic Books.

Guyer, Jane, and Kabiru Salami. 2013. "Life Courses of Indebtedness." In *Transitions and Transformations: Cultural Perspectives on Aging and the Life Course*, Caitrin Lynch and Jason Danely, eds. Pp. 206–217. New York: Berghahn Books.

Hallam, Elizabeth, Jennifer L. Hockey, and Glennys Howarth. 1999. *Beyond the Body: Death and Social Identity*. New York: Routledge.

Hallowell, Irving. 1937. "Temporal Orientation in Western Civilization and in Pre-literate Society." *American Anthropologist* 39 (4) (October–December): 647–670.

Hamabata, Mathew. 1990. *The Crested Kimono: Power and Love in the Japanese Business Family*. Ithaca, NY: Cornell University Press.

Han, Clara. 2011. "Symptoms of Another Life: Time, Possibility, and Domestic Relations in Chile's Credit Economy." *Cultural Anthropology* 26 (1): 7–32.

Han, Shin-Kap, and Phyllis Moen. 1999. "Clocking Out: Temporal Patterning of Retirement 1." *American Journal of Sociology* 105 (1): 191–236.

Hardacre, Helen. 1989. *Shintō and the State, 1868–1988*. Princeton, NJ: Princeton University Press.

———. 1997. *Marketing the Menacing Fetus in Japan*. Berkeley: University of California Press.

Hareven, Tamara K. 2002. *Silk Weavers of Kyoto: Family and Work in a Changing Traditional Industry*. Berkeley: University of California Press.

Hart, Keith, Jean-Louis Laville, and Antonio David Cattani. 2010. *The Human Economy*. Cambridge: Polity.

Hashimoto, Akiko. 1996. *The Gift of Generations: Japanese and American Perspectives on Aging and the Social Contract*. Cambridge: Cambridge University Press.

———. 2009. "Blondie, Sazae, and Their Storied Successors: Japanese Families in Newspapers Comics." In *Imagined Families, Lived Families: Culture and Kinship in Contemporary Japan*, Akiko Hashimoto and John W. Traphagan, eds. Pp. 15–32. Albany: State University of New York Press.

Hattori, K., M. A. McCubbin, and D. N. Ishida. 2006. "Concept Analysis of Good Death in the Japanese Community." *Journal of Nursing Scholarship* 38 (2): 165–170.

Hazan, Haim. 1980. *The Limbo People: A Study of the Constitution of the Time Universe among the Aged.* Boston: Routledge Kegan Paul.

Hendricks, Jon. 2003. "Structure and Identity—Mind the Gap: Toward a Personal Resource Model of Successful Aging." In *The Need for Theory: Critical Approaches to Social Gerontology*, Simon Biggs, Ariella Lowenstein, and Jon Hendricks, eds. Pp. 63–87. Amityville, NY: Baywood.

Hendricks, Jon, and Mildred Seltzer. 1986. "Explorations in Time." *American Behavioral Scientist* 29 (6): 653–661.

Hendry, Joy. 1986. *Becoming Japanese.* Honolulu: University of Hawaii Press.

———. 1995. *Wrapping Culture: Politeness, Presentation, and Power in Japan and Other Societies.* Oxford: Clarendon.

Hertz, Richard. 1960. *Death and the Right Hand.* B. Needham and C. Needham, trans. Glencoe, IL: Free Press.

Hiratate, Hideaki. 2008. "Patients Adrift: The Elderly and Japan's Life-Threatening Health Reforms." *Japan Focus*, March 11. http://japanfocus.org/-Hiratate-Hideaki/2693, accessed July 16, 2012.

Hirato, Dennis. 1999. "Plain Words on the Pure Land Way." In *Religions of Japan in Practice*, George J. Tanabe Jr., ed. Pp. 269–279. Princeton, NJ: Princeton University Press.

Hockey, Jenny, and Allison James. 1993. *Growing Up and Growing Old: Ageing and Dependency in the Life Course.* London: Sage.

Hockey, Jenny, Jeanne Katz, and Neil Small, eds. 2001. *Grief, Mourning, and Death Ritual.* Hull, UK: Open University Press.

Hoffman, Michael. 2010. "From Being Accorded the Highest Confucian Respect to Being Left to Die, the Historical Lot of Japan's Elderly Makes an Eye-opening Tale." *Japan Times*, September 12.

Hollan, Douglas W., and Jane C. Wellenkamp. 1994. *Contentment and Suffering: Culture and Experience in Toraja.* New York: Columbia University Press.

Hori, Ichiro. 1959. "Japanese Folk Beliefs." *American Anthropologist* 61 (3): 405–424.

———. 1968. *Folk Religion in Japan: Continuity and Change.* Chicago: University of Chicago Press.

Hosoda, Ayako. 2012. "Women's Life Cycles Depicted in Kumano Beliefs." *Annual of the Institute of Thanatology, Toyo Eiwa University* 145–183.

Hozumi, Nobushige. 1901. *Ancestor-Worship and Japanese Law.* Tokyo: Z.P. Maruya.

Huang, Evelyn. 2011. "Obasuteyama: Care or Abandonment?" Paper presented at the conference of the Association of Japanese Literature Studies, November 5.

I Ching or Book of Changes. [1950] 1967. R. Wilhelm and C. F. Baynes, trans. Princeton, NJ: Princeton University Press.

Iida Fumihiko. 1999. *Ikigai no Sozo "Umarekawari no Kagaku" ga Jinsei wo Kaeru* [The creation of Ikigai: "The science of reincarnation" will change your life]. Tokyo: PHP Kenkyūjo.

Ikegami, Naoki, Byung-Kwang Yoo, Hideki Hashimoto, Masatoshi Matsumoto, Hiroya Ogata, Akira Babazono, Ryo Watanabe, et al. 2011. "Japanese Universal Health Coverage: Evolution, Achievements, and Challenges." *Lancet* 378 (9796): 1106–15.

Ilye Athico. 2001. *Kyotojin Dake ga Shitteiru* [Only Kyoto people know]. Tokyo: Yōsensha.

Imamura, Emiko. 2009. "Older Japanese Adults' Religiosity: Relationship with Age; Gender; Physical, Mental, and Cognitive Health; Social Support/Integration; and Health Promotion Behaviors." PhD dissertation, Department of Nursing, University of Michigan.

Imamura Shohei (Director). 1983. *The Ballad of Narayama* [Motion picture]. Japan: Toei Co. Ltd.

Inoue Haruyo. 2000. *Haka wo Meguru Kazokuron* [Family theory through the grave]. Tokyo: Heibonsha.

———. 2003. *Haka to Kazoku no Hen'yo* [Changes in graves and the family]. Tokyo: Iwanami Shoten.

———. 2004. "Haiguusha Sōshitsu to Kakukazoku no Shisha Saishi" [Partner loss and mortuary rituals of nuclear families]. *Ikigai Kenkyuu* 10: 65–82.

Inoue, Jun. 2010. "Migration of Nurses in the EU, the UK, and Japan: Regulatory Bodies and Push-Pull Factors in the International Mobility of Skilled Practitioners." Discussion Paper Series A No. 526, Institute of Economic Research Hitotsubashi University, Tokyo.

Inoue Tomohiro. 2013. "Suruganokuni Double Suicide Pact: Son Burns the Wheelchair, Arrested as a Suspect in His Mother's Murder." *Mainichi Shinbun*, November 8. http://mainichi.jp/area/shizuoka/news/20131108ddlk22040583000c.html, accessed November 28, 2013.

Inoue Yasushi. 1965. "Obasute." In *The Counterfeiter and Other Stories*, Leon Picon, trans. Pp. 73–96. Rutland, VT: Charles E. Tuttle.

———. 1982. *Chronicle of My Mother*. J. O. Moy, trans. New York: Kodansha International.

Itō Masaharu. 2006. *Nihonjin no Jinruigakuteki Jigazō* [Anthropological self-portrait of the Japanese]. Tokyo: Kikuike Meiro.

Ivy, Marylin. 1995. *Discourses of the Vanishing: Modernity, Phantasm, Japan*. Chicago: University of Chicago Press.

Iwasaka, Michiko, and Barre Toelken. 1994. *Ghosts and the Japanese: Cultural Experience in Japanese Death Legends*. Logan: Utah State University Press.

Jackson, Michael. 2002. *The Politics of Storytelling: Violence, Transgression, and Intersubjectivity*. Portland, OR: Museum Tusculanum Press.

Jacoby, Susan. 2011. *Never Say Die: The Myth and Marketing of the New Old Age*. New York: Pantheon Books.

Japan Times. 2010a. "Cities Scrambling to Find Centenarians but Privacy Law, Reliance on Volunteers Hamper Effort." August 6.

———. 2010b. "Daughter of '102-Year-Old Woman' Facing Fraud Charges in Fukushima." August 29. http://search.japantimes.co.jp/cgi-bin/nn20100829x2.html, accessed August 29, 2010.

———. 2012. "Foreign Pass Rate for Nurses Triples." March 27. http://www.japantimes.co.jp/news/2012/03/27/national/foreign-pass-rate-for-national-nurse-exam-triples/#.UhuuVD81Fxo, accessed August 25, 2013.

Jenike, Brenda Robb. 1997. "Home-Based Health Care for the Elderly in Japan: A Silent System of Gender and Duty." In *Aging Asian Concepts and Experiences Past and Present*, Susan Formanek and Sepp Linhart, eds. Pp. 329–346. Vienna: Österreichische Akademie der Wissenschaften.

———. 2003. "Parent Care and Shifting Family Obligations in Urban Japan." In *Demographic Change and the Family in Japan's Aging Society*, John W. Traphagan and John C. Knight, eds. Pp. 177–202. Albany: State University of New York Press.

Jenike, Brenda R., and John W. Traphagan. 2009. "Transforming the Cultural Scripts of Aging and Elder Care in Japan." In *The Cultural Context of Aging: Worldwide Perspectives*, 3rd ed., Jay Sokolovsky, ed. Pp. 240–259. Westport, CT: Greenwood.

Johnson, Frank. A. 1993. *Dependency and Japanese Socialization: Psychoanalytic and Anthropological Investigations into Amae*. New York: New York University Press.

Johnson-Hanks, Jennifer. 2002. "On the Limits of Life Stages in Ethnography: Toward a Theory of Vital Conjunctures." *American Anthropologist* 104 (3): 865–880.

Josephson, Jason Ananda. 2012. *The Invention of Religion in Japan*. Chicago: University of Chicago Press.

Kabir, Russell. 2011. "Narrative Medicine and Japan—Canonizing Curricula, Creating Applications, and Reacting to Rapid Professionalization." Honors thesis, Department of International Studies, University of Oklahoma.

Kalland, Arne. 1991. *Facing the Spirits: Illness and Healing in a Japanese Community* (NIAS Reports). Copenhagen: Nordic Institute of Asian Studies.

Kalmanson, Leah. 2010. "Levinas in Japan: The Ethics of Alterity and the Philosophy of No-Self." *Continental Philosophy Review* 43 (2): 193–206.

Kameoka, Hideta. 2013. "Kaigo Hoken Minaoshi (N.473) Tokuyou no nyuujo ha youkaigo 3 ijou" [Admittance to nursing homes, over level 3 need for care]. *Tokyo Shinbun*, November 6. http://www.tokyo-np.co.jp/article/seikatuzukan/2013/CK2013110602000187.html, accessed November 28, 2013.

Kamiya, Sestsuko. 2006. "Ceremonies to Say 'Thanks and Goodbye': Last Rites for the Memories as Beloved Dolls Pass Away." *Japan Times*, October 15.

Katz, Stephen. 2000. "Busy Bodies: Activity, Aging, and the Management of Everyday Life." *Journal of Aging Studies* 14 (2): 135–152.

Kaufman, Sharon. 1986. *The Ageless Self: Sources of Meaning in Later Life*. Madison: University of Wisconsin Press.

———. 2005. *And a Time to Die: How American Hospitals Shape the End of Life*. Chicago: University of Chicago Press.

Kawabata, O., K. Atsumi, and S. Shimura. 2001. *Kōreisha Seikatsu Hyō 1925–2001* [Table of senior citizen lifestyle 1925–2001]. Tokyo: Japan Editors School.

Kawada, Minoru. 1993. *The Origin of Ethnography in Japan: Yanagita Kunio and His Times*. Toshiko Kishida-Ellis, trans. New York: Kegan Paul.

Kawanishi, Yuko. 2009. *Mental Health Challenges Facing Contemporary Japanese Society: The "Lonely People."* Kent, UK: Global Oriental.

Kawano, Satsuki. 2003. "Finding Common Ground: Family, Gender, and Burial in Contemporary Japan." In *Demographic Change and the Family in Japan's Aging Society*, John W. Traphagan and John C. Knight, eds. Pp. 125–144. Albany: State University of New York Press.

———. 2005. *Ritual Practice in Modern Japan*. Honolulu: University of Hawaii Press.

———. 2010. *Nature's Embrace: Japan's Aging Urbanites and New Death Rites*. Honolulu: University of Hawaii Press.

Keene, Donald, ed. 1970. *Twenty Plays of the Nō Theater*. New York: Columbia University Press.

Kellehear, Allan. 2007. *A Social History of Dying*. New York: Cambridge University Press.

Kelly, Tim. 2011. "Death Industry Reaps Grim Profit as Japan Dies." *Reuters*, September 12.

Kenny, E., and E. T. Gilday. 2000. "Mortuary Rites in Japan." *Japanese Journal of Religious Studies* 27 (3–4): 163–178.

Kenyon, Gary M., Phillip G. Clark, and Brian De Vries. 2001. *Narrative Gerontology: Theory, Research, and Practice*. New York: Springer.

Kierkegaard, Søren. [1843] 2013. *Kierkegaard's Writings, VI: Fear and Trembling/Repetition.* New ed. Edna H. Hong and Howard V. Hong, trans. Princeton, NJ: Princeton University Press.

Kilborne, Benjamin. 2002. *Disappearing Persons: Shame and Appearance.* Albany: State University of New York Press.

Kim, H. S., D. K. Sherman, D. Ko, and S. E. Taylor. 2006. "Pursuit of Comfort and Pursuit of Harmony: Culture, Relationships, and Social Support Seeking." *Personality and Social Psychology Bulletin* 32 (12) (December 1): 1595–1607.

Kimble, Melvin E., and Susan H. McFadden, eds. 2003. *Aging, Spirituality and Religion.* Vol. 2. Minneapolis: Fortress Press.

Kinoshita, Keisuke (Director). 1958. *Narayama Bushikō* [The ballad of Narayama] [Motion picture]. Tokyo: Shochiku.

Kinoshita, Yasushito, and Christie W. Kiefer. 1992. *Refuge of the Honored: Social Organization in a Japanese Retirement Community.* Berkeley: University of California Press.

Kitayama Osamu. 1998. "Transience: Its Beauty and Danger." *International Journal of Psycho-analysis* 79 (5) (October): 937–953.

———. 2007. "Psychoanalysis in the 'Shame Culture' of Japan: A Dramatic Point of View." In *Freud and the Far East: Psychoanalytic Perspectives on the People and Culture of China, Japan, and Korea,* Salman Akhtar, ed. Pp. 89–104. Northvale, NJ: Jason Aronson.

Kleinman, Arthur. 1988. *The Illness Narratives: Suffering, Healing, and the Human Condition.* New York: Basic Books.

Knight, John C., and John W. Traphagan. 2003. "The Study of the Family in Japan: Integrating Anthropological and Demographic Approaches." In *Demographic Change and the Family in Japan's Aging Society,* John W. Traphagan and John C. Knight, eds. Pp. 3–23. Albany: State University of New York Press.

Kojima, Hiroshi. 2000. "Japan: Hyper-aging and Its Policy Implications." In *Aging East and West: Families, States, and the Elderly,* Vern L. Bergston, Kyong-Dong Kim, George C. Myers, and Ki-Soo Eun, eds. Pp. 95–120. New York: Springer.

Kōmoto, Mitsugi. 2001. *Gendai Nihon ni okeru Senzo Saishi* [Ancestor worship in contemporary Japan]. Tokyo: Ochanomizu Shobo.

Komparu, Kunio. 2005. *The Noh Theater: Principles and Perspectives.* Warren, CT: Floating World Editions.

Kondo, Dorinne. 1990. *Crafting Selves: Power, Gender, and Discourses of Identity in a Japanese Workplace.* Chicago: University of Chicago Press.

Kondo, Megumi. 2012. "A Terminal Patient's Hopes for Connections Transcending Time." *Anthropology and Aging Quarterly* 33 (2): 44–52.

Kotsuji, Hisanori, and Muneyuki Kobayashi. 2011. "Kodokushi Hōdō no Rekishi" [The history of media reports on Kodokushi]. *Core Ethics* 7: 121–130.

Koyano, Wataru. 1989. "Japanese Attitudes toward the Elderly: A Review of Research Findings." *Journal of Cross-Cultural Gerontology* 4 (4) (October 1): 335–345.

Krämer, Hans Martin. 2013. "How 'Religion' Came to Be Translated as Shukyo: Shimaji Mokurai and the Appropriation of Religion in Early Meiji Japan." *Japan Review* 25: 89–111.

Krause, Neal, Jersey Liang, Joan Bennett, Erika Kobayashi, Hiroko Akiyama, and Taro Fukaya. 2010. "A Descriptive Analysis of Religious Involvement among Older Adults in Japan." *Ageing and Society* 30 (4) (March 17): 671–696.

Krause, Neal, Jersey Liang, Benjamin A. Shaw, Hidehiro Sugisawa, Hye-Kyung Kim, and Yoko Sugihar. 2002. "Religion, Death of a Loved One, and Hypertension among Older Adults in Japan." *Journal of Gerontology* 57B (2): S96–S107.

Kundera, Milan. 1991. *Immortality*. New York: Grove Press.

Kurahashi, Yumiko. 2003. *Otona no tame no Zankoku Dōwa* [Tales of misery]. Tokyo: Kodansha.

Kurihara, Akira. 1986. "'Oi' to 'Oiru' no Doramatourugii" [Drammatology of "oi" and "Oiru"]. In *Oi no Jinruigaku, Oi no Hakken, 1* [The anthropology of aging, discovering of aging, vol. 1], Kurihara Akira, ed. Pp. 11–48. Tokyo: Iwanami Shoten.

Kuwayama, Takami. 2004. *Native Anthropology: The Japanese Challenge to Western Academic Hegemony*. Melbourne: Trans Pacific Press.

Kyoto City General Planning Bureau Information Office of Statistical Data. 2012. "Kyoto Estimated Demography October 2011–October 2012." http://www.city.kyoto.jp/html/html/sogo/toukei/Population/Estimate/report.html, accessed November 28, 2013.

———. 2013. "Nenreibetsu Suikei Jinkō" [Estimated population by age]. http://www.city.kyoto.jp/html/html/sogo/toukei/Population/Data/Estimate/Each_Age/Each_Age_2013.xls, accessed April 30, 2014.

LaFleur, William. 1992. *Liquid Life: Abortion and Buddhism in Japan*. Princeton, NJ: Princeton University Press.

Lamb, Sarah. 2000. *White Saris, Sweet Mangoes: Aging, Gender, and the Body in Northern India*. Berkeley: University of California Press.

———. 2009. *Aging and the Indian Diaspora: Cosmopolitan Families in India and Abroad*. Bloomington: Indiana University Press.

———. 2014. "Permanent Personhood or Meaningful Decline? Toward a Critical Anthropology of Successful Aging." *Journal of Aging Studies* 29 (April): 41–52.

Lambek, Michael. 1996. "The Past Imperfect: Remembering as a Moral Practice." In *Tense Past: Cultural Essays in Trauma and Memory*, P. Antze and M. Lambek, eds. Pp. 235–254. New York: Routledge.

Langford, Jean M. 2009. "Gifts Intercepted: Biopolitics and Spirit Debt." *Cultural Anthropology* 24 (4): 681–711.

Leavitt, Steven. C. 1995. "Seeking Gifts from the Dead: Long-Term Mourning in a Bumbita Arapesh Cargo Narrative." *Ethos* 23 (4): 453–473.

Lebra, Takie S. 1976. *Japanese Patterns of Behavior*. Honolulu: University of Hawaii Press.

———. 1979. "The Dilemma and Strategies of Aging among Contemporary Japanese Women." *Ethnology* 18 (4): 337–353.

———. 1983. "Shame and Guilt: A Psychocultural View of the Japanese Self." *Ethos* 11 (3): 192–209.

Leckman, J. F., D. E. Grice, J. Boardman, H. Zhang, A. Vitale, C. Bondi, J. Alsobrook, B. S. Peterson, D. J. Cohen, S. A. Rasmussen, W. K. Goodman, C. J. McDougle, and D. L. Paulis. 1997. "Symptoms of Obsessive Compulsive Disorder." *American Journal of Psychiatry* 154: 911–917.

Lester, Rebecca. 2005. *Jesus in Our Wombs Embodying Modernity in a Mexican Convent*. Berkeley: University of California Press.

Levy, Robert I., and Douglas W. Hollan. 1998. "Person Centered Interviewing and Observation." In *Handbook of Methods in Cultural Anthropology*, Russell H. Bernard, ed. Pp. 333–364. Walnut Creek, CA: AltaMira Press.

Liang, Jersey. 2003. "Changes in Health and Well-Being among Older Japanese." *Social Science Japan* 27 (November): 6–8.

Livingston, Julie. 2007. "Maintaining Local Dependencies: Elderly Women and Global Rehabilitation Agendas in Southeastern Botswana." In *Generations and Globalization: Youth, Age, and Family in the New World Economy*, Jennifer Cole and Deborah Durham, eds. Pp. 164–189. Bloomington: Indiana University Press.

Lock, Margaret. 1982. "Popular Conceptions of Mental Health in Japan." In *Cultural Conceptions of Mental Health and Therapy*, Anthony J. Marsella and Geoffrey M. White, eds. Pp. 215–233. Dordrecht: Reidel.

———. 1993. *Encounters with Aging: Mythologies of Menopause in Japan and North America*. Berkeley: University of California Press.

Loe, Meika. 2011. *Aging Our Way: Lessons for Living from 85 and Beyond*. New York: Oxford University Press.

Lohmann, Roger Ivar. 2003. *Dream Travelers: Sleep Experiences and Culture in the Western Pacific*. New York: Palgrave Macmillan.

Long, Susan O., ed. 2000. *Caring for the Elderly in Japan and United States: Practices and Policies*. London: Routledge.

———. 2005. *Final Days: Japanese Culture and Choice at the End of Life*. Honolulu: University of Hawaii Press.

———. 2009. "'Someone's Old, Something's New, Someone's Borrowed, Someone's Blue': Changing Elder Care at the Turn of the 21st Century." In *Imagined Families, Lived Families: Culture and Kinship in Contemporary Japan*, Akiko Hashimoto and John W. Traphagan, eds. Pp. 137–157. Albany: State University of New York Press.

———. 2012a. "Bodies, Technologies, and Aging in Japan: Thinking about Old People and Their Silver Products." *Journal of Cross-Cultural Gerontology* 27 (2) (May 8): 119–137.

———. 2012b. "Ruminations on Study of Late Life in Japan." *Anthropology and Aging Quarterly* 33 (2): 31–37.

Long, Susan O., and Phyllis B. Harris. 1997. "Caring for Bedridden Elderly: Ideals, Realities, and Social Change in Japan." In *Aging Asian Concepts and Experiences Past and Present*, Susan Formanek and Sepp Linhart, eds. Pp. 347–367. Vienna: Österreichische Akademie der Wissenschaften.

Luhrman, Tanya M. 2006. "Subjectivity." *Anthropological Theory* 6: 345–361.

Lynch, Caitrin, and Jason Danely, eds. 2013. *Transitions and Transformations: Cultural Perspectives on Aging and the Life Course*. New York: Berghahn Books.

Maeda Daisaku. 2000. "The Socioeconomic Context of Japanese Social Policy for Aging." In *Caring for the Elderly in Japan and United States: Practices and Policies*, Susan O. Long, ed. Pp. 28–51. London: Routledge.

Mageo, Jeannette Marie. 2003. *Dreaming and the Self: New Perspectives on Subjectivity, Identity, and Emotion*. Albany: State University of New York Press.

Mainichi Shinbun. 2013. "Suruga no murishinchu. Shobun horyu haha shakuho" [Suicide pact in Suruga: Ruling postponed. Mother released]. November 29. http://mainichi.jp/area/shizuoka/news/20131129ddlk22040269000c.html, accessed December 1, 2013.

Manning, Lydia. 2012. "Spirituality as a Lived Experience: Exploring the Essence of Spirituality in Late Life." *International Journal of Aging and Human Development* 75 (2): 95–113.

Markus, Hazel R., and A. R. Herzog. 1991. "The Role of the Self Concept in Aging." *Annual Review of Gerontology and Geriatrics* 11: 110–143.

Markus, Hazel R., and Paul Nurius. 1986. "Possible Selves." *American Psychologist* 41 (9): 954–969.

Mataix-Cols, David, Randy O. Frost, Alberto Pertusa, Lee Anna Clark, Sanjaya Saxena, James F. Leckman, Dan J. Stein, Hisato Matsunaga, and Sabine Wilhelm. 2010. "Hoarding Disorder: A New Diagnosis for DSM-V?" *Depression and Anxiety* 27 (6): 556–572.

Mathews, Gordon. 1996. *What Makes Life Worth Living? How Japanese and Americans Makes Sense of Their Worlds*. Berkeley: University of California Press.

Matsumoto, Yoshiko, ed. 2011. *Faces of Aging: The Lived Experiences of the Elderly in Japan.* Stanford, CA: Stanford University Press.

Matsunaga, A. O., and D. Matsunaga. 1974. *Foundation of Japanese Buddhism Volume 1: The Aristocratic Age.* Los Angeles: Buddhist Books International.

Matsunaga, H., K. Maebayashi, K. Hayashida, K. Okino, T. Matsui, T. Iketani, N. Kiriike, and D. J. Stein. 2008. "Symptom Structure in Japanese Patients with Obsessive Compulsive Disorder." *American Journal of Psychiatry* 165: 252–253.

Matsutani, Akihito. 2006. *Shrinking Population Economics: Lessons from Japan.* Tokyo: International House of Japan.

Mattingly, Cheryl. 2010. *The Paradox of Hope: Journeys through a Clinical Borderland.* Berkeley: University of California Press.

Mauss, Marcel. 1990. *The Gift: The Form and Reason for Exchange in Archaic Societies.* W. D. Halls, trans. London: Routledge.

Mazuz, Keren. 2013. "Folding Paper Swans, Modeling Lives." *Medical Anthropology Quarterly* 27 (2): 215–232.

McAdams, Dan P. 1996. "Narrating the Self in Adulthood." In *Aging and Biography: Explorations in Adult Development,* James E. Birre, Gary M. Kenyon, Jan-Erik Ruth, Johannes J. F. Schroots, and Torbjorn Svensson, eds. Pp. 131–148. New York: Springer.

———. 2005. "Studying Lives in Time: A Narrative Approach." *Advances in Life Course Research* 10: 237–258.

McAdams, Dan P., Jeffrey Reynolds, Martha Lewis, Allison H. Patten, and Phillip J. Bowman. 2001. "When Bad Things Turn Good and Good Things Turn Bad: Sequences of Redemption and Contamination in Life Narrative and Their Relation to Psychosocial Adaptation in Midlife Adults and in Students." *Personality and Social Psychology Bulletin* 27 (4): 474–485.

McFadden, Susan H., and Robert C. Atchley. 2001. *Aging and the Meaning of Time: A Multidisciplinary Exploration.* New York: Springer.

McLaughlin, Levi. 2013. "What Have Religious Groups Done after 3.11? Part 2: From Religious Mobilization to 'Spiritual Care.'" *Religion Compass* 7 (8) (August): 309–325.

Metcalf, Peter, and Richard Huntington. 1991. *Celebrations of Death: The Anthropology of Mortuary Ritual.* New York: Cambridge University Press.

Ministry of Health, Labor and Welfare (MHLW). 2005. "Statistics and Information Department, Minister's Secretariat, Ministry of Health, Labor and Welfare, 2–26 Infant Deaths by Sex, Infant Death Rate, Sex Ratio of Infant Death and Infant Death Rate among Total Death (1899–2004)." http://www.mhlw.go.jp/toukei/list/81-1.html, accessed November 28, 2013.

———. 2010. "Heisei 23 Nenban Koseirodo Hakusho" [2010 Ministry of Health, Labor and Welfare white paper]. http://www.mhlw.go.jp/wp/hakusyo/kousei/11/, accessed April 30, 2014.

———. 2011. "Kokumin Seikatsu Kiso Chosa" [Comprehensive survey of people's living conditions]. http://www.mhlw.go.jp/toukei/list/20-19-1.html, accessed November 25, 2013.

———. 2012. "Abridged Life Tables for Japan 2012." http://www.mhlw.go.jp/english/database/db-hw/lifetb12/dl/lifetb12-01.pdf, accessed May 2, 2014.

Mishra, Swasti Vardhan. 2011. "The Elderly Dependents in India: A Critical Review." *Indian Journal of Spatial Science* 2 (2): Article 5.

Mittermaier, Amira. 2010. *Dreams That Matter: Egyptian Landscapes of the Imagination.* Berkeley: University of California Press.

Miyake, K., and K. Yamazaki. 1995. "Self Conscious Emotions, Child Rearing Psychopathology in Japanese Culture." In *Self-Conscious Emotions: The Psychology of*

Shame, Guilt, Embarrassment, and Pride, J. P. Tangney and K. W. Fischer, eds. Pp. 488–504. New York: Guilford.

Miyazaki, Hirokazu. 2004. *The Method of Hope: Anthropology, Philosophy, and Fijian Knowledge.* Stanford, CA: Stanford University Press.

Moberg, David O. 2001. *Aging and Spirituality: Spiritual Dimensions of Aging Theory, Research, Practice, and Policy.* New York: Haworth Pastoral Press.

Moore, Katrina, and Ruth Campbell. 2009. "Mastery with Age: The Appeal of the Traditional Arts to Senior Citizens in Contemporary Japan." *Japanstudien* 21: 223–251.

MSN Sankei News. 2013. "Kaigotsukare de 75sai tsuma wo satsugaika 79sai oto, Sumidagawa de jisatsu misui" [79 year old husband, suspected of murdering 75 year old wife due to caregiver exhaustion, suicide attempt in the Sumida river ends in failure]. July 9. http://sankei.jp.msn.com/affairs/news/130709/crm13070914010006-n1.htm, accessed May 2, 2014.

Mullins, Mark R. 1998. *Christianity Made in Japan: A Study of Indigenous Movements.* Honolulu: University of Hawaii Press.

Munn, Nancy. 1986. *The Fame of Gawa: A Symbolic Study of Value Transformation in a Massim (Papua New Guinea) Society.* Durham, NC: Duke University Press.

Murakami, K. 2005. "Shisha saishi, kuyō no toshika, kindaika ni okery shudansei to kojinsei" [Death rites, urbanization of memorial, modernization, collectivity and individuality]. Paper presented at CSJR 2005: The 64th Annual Conference on the Study of Japanese Religion, Osaka.

Muramatsu, Naoko, and Hiroko Akiyama. 2011. "Japan: Super-Aging Society Preparing for the Future." *Gerontologist* 51 (4): 425–432.

Murayama, K. 2001. *Senzo wo Matsuru* [Venerating the ancestors]. Osaka: Hikari No Kuni.

Myerhoff, Barbara. 1978. *Number Our Days.* New York: E. P. Dutton.

Nakagawa, G. 1980. *Chōnaikai: Nihonjin no Jichikankanku* [Block associations: The self-governing sentiment of the Japanese]. Tokyo: Chūōkōronsha.

Nakane, Chie. 1970. *Japanese Society.* Berkeley: University of California Press.

Nakanishi, Miharu, Taeko Nakashima, and Tatsuo Honda. 2010. "Disparities in Systems Development for Elder Abuse Prevention among Municipalities in Japan: Implications for Strategies to Help Municipalities Develop Community Systems." *Social Science & Medicine* 71 (2) (July): 400–404.

National Institute of Population and Social Security Research in Japan. 2012. "Population Projections for Japan 2011–2060." http://www.ipss.go.jp/site-ad/index_english/esuikei/econ2.html, accessed May 22, 2014.

Neilson, Brett. 2003. "Globalization and the Biopolitics of Aging." *CR: The New Centennial Review* 3 (2): 161–186.

———. 2006. "Anti-ageing Cultures, Biopolitics and Globalisation." *Cultural Studies Review* 12 (2): 149–164.

———. 2012. "Ageing, Experience, Biopolitics: Life's Unfolding." *Body and Society* 18 (3–4) (September 1): 44–71.

Nelson, John. 2003. "Social Memory as Ritual Practice: Commemorating Spirits of the Military Dead at Yasukuni Shinto Shrine." *Journal of Asian Studies* 62 (2): 443–467.

Ngai, Sianne. 2005. *Ugly Feelings.* Cambridge, MA: Harvard University Press.

Niiya, Yu, Phoebe C. Ellsworth, and Susumu Yamaguchi. 2006. "Amae in Japan and the United States: An Exploration of a 'Culturally Unique' Emotion." *Emotion* 6 (2): 279–295.

Nikkan Sports. 2010. "Kōreisha shozai Fumei 70 nin koe Ishihara tochiji 'gendai no kaidan'" [Over 70 senior citizens whereabouts unknown, governor Ishihara "modern ghost story"]. August 6.

Nishizawa Shigejirō. 1936. *Obasuteyama shinkō* [The evolution of Obasuteyama]. Nagano: Shinano Kyōdoshi Kankōkai.

Niwa Fumio. 1962. "The Hateful Age." In *Modern Japanese Stories, an Anthology*, I. Morris, ed. Pp. 320–348. Rutland, VT: Charles Tuttle.

Nobel, Justin. 2010. "Japan's 'Lonely Deaths': A Business Opportunity." *Time*, April 6.

Nussbaum, Jon F., and Clara L. Fisher. 2011. "Successful Aging and Communication Wellness: A Process of Transition and Continuity." In *Faces of Aging: The Lived Experiences of the Elderly in Japan*, Y. Matsumoto, ed. Pp. 263–272. Palo Alto, CA: Stanford University Press.

Obara, Sawako. 2010. "Abuse of Elderly Up, Said Often Unintended." *Japan Times*, January 30, 2010. http://www.japantimes.co.jp/text/nn20100130fi.html#.T-H2VxdSRIE, accessed June 20, 2012.

Ochs, Elinor, and Lisa Capps. 1996. "Narrating the Self." *Annual Review of Anthropology* 25: 19–43.

———. 2002. *Living Narrative: Creating Lives in Everyday Storytelling*. Cambridge, MA: Harvard University Press.

Ogawa, Naohiro, and Robert D. Retherford. 1997. "Shifting Costs for the Elderly Back to Families in Japan: Will It Work?" *Population and Development Review* 23 (1): 59–94.

Ōguma, K. 1996. "Kono yo no Jigoku" [Hell on Earth]. In *Kono Yo to Ano Yo*, N. Masaaiki, ed. Pp. 179–206. Tokyo: Shōgakkan.

Ohnuki-Tierney, Emiko. 1984. *Illness and Culture in Contemporary Japan*. Cambridge: Cambridge University Press.

———. 2002. *Kamikaze, Cherry Blossoms, and Nationalisms: The Militarization of Aesthetics in Japanese History*. Chicago: University of Chicago Press.

Ohta Tenrei. [1970] 1984. *Rōjin-tō* [Island of the old]. Tokyo: Ohta Publishing.

Olivares-Tirado, Pedro, and Nanako Tamiya. 2014. *Trends and Factors in Japan's Long-Term Care Insurance System* (Springer Briefs in Aging). New York: Springer.

Oliver, Caroline. 2008. *Retirement Migration: Paradoxes in Ageing*. New York: Routledge.

Ooms, Herman. 1977. "Structural Analysis of Japanese Ancestral Rites and Beliefs." In *Ancestors*, William H. Newell, ed. Pp. 61–90. Chicago: Mouton.

O'Rand, Angela M. 1996. "The Precious and the Precocious: Understanding Cumulative Disadvantage and Cumulative Advantage over the Life Course." *Gerontologist* 36 (2): 230–238.

Otani, Izumi. 2010. "'Good Manner of Dying' as a Normative Concept: 'Autocide,' 'Granny Dumping,' and Discussions on Euthanasia/Death with Dignity in Japan." *International Journal of Japanese Sociology* 19 (1) (November): 49–63.

Otto, Lene. 2013. "Negotiating a Healthy Body in Old Age: Preventive Home Visits and Biopolitics." *International Journal of Ageing and Later Life* 8 (1): 111–135.

Ozawa, Itami. 2010. "'Good Manner of Dying' as a Normative Concept: 'Autocide,' 'Granny-Dumping' and Discussions of Euthanasia/Death with Dignity in Japan." *International Journal of Japanese Sociology* 19: 49–63.

Ozawa de-Silva, Chikako. 2005. *Psychotherapy and Religion in Japan: The Japanese Introspection Practice of Naikan*. New York: Routledge.

———. 2007. "Demystifying Japanese Therapy: An Analysis of Naikan and the Ajase Complex through Buddhist Thought." *Ethos* 35 (4): 411–446.

Palmore, Ernest B., and Daisuke Maeda. 1975. *The Honorable Elders: A Cross-Cultural Analysis of Aging in Japan*. Durham, NC: Duke University Press.

———. 1985. *The Honorable Elders Revisited—Otoshiyori saikō: A Revised Cross-Cultural Analysis of Aging in Japan*. Durham, NC: Duke University Press.

Parish, Steven M. 2008. *Subjectivity and Suffering in American Culture: Possible Selves*. New York: Palgrave MacMillan.

Peak, Lois. 1991. *Learning to Go to School in Japan: The Transition from Home to Preschool Life*. Berkeley: University of California Press.

Petryna, Adriana. 2002. *Life Exposed: Biological Citizens after Chernobyl*. Berkeley: University of California Press.

Pilgrim, Richard B. 1986. "Intervals ('Ma') in Space and Time: Foundations for a Religio-Aesthetic Paradigm in Japan." *History of Religions* 25 (3): 255–277.

Pitelka, Morgan. 2005. *Handmade Culture: Raku Potters, Patrons, and Tea Practitioners in Japan*. Honolulu: University of Hawaii Press.

Plath, David W. 1964. "Where the Family of God Is the Family: The Role of the Dead in Japanese Households." *American Anthropologist* 66 (2): 300–317.

———. 1980. *Long Engagements: Maturity in Modern Japan*. Stanford, CA: Stanford University Press.

———. 1982. "Resistance at Forty-Eight: Old Age Brinksmanship and Japanese Life Course Pathways." In *Aging and Life Course Transitions: An Interdisciplinary Perspective*, Tamara K. Hareven and K. J. Adams, eds. Pp. 109–125. New York: Guilford.

Pollock, George H. 1989. *The Mourning-Liberation Process*. Madison, CT: International Universities Press.

Pols, Jeannette. 2012. *Care at a Distance on the Closeness of Technology*. Amsterdam: Amsterdam University Press.

Portacolone, Elena. 2013. "The Notion of Precariousness among Older Adults Living Alone in the U.S." *Journal of Aging Studies* 27 (2) (April): 166–174.

Randall, William L., and Gary M. Kenyon. 2004. "Time, Story, and Wisdom: Emerging Themes in Narrative Gerontology." *Canadian Journal of Aging* 23 (4): 333–346.

Razavi, Shahra. 2007. "The Political and Social Economy of Care in a Development Context: Conceptual Issues, Research Questions and Policy Options." Gender and Development Programme Paper No. 3 (June), United Nations Research Institute for Social Development, Geneva.

Reader, Ian. 1991. *Religion in Contemporary Japan*. Honolulu: University of Hawaii Press.

———. 1995. "Social Action and Personal Benefits in Contemporary Japanese Buddhism." *Buddhist Christian Studies* 15 (1): 3–17.

Reader, Ian, and George Tanabe Jr. 1998. *Practically Religious: Worldly Benefits and the Common Religion of Japan*. Honolulu: University of Hawaii Press.

Reider, Noriko T. 2011. "'Hanayo no hime,' or 'Blossom Princess': A Late-Medieval Japanese Stepdaughter Story and Provincial Customs." *Asian Ethnology* 70 (1): 59–80.

Robben, Antonius C. G. M. 2004. *Death, Mourning, and Burial: A Cross-Cultural Reader*. Malden, MA: Blackwell.

Robertson, Jennifer. 1994. *Native and Newcomer: Making and Remaking a Japanese City*. Berkeley: University of California Press.

Roemer, Michael K. 2007. "Ritual Participation and Social Support in a Major Japanese Festival." *Journal for the Scientific Study of Religion* 46 (2): 185–200.

———. 2012. "Thinking of Ancestors (and Others) at Japanese Household Altars." *Journal of Ritual Studies* 26 (1): 33–45.

Rohlen, Thomas P. 1978. "The Promise of Adulthood in Japanese Spiritualism." In *Adulthood: Essays*, Erik H. Erikson, ed. Pp. 129–147. New York: Norton.

Rosaldo, Michelle. 1983. "The Shame of Headhunters and the Autonomy of Self." *Ethos* 11 (3): 135–151.

Rose, Nikolas S. 2007. *Politics of Life Itself: Biomedicine, Power, and Subjectivity in the Twenty-First Century.* Princeton, NJ: Princeton University Press.

Rosenberger, Nancy Ross, ed. 1994. *Japanese Sense of Self.* New York: Cambridge University Press.

Rowe, J. W., and R. L. Kahn. 1987. "Human Aging: Usual and Successful." *Science* 237 (4811): 143–149.

Rowe, Mark Michael. 2000. "Stickers for Nails: The Ongoing Transformation of Roles, Rites, and Symbols in Japanese Funerals." *Japanese Journal of Religious Studies* 27 (3–4): 353–378.

———. 2003. "Grave Changes: Scattering Ashes in Contemporary Japan." *Journal of Japanese Studies* 30 (1–2): 85–118.

———. 2011. *Bonds of the Dead: Temples, Burial, and the Transformation of Contemporary Japanese Buddhism.* Chicago: University of Chicago Press.

Ryang, Sonia. 2002. "Chrysanthemum's Strange Life: Ruth Benedict in Postwar Japan." *Asian Anthropology* 1: 87–116.

Saito, Yuriko. 2005. "The Aesthetics of Weather." In *The Aesthetics of Everyday Life*, Andrew Light and Jonathan Smith, eds. Pp. 157–176. New York: Columbia University Press.

———. 2007. "The Moral Dimension of Japanese Aesthetics." *Journal of Aesthetics and Art Criticism* 65 (1): 85–97.

———. 2010. *Everyday Aesthetics.* New York: Oxford University Press.

Sasaki, K. 2002. *Sei to shi no Nihon shisō* [Japanese thoughts on life and death]. Tokyo: Transview.

Saxena, S., A. L. Brody, K. M. Maidment, E. C. Smith, N. Zohrabi, E. Katz, S. K. Baker, and L. R. Baxter. 2004. "Cerebral Glucose Metabolism in Obsessive-Compulsive Hoarding." *American Journal of Psychiatry* 161 (6): 1038–1048.

Saxena, S., and K. M. Maidment. 2007. "Treatment of Compulsive Hoarding." *Journal of Lifelong Learning in Psychiatry* 5 (3): 381–387.

Schattschneider, Ellen. 2003. *Immortal Wishes: Labor and Transcendence on a Japanese Sacred Mountain.* Durham, NC: Duke University Press.

———. 2004. "Family Resemblances: Memorial Images and the Face of Kinship." *Japanese Journal of Religious Studies* 31 (1): 141–162.

Scheper-Hughes, Nancy. 1993. *Death Without Weeping: The Violence of Everyday Life in Brazil.* Berkeley: University of California Press.

Scheper-Hughes, Nancy, and Margaret Lock. 1987. "The Mindful Body: A Prolegomenon to Future Work in Medical Anthropology." *Medical Anthropology Quarterly* 1: 6–41.

Schnell, Scott. 2007. "Are Mountain Gods Vindictive? Competing Images of the Japanese Alpine Landscape." *Journal of the Royal Anthropological Institute* 13 (4): 863–80.

Sekoff, Jed. 1999. "The Undead: Necromancy and the Inner World." In *The Dead Mother: The Work of Andre Green*, G. Kohon, ed. Pp. 109–127. New York: Routledge.

Sherman, E. 1995. "Reminiscentia: Cherished Objects as Memorabilia in Late-Life Reminiscence." In *The Meaning of Reminiscence and Life-Review*, Jon Hendricks, ed. Pp. 193–204. Amityville, NY: Baywood.

Shibata, Takanori, and Kazuyoshi Wada. 2011. "Robot Therapy: A New Approach for Mental Healthcare of the Elderly—A Mini-Review." *Gerontology* 57 (4): 378–386.

Shimazono, Susumu. 2004. *From Salvation to Spirituality: Popular Religious Movements in Modern Japan*. Portland, OR: Trans Pacific Press.

Shirasaki, Asako. 2009. *Kaigo Rōdō wo Ikiru* [Living in caregiving labor]. Tokyo: Gendai Shokan.

Skord, Virginia. 1989. "Withered Blossoms: Aging in Japanese Literature." In *Perceptions of Aging in Literature: A Cross-Cultural Study*, P. von Dorotka Bagnell and P. Spencer Soper, eds. Pp. 131–143. New York: Greenwood.

Smith, Robert J. 1974. *Ancestor Worship in Contemporary Japan*. Stanford, CA: Stanford University Press.

———. 1999. "The Living and the Dead in Japanese Popular Religion." In *Lives in Motion: Composing Circles of Self and Community in Japan*, Susan O. Long, ed. Pp. 255–281. Ithaca, NY: Cornell University East Asia Program.

Somers, Margaret R. 1994. "The Narrative Constitution of Identity: A Relational and Network Approach." *Theory and Society* 23 (5): 605–649.

Sōmucho Tōkeikyoku. 2010. *Japan Statistical Yearbook*. Tokyo: Sōmucho Tōkeikyoku. http://www.stat.go.jp/data/nenkan/pdf/y2800000.pdf, accessed April 30, 2014.

Sorgenfrei, C. F. 1994. "Deadly Love: Mothers, Whores, and Other Demonic Females in Japanese Theater." *Contemporary Theater Review* 1 (2): 77–84.

Spiro, Melford. 1994. "Some Reflections on Family and Religion in East Asia." In *Culture and Human Nature*, Benjamin Kilborne and Lewis L. Landness, eds. Pp. 262–285. New Brunswick, NJ: Transaction.

Stabile, Susan M. 2004. *Memory's Daughters: The Material Cultural of Remembrance in Eighteenth Century America*. Ithaca, NY: Cornell University Press.

Stafford, Phillip. 2009. "Aging in the Hood: Creating and Sustaining Elder-friendly Environments." In *The Cultural Context of Aging: Worldwide Perspectives*, 3rd ed., Jay Sokolovsky, ed. Pp. 441–452. Westport, CT: Greenwood.

Stasch, Rupert. 2009. *Society of Others: Kinship and Mourning in a West Papuan Place*. Berkeley: University of California Press.

Stone, Jacqueline, and Mariko Namba Walter. 2008. *Death and the Afterlife in Japanese Buddhism*. Honolulu: University of Hawaii Press.

Straight, Belinda. 2006. "Becoming Dead: The Entangled Agencies of the Dearly Departed." *Anthropology and Humanism* 31 (2): 101–110.

Sung, Kyu-taik. 2001. "Elder Respect: Exploration of Ideals and Forms in East Asia." *Journal of Aging Studies* 15 (1): 13–26.

Suzuki, Hikaru. 2000. *The Price of Death: The Funeral Industry in Contemporary Japan*. Stanford, CA: Stanford University Press.

———. 2005. "Shifting Lives of Japanese Elders: Emerging Communal Relationships with Funeral Companies." SMU Social Science and Humanities Working Paper Series No. 14-2005, Southern Methodist University.

———, ed. 2013. *Death and Dying in Contemporary Japan*. New York: Routledge.

Swyngedouw, Jan. 1993. "Religion in Contemporary Japanese Society." In *Religion and Society in Modern Japan*, Mark R. Mullins, Shimazono Susumu, and Paul L. Swanson, eds. Pp. 49–72. Berkeley, CA: Asian Humanities Press.

Takagi, Emiko, and Merril Silverstein. 2006. "Intergenerational Coresidence of the Japanese Elderly: Are Cultural Norms Proactive or Reactive?" *Research on Aging* 28 (4): 473–492.

Takahashi, Shigeyuki. 2004. *Sōsai no Nihon Shi* [History of Japanese funerals]. Tokyo: Kodansha.

Takenaka, Ayumi. 2012. "Demographic Challenges for the 21st Century." *Anthropology and Aging Quarterly* 33 (2): 38–43.

Takenaka, Hoshirō. 2000. *Kōreisha no Kodoku to Yutakasa* [The solitude and richness of the elderly]. Tokyo: Nihon Hōsō Shuppan Kyōkai.

Talmadge, Eric. 2010. "Where Are Japan's Missing Centenarians?" Associated Press, August 12, 2010. http://msnbc.msn.com/id/38678356/ns/world_news-asiapacific/#.UAGcdfXEEdU, accessed July 10, 2012.

Tamiya, Nanako, Haruko Noguchi, Akihiro Nishi, Michael R. Reich, Naoki Ikegami, Hideki Hashimoto, Kenji Shibuya, Ichiro Kawachi, and John Creighton Campbell. 2011. "Population Ageing and Wellbeing: Lessons from Japan's Long-Term Care Insurance Policy." *Lancet* 378 (9797): 1183–1192.

Tanaka, Jiro, and Yamaori Tetsuo. 2005. *Omoshiroi Hodo Yoku Wakaru Nihon Shūkyō: Shinto, Bukkyō, Shinshukyō-Gurashi ni Yakutatsu Chishiki* [The more interesting, the more you understand: Shinto, Buddhism, new religions—Practical knowledge for everyday life]. Tokyo: Nippon Bungeisha.

Tanizaki, Junichirō. 1977. *In Praise of Shadows*. Stony Creek: Leete's Island Books.

Tatsumi Yoshihiro. [1970] 2006. *Abandon the Old in Tokyo*. Montreal: Drawn and Quarterly.

Taylor, Janelle. 2008. "On Recognition, Caring, and Dementia." *Medical Anthropology Quarterly* 22 (4): 313–335.

Taylor, Mark C. 2009. *Fieldnotes from Elsewhere: Reflections on Dying and Living*. New York: Columbia University Press.

Tedlock, Barbara. 2001. "Divination as a Way of Knowing: Embodiment, Visualization, Narrative, and Interpretation." *Folklore* 112: 189–197.

Thang, Leng Leng. 2001. *Generations in Touch: Linking the Old and Young in a Tokyo Neighborhood*. Ithaca, NY: Cornell University Press.

Thomas, Gary. 2010. "Doing Case Study: Abduction Not Induction, Phronesis Not Theory." *Qualitative Inquiry* 16 (7): 1–8.

Thomas, L. Eugene. 1999. *Religion, Belief, and Spirituality in Late Life*. New York: Springer.

Ticktin, Miriam Iris. 2011. *Casualties of Care: Immigration and the Politics of Humanitarianism in France*. Berkeley: University of California Press.

Tobin, Joseph. 1994. "Japanese Preschools and Pedagogy of Selfhood." In *Japanese Sense of Self*, Nancy R. Rosenberger, ed. Pp. 21–39. Cambridge: Cambridge University Press.

Tomita, Susan. 1994. "The Consideration of Cultural Factors in the Research of Elder Mistreatment with an In-Depth Look at the Japanese." *Journal of Cross-Cultural Gerontology* 9: 39–52.

Traphagan, John W. 2000. *Taming Oblivion: Aging Bodies and the Fear of Senility in Japan*. Albany: State University of New York Press.

———. 2003. "Older Women as Caregivers and Ancestral Protection in Rural Japan." *Ethnology* 42 (2): 127–139.

———. 2004. *The Practice of Concern: Ritual, Well-Being, and Aging in Rural Japan*. Durham, NC: Carolina Academic Press.

———. 2006. "How to Be a Good Rōjin: Senility, Power, and Self-Actualization in Japan." In *Thinking about Dementia: Culture, Loss, and the Anthropology of Senility*, Annette Leibing and Lawrence Cohen, eds. Pp. 269–287. New Brunswick, NJ: Rutgers University Press.

———. 2010. "Intergenerational Ambivalence, Power, and Perceptions of Elder Suicide in Rural Japan." *Journal of Intergenerational Relationships* 8 (1): 21–37.

———. 2011. "Generations Apart: Burdens, Bad Families, and Elder Suicide in Rural Japan." In *Faces of Aging: The Lived Experiences of the Elderly in Japan*, Yoshiko Matsumoto, ed. Pp. 87–108. Stanford, CA: Stanford University Press.

———. 2013. *Rethinking Autonomy: A Critique of Principlism in Biomedical Ethics*. Albany: State University of New York Press.

Traphagan, John W., and John C. Knight, eds. 2003. *Demographic Change and the Family in Japan's Aging Society*. Albany: State University of New York Press.

Tsu, Yun Hui. 1984. "Post-mortem Identity and Burial Obligation: On Blood Relations, Place Relations, and Associational Relations in the Japanese Community in Singapore." *Senri Ethnological Studies* 16: 93–114.

Tsuji, Yohko. 1997. "Continuities and Changes in the Conceptions of Old Age in Japan." In *Aging Asian Concepts and Experiences Past and Present*, Susan Formanek and Sepp Linhart, eds. Pp. 197–210. Vienna: Österreichische Akademie der Wissenschaften.

———. 2002. "Death Policies in Japan: The State, the Family, and the Individual." In *Family and Social Policy in Japan: Anthropological Approaches*, R. Goodman, ed. Pp. 177–199. Cambridge: Cambridge University Press.

———. 2005. "Time Is Not Up: Temporal Complexity of Older Americans' Lives." *Journal of Cross-Cultural Gerontology* 20 (1) (March 1): 3–26.

———. 2006. "Mortuary Rituals in Japan: Hegemony of Tradition and Motivations of Individuals." *Ethos* 34 (3): 391–431.

Tulle-Winton, Emmanuelle. 1999. "Growing Old and Resistance: Towards a New Cultural Economy of Old Age?" *Ageing and Society* 19 (3): 281–299.

Turner, Victor. 1967. *Forest of Symbols*. Ithaca, NY: Cornell University Press.

Twigg, Julia. 2000. *Bathing, the Body, and Community Care*. London: Routledge.

Ushikubo, Mitsuko. 1998. "A Study of Factors Facilitating and Inhibiting the Willingness of the Institutionalized Disabled Elderly for Rehabilitation: A United States-Japanese Comparison." *Journal of Cross-Cultural Gerontology* 13: 127–157.

Valentine, Christine. 2009. "Negotiating a Loved One's Dying in Contemporary Japanese Society." *Mortality* 14 (1) (February): 34–52.

———. 2010. "The Role of the Ancestral Tradition in Bereavement in Contemporary Japanese Society." *Mortality* 15 (4): 275–293.

Van Bremen, Jan. 1998. "Death Rites in Japan in the Twentieth Century." In *Interpreting Japanese Society: Anthropological Approaches*, 2nd ed., J. Hendry, ed. Pp. 131–144. New York: Routledge.

Vartanian, Ivan, and Kyoko Wada. 2011. *See/Saw: Connections between Japanese Art Then and Now*. San Francisco: Chronicle Books.

Wada, Shuichi. 1995. "The Status and Image of the Elderly in Japan: Understanding the Paternalistic Ideology." In *Images of Aging: Cultural Representations of Later Life*, M. Featherstone and A. Wernick, eds. Pp. 47–58. New York: Routledge.

Washburn, Dennis. 2011. "Transfiguration of Loss: Grief and Aging in the Maboroshi (Spirit Summoner) Chapter of The Tale of Genji." Paper presented at the conference of the Association of Japanese Literature Studies, November 5.

Weiler, A. H. 1961. "Screen: Taken from Japanese Legend; 'Ballad of Narayama' Is Import at Carnegie, Drama Is Stylized and Occasionally Graphic." *New York Times*, June 20, 27.

Wentzell, Emily. 2013. "Aging Respectably by Rejecting Medicalization: Mexican Men's Reasons for Not Using Erectile Dysfunction Drugs." *Medical Anthropology Quarterly* 27 (1) (March): 3–22.

White, Merry Isaacs. 2002. *Perfectly Japanese: Making Families in an Era of Upheaval*. Berkeley: University of California Press.

Wierzbicka, Anna. 1996. "Japanese Cultural Scripts: Cultural Psychology and 'Cultural Grammar.'" *Ethos* 24 (3): 527–555.

Wikan, Unni. 1990. *Managing Turbulent Hearts: A Balinese Formula for Living*. Chicago: University of Chicago Press.

Wilińska, Monika, and Els-Marie Anbäcken. 2013. "In Search of the Everyday Life of Older People in Japan: Reflections Based on Scholarly Literature." *Journal of Cross-Cultural Gerontology* 28 (4) (August 14): 435–451.

Willerslev, Rane. 2009. "The Optimal Sacrifice: A Study of Voluntary Death among the Siberian Chukchi." *American Ethnologist* 36 (4): 693–704.

Woodward, Kathleen. 1991. *Aging and Its Discontents: Freud and Other Fictions*. Bloomington: Indiana University Press.

———. 1999. "The Mirror Stage of Old Age." In *Figuring Age: Women, Bodies, Generations*, Kathleen Woodward, ed. Pp. 98–113. Bloomington: Indiana University Press.

———. 2012. "Assisted Living: Aging, Old Age, Memory, Aesthetics." *Occasion: Interdisciplinary Studies in the Humanities* 4 (May 31): 1–13.

Yajima, Kazuyoshi. 2009. "Training and Supply of Japanese Physicians: An Impending Crisis?" *World Medical and Health Policy* 1 (1): 57–62.

Yamada, Masahiro. 2001. *Kazoku to iu risuku* [Family risk]. Tokyo: Keiso Shobo.

Yamada, Yoko. 2002. "Models of Life-Span Developmental Psychology: A Construction of the Generative Life Cycle Model Including the Concept of 'Death.'" *Kyoto University Graduate School of Education Research Bulletin* 48: 39–62.

———. 2003. "The Generative Life Cycle Model: Integration of Japanese Folk Images and Generativity." In *The Generative Society: Caring for Future Generations*, E. de St. Aubin, Dan P. McAdams, and T. C. Kim, eds. Pp. 97–112. Washington, DC: American Psychological Association.

Yamada Yoko and Yoshinobu Kato. 2006. "Images of Circular Time and Spiral Repetition: The Generative Life Cycle Model." *Culture and Psychology* 12 (2): 143–160.

Yamaori Tetsuo. 1990. "The Religious Identity of the Japanese." In *Japanese Civilization in the Modern World VI: Religion* (Senri Ethnological Studies No. 29), Umesao Tadao, ed. Pp. 63–74. Osaka: National Museum Ethnology.

———. 1997a. "Buddha and Okina ('Aged Man'): The Expression of Dying and Maturity." In *Aging Asian Concepts and Experiences Past and Present*, Susan Formanek and Sepp Linhart, eds. Pp. 76–96. Vienna: Österreichische Akademie der Wissenschaften.

———. 1997b. "The Image of Rōjō or Elderly Women in Japanese Legend." *Nichibunken Japan Review* 9: 20–40.

———. 2004. *Wandering Spirits and Temporary Corpses Studies in the History of Japanese Religious Traditions*. Denis Hirota, trans. Kyoto: International Research Center for Japanese Studies.

Yanagita Kunio. [1946] 1970. *About Our Ancestors*. Fanny Hagen Meyer and Ishikawa Yasuyo, trans. Tokyo: Japan Society for the Promotion of Science.

———. [1945] 1979. *Teihon Yanagita Kunio shū*. Vol. 21. Tokyo: Chikuma Shobo.

Yano, Christine Reiko. 2002. *Tears of Longing: Nostalgia and the Nation in Japanese Popular Song*. Cambridge, MA: Harvard University Asia Center.

Yasuhiro Yuki. 2012. *Kaigo: Genba kara no Chōsa* [Caregiving: A survey from the ground]. Tokyo: Iwanami Shinsho.

Yomiuri Shinbun. 1933. *Kuka ni Obaasan—Hikkoshi wo Saiwai ni Fukosha no Kyōdai—sobo wo oitekebori—Kono yo Ubasuteyama* [Old woman in an empty room—A fortuitous relocation for unfilial brothers—Grandmother left behind Obasuteyama in this world]. September 6.

————. 2014. "'Honnin ga nozomu saiki' sonchō" [Respect for "personal hopes for end of life"]. April 14, 10.

Yoshikawa, Yūko. 1998. "Umare kiyomari no minkan setsuwa—kirō tan no shūkyō minzoku" [Folklore of birth and purification—Religious folklore of tales of deserting old people]. *Setsuwa Denshōgaku* 6: 117–136.

Young, Richard, and Ikeuchi Emiko. 1997. "Geriatric Rituals in Japan." In *Aging Asian Concepts and Experiences Past and Present*, Susan Formanek and Sepp Linhart, eds. Pp. 229–255. Vienna: Österreichische Akademie der Wissenschaften.

Zhang, H., J. F. Leckman, D. L. Pauls, C. P. Tsai, K. K. Kidd, M. Rosario Campos, and the Tourette Syndrome Association International Consortium for Genetics. 2002. "Genome-wide Scan of Hoarding in Sib Pairs in Which Both Sibs Have Gilles de la Tourette Syndrome." *American Journal of Human Genetics* 70: 896–904.

Index

About the Author

JASON DANELY earned a bachelor's in comparative religion from Western Michigan University and a PhD in anthropology from the University of California, San Diego. He is recipient of an IIE Fulbright Research Grant, the Melford E. Spiro Dissertation Award, the University of Wisconsin–Milwaukee Center on Age and Community Postdoctoral Research Fellowship, and the Japan Society for the Promotion of Science Postdoctoral Research Fellowship. He is co-editor, with Caitrin Lynch, of *Transitions and Transformations: Cultural Perspectives on Aging and the Life Course* (2013, Berghahn Books) and editor-in-chief of *Anthropology and Aging*. He is currently a senior lecturer of anthropology at Oxford Brookes University.

CPSIA information can be obtained
at www.ICGtesting.com
Printed in the USA
LVOW11s2309180118

563148LV00001B/99/P